www.wadsworth.com

wadsworth.com is the World Wide Web site for Wadsworth and is your direct source to dozens of online resources.

At *wadsworth.com* you can find out about supplements, demonstration software, and student resources. You can also send email to many of our authors and preview new publications and exciting new technologies.

wadsworth.com
Changing the way the world learns®

A Concise Introduction to Computer Languages

Design, Experimentation, and Paradigms

Daniel E. Cooke

Texas Tech University

THOMSON

™

BROOKS/COLE

Australia • Canada • Mexico • Singapore • Spain
United Kingdom • United States

THOMSON
™
BROOKS/COLE

Editor: *Kallie Swanson*
Senior Editorial Assistant: *Carla Vera*
Technology Project Manager: *Burke Taft*
Marketing Director: *Tom Ziolkowski*
Marketing Assistant: *Darcie Pool*
Advertising Project Manager: *Laura Hubrich*
Project Manager, Editorial Production: *Kelsey McGee*
Print/Media Buyer: *Vena M. Dyer*
Permissions Editor: *Connie Dowcett*

Production Service: *Matrix Productions*
Text Designer: *Roy R. Neuhaus*
Copy Editor: *Frank Hubert*
Cover Designer: *Linda Harper*
Cover Illustration: *Diane Fenster*
Cover Printing, Printing, and Binding:
  Phoenix Color Corp
Compositor: *Parkwood Composition Service*

For more information about our products, contact us at:
Thomson Learning Academic Resource Center
1-800-423-0563

For permission to use material from this text,
contact us by: **Phone:** 1-800-730-2214
Fax: 1-800-730-2215
Web: http://www.thomsonrights.com

Library of Congress Cataloging-in-Publication Data
Cooke, D. (Daniel)
  A concise introduction to computer languages:
design, experimentation, and paradigms
/Daniel E. Cooke.—[1st ed.]
    p. cm.
  Includes bibliographical references and index.
  ISBN 0-534-37695-9
    1. Programming languages (Electronic computers)
I. Title.

QA76.7 .C665 2003
005.13--dc21   2002022631

Brooks/Cole—Thomson Learning
511 Forest Lodge Road
Pacific Grove, CA 93950
USA

Asia
Thomson Learning
5 Shenton Way #01-01
UIC Building
Singapore 068808

Australia
Nelson Thomson Learning
102 Dodds Street
South Melbourne, Victoria 3205
Australia

Canada
Nelson Thomson Learning
1120 Birchmount Road
Toronto, Ontario M1K 5G4
Canada

Europe/Middle East/Africa
Thomson Learning
High Holborn House
50/51 Bedford Row
London WC1R 4LR
United Kingdom

Latin America
Thomson Learning
Seneca, 53
Colonia Polanco
11560 Mexico D.F.
Mexico

Spain
Paraninfo Thomson Learning
Calle/Magallanes, 25
28015 Madrid, Spain

For Kathy

CONTENTS

PREFACE

Recently some have suggested that there is no need to develop new computer languages nor even to teach language design and compiler theory. This point of view ignores the true essence of computer science and software engineering: to solve complicated problems—to find order in chaos and complexity. Put another way, the end goal of computer science is to contribute to the reverse of entropy. Computer languages are necessary for this endeavor, and improved languages are necessary for continued progress.

Languages provide the framework for the way we organize complexity in our own minds. We use languages to build the mental models that aid us in understanding complicated ideas and phenomena. *Languages are also the means by which we communicate our understanding.* Whether we realize it or not, dialogues are taking place among parts of our nervous system responsible for the levels of reasoning we constantly perform. From the most basic reflexive activities that rarely enter our awareness to the so-called off-line reasoning that permits humans to reflect, analyze, and solve problems, there are language translations occurring.

Thus, languages are central to the investigations and discoveries required of computer scientists. The goal of this book is to provide a concise introduction to the basic knowledge a computer scientist should have concerning language and language design and to provide inspiration to students in this field. The content of this book is a product of more than fifteen years of teaching classes variously called "Survey of Programming Languages," "Design and Implementation of Programming Languages," and "Concepts of Programming Languages." These classes were taught to undergraduates at the junior level at the University of Texas at El Paso and more recently at Texas Tech University. Students at this level are capable of learning the semantics of the executable language constructs. Thus, this text teaches formal approaches to syntax and semantic definition. However, the semantics of function or procedure definition or invocation are not covered. With this approach, we can avoid the more sophisticated semantic operators (e.g., the denotational projection and injection), which are better left to a more advanced level.

Students find that their understanding of languages is enhanced by the formal semantic definitions. Prior to learning this material, students mainly learn about language statements through observation. They write, compile, and execute codes, and by doing so, it is hoped, they observe the operational semantics of language statements. In addition to these experiments, students who learn semantic definitions of statements improve their understanding through a careful analysis of semantic equations. Often subtleties in language statements become obvious after one studies the equations that define them. The formalisms developed to describe languages are analogous to the differential equations employed in describing and modeling physical phenomena. Just as the study of the models of physical phenomena has led to breakthroughs in physics, so the study of mathe-matical models describing language approaches will likely advance our under-standing of problem solving.

This book also describes how to write a simple interpreter so that students can observe the transition from language design to language implementation. The language design and implementation material presented here provide the basis for understanding the language paradigms. Peppered throughout the chapters on procedural, object-oriented, functional, and logic programming languages are syntactic and semantic definitions. Furthermore, language translation and imple-mentation are investigated in these languages.

The final chapter presents the observations and thinking that went into the definition of SequenceL declarative language. I view this chapter as a case study in language design, intended to clarify how the languages described in the book influenced the development of SequenceL and, more than that, to tie the book together and provide the reader with further insight into language design.

DESIGN OF THE TEXT

In this book the reader will study the methods and mathematical tools employed to design a language. The first section presents the methods to define a language syntactically and semantically and then explains how to develop a simple inter-preter for a small language. The second section shows how to learn a new lan-guage. This section will be based upon the constructs for procedural languages by means of which the reader will explore each of the paradigms: the imperative (or procedural), object-oriented, functional, and logical.

Readers of this text are expected to know discrete mathematics and program-ming through data structures. It is desirable, but not mandatory, that they also know the theory of automata.

ACKNOWLEDGMENTS

People who contributed immensely to the writing of this book are Richard Watson, Vladik Kreinovich, Michael Gelfond, and Joseph Urban. Moreover, during the 15 years I have been teaching this material, both at Texas Tech University and the University of Texas at El Paso, many wonderful students have provided feedback and questions that were of great value. Specifically in regard to the SequenceL work, I want to acknowledge the efforts of current and former graduate students Ann Gates, Miguel Pedroza, Aida Gutierrez, Bassam Chokr, Richard Duran, Bo Friesen, Joseph Pizzi, and Per Andersen. I am also very grateful for the editorial assistance provided by the reviewers of the text—John B. Connely, California Polytechnic State University; Thomas W. Christopher, Illinois Institute of Technology; Roger Hartley, New Mexico State University; Rachelle Heller, George Washington University; and Robert Moll, University of Massachusetts—and by Kallie Swanson and Carla Vera.

Daniel Cooke

1

AN INTRODUCTION TO LANGUAGE DESIGN

MOTIVATION FOR LANGUAGE RESEARCH

> Early in my experiences with computers, I saw some of these . . . "programs," as they are called—and because they seemed to be an unintelligible array of letters and numbers, arranged in patterns quite unrelated to those in English, or in arithmetic or algebra, I came to think of programming as a black art, best left to the professionals. For several years, I prepared my problems, and the instructions for solving them, in a language that I knew, and handed the lot over to a programmer, who went on from there. Together, programmers and computers relieved me of a great deal of drudgery, but they also gave me a feeling I didn't like—a feeling of remoteness from my problems. [Bernstein]

Jeremy Bernstein, a physicist, published these remarks in the early 1960s. Amazingly, the words ring as true today as they did some 40 years ago. These words seem to summarize the motivation behind the continual quest for new languages—languages that bring the "user" closer to the problem solution.

The answer to Bernstein's lament was FORTRAN. Why is it that FOR-TRAN sufficed for his problems but does not hit the mark for many present-day users and problem solvers? Is it because we eventually ask new abstractions to solve more and more complicated problems and consequently stress them to the point that we end up, in some manner, where we started—needing a more capable language? Quite a bit of history and experience supports this view.

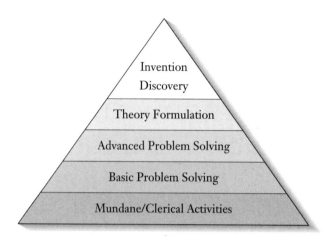

FIGURE 1.1

Consider all of the activities involved in doing research before computers were invented. As the pyramid shown in Figure 1.1 indicates, the bulk of a scientist's time was devoted to mundane or clerical activities that are now typically handled by the computer. The amount of available time as depicted in the pyramid is based upon the dependencies that exist between one category and another. For example, before doing theory formulation, a researcher will probably need to perform data analysis requiring some basic and advanced problem solving. The time spent on these activities causes the available time for theory formulation and invention and discovery to dwindle.

As more and more of these lower-level efforts are handled quickly through the use of computers, the time allotted to these efforts and the delays caused by the dependencies among the categories are reduced, and higher-level efforts proceed more quickly. Furthermore, time is provided for exploring the varied ways in which results can be presented, potentially providing greater insight into problem understanding.

When FORTRAN was introduced, scientists were elated by the fact that they could themselves write the programs that perform simple, basic calculations quickly. Gradually, the elation over this accomplishment subsided, and demands for solutions that moved the field up the pyramid were heard. As these demands increased, FORTRAN was viewed more and more the way Bernstein was viewing assembly language, or machine code. The field, in a sense, turned back to where it began.

Now the goal is to achieve a grand level of capability termed *human-centered computing*, wherein the computer extends the reasoning power of the human to the point that the human is free to concentrate on the creative efforts involved in invention and discovery.

Wojciech Cellary, of the Poznan University of Economics in Poland, provides a historical context that supports the current goal. His view is based upon the role humans and knowledge have played in each of the major societal epochs: the agrarian, industrial, and information. In the agrarian society *humans = physical labor* and *work*. The application of knowledge was performed by a small number of so-called masters, who knew how to apply knowledge in essentially one area. A boot maker or blacksmith would be an example. But in the Industrial Age machines began to perform more of the physical labor previously done by humans and, in fact, magnified and extended the physical capabilities of the humans who used them. With a steam shovel a person can create excavations many times greater than could be performed with cruder tools. Humans provided the brains for the machines that performed the work, enabling more work to be performed. As a result, more people developed skills, and more people could apply knowledge in one area than had been the case in the agrarian society. The human role was characterized as *human = intelligence* during this age.

In the Information Age much of the skill involved in the application of knowledge is embodied in computer programs. Software allows people to do their own taxes, accounting, inventory, and so forth. Thus, more people can apply knowledge in more areas than previously. In the Information Age *human = creativity*. Whereas humans provided the brains for the machines of the Industrial Age, the computer now extends and magnifies the ability of the brain of the individual human. To capture the essence of the term *human-centered computing*, Kenneth Ford of the Institute for Human & Machine Cognition, coined the term *cognitive prostheses*. Just as eyeglasses serve as ocular prostheses, the computer can provide the human with assistance in cognition.

As society demands higher levels of capabilities from computers—as the work of the computer ascends the pyramid presented earlier—more sophisticated languages are required. Instead of satisfying the users, these improved languages whet their appetite for even better languages. With this motivational backdrop in mind, we will now explore the field of computer language research.

LANGUAGE RESEARCH IN THE CONTEXT OF COMPUTER SCIENCE

In a broad sense *computer science* can be viewed as the science of problem solving using computers. The beginning of modern computer science was marked by Alan Turing's paper, which, among other insights, showed that there are unsolvable problems. That is, within the infinite set of solvable problems there is an infinite set of tractable problems (problems for which technically feasible solutions exist) and an infinite set of intractable problems (problems that it would take a supercomputer an unavailable amount of time to solve). See Figure 1.2 for the relationships among these sets.

One category of computer science research is devoted to decreasing the set of intractable problems. Advances in computer hardware, for example, lead to

FIGURE 1.2 Set of all possible problems.

more powerful computers that execute faster and have larger stores of memory. The resulting increase in raw computing power lets us solve more complex problems, including some that were formerly not feasible.

Computer architecture, which is concerned with the manner in which hardware devices are organized, is intended to find new ways to effectively employ the raw computer power we possess. Supercomputers are developed to execute—in parallel—the pieces of a problem that can be solved concurrently (at the same time). In addition to hardware and architecture research, some computer scientists are devoted to the development of improved algorithmic solutions to complex problems.

Suppose known solutions to problem X are intractable. Sometimes it turns out that there is an equivalent tractable solution (i.e., an algorithm that solves exactly the same problem). From earlier courses in computer science, you have learned that there are several approaches to the sorting problem, ranging in efficiency from $O(n^2)$ to $O(n \log_2 n)$. All the algorithms are equivalent in that they all solve the same problem—they sort items. The range in efficiency among the approaches, however, is wide.

Consider, as an example, the problem of sorting the items for a phone book. Suppose that there are $n = 500,000$ entries to be ordered. Assume that on average it takes 1 microsecond (µs) to perform the test and (if need be) exchange for each of the $n - 1$ items. If we employ the *bubble sort,* it will take $500,000^2 = 250,000,000,000$ (µs) $= 250,000$ seconds $= 4,166.66$ mins $= 69.4$ hrs $= 2.89$ days to sort the items for the phone book. If instead we choose the *heap sort,* we can expect an average case of $500,000 \log_2 500,000 = 500,000 \cdot 18.932 = 9,466,000$ µs $= 9.46$ seconds to perform the sort.

In general, the first category of computer science research is devoted to making complicated problems more *technically feasible* to solve. The second category of research has to do with making it *humanly feasible* to solve more complicated problems. Some of the efforts in the second category of research focus on ways to delegate some of the complexity of certain activities to easy-to-use tools such as database management systems, operating systems, networking tools, and so forth. Other efforts in the second category focus on problem representation as in artificial intelligence and software engineering. But central to all efforts to improve upon the human's ability to solve more complicated problems is computer language research.

■ ■

THEORETICAL LANGUAGE RESEARCH

A programming language can be viewed as the central part of a problem-solving theory. The language is central to the theory because it is the basis for communicating problem solutions to machines or other people. Let us consider the features of a programming language that make it effective in this role.

ABSTRACTION

Possibly the most important aspect of a programming language is the fact that it alone manifests the *abstraction*—or the approach to problem solving—provided by the theory. "One of the most crucial steps in the design of a language is the choice of abstraction upon which programs are to base." [Wirth74] Abstraction is key to an understanding of language and language design.

An abstraction is commonly viewed as the act of taking away—the formation of an idea apart from the concrete existence or specification thereof. A computer abstraction can be viewed as the result of dropping out nonessential, complicating details. Hence, an abstraction defines both that which is salient to the problem solution and that which constitutes extraneous details that can be ignored.

The original model of computing required the physical rewiring of the CPU to alter the CPU's actions. A revolution in abstraction came with the *stored-program concept*, also known as the *Von Neumann architecture*. The Von Neumann approach dropped out the original distinction between the storage of data and the storage of a program. Assembler languages quickly followed. These languages dropped out many nonessential details, including the need to keep track of physical addresses. Macro definitions for oft repeated functions such as input-output (I/O) improved the assembler abstraction by removing many nonessential details from the programmer's concern. In the case of I/O on the IBM 360/370, the details hidden are those involved in executing channel programs. The GET and PUT macros essentially hide a surfeit of nonessential details: without these macros the programmer has to write programs that run on the I/O channel processors together with the mainframe program code required to initiate the I/O transfers.

FORTRAN was a major step in abstraction improvement because it provided a view of problem solving in which many machine-level details, such as register usage and memory management, could be ignored. FORTRAN's abstraction moves the programmer away from machine operations, pointing toward algebraic operations instead. Languages like Algol and Pascal in turn improved the FORTRAN abstraction in a significant way by adding prominent control structures and placing data structure design on a level equal to algorithm design. In other words, with the newer abstractions the design of the data structure comes to be viewed as a critical element in problem solving. To illustrate the significance of the data structure, imagine trying to convert an arbitrary postfix expression into an equivalent prefix expression without the use of an advanced data structure. The Pascal abstraction eventually led to the view that the programmer's product is a data product rather than a program that produces that data product.

The object-oriented approach to programming is not an abstraction change; it adds rather than deletes technical detail. The approach was motivated by the fact that procedural languages lacked a "middle ground" between local and global variables. The lack of this middle ground led to technical difficulties in the implementation and reusability of data structures. The difficulty was addressed by David Parnas's definition of *information hiding*, a form of hiding variables beyond the hiding afforded by local variables. These problems were solved by adding features to encapsulate data structures. Once one encapsulates data structures, it is a logical step to encapsulate program structures and provide access to the so-called objects via an inheritance mechanism. Object-oriented programming is a natural, evolutionary step that adds features to the procedural language abstraction in order to solve technical problems that arise in the use and reuse of data and program structures.

Other changes to the procedural abstraction have been made to accommodate concurrent programming. Languages like Ada, Modula, and Linda have added some notion of multitasking in a manner that interacts with existent program structures for procedures and functions.

Apart from the evolution of procedural programming, important abstraction improvements have been made in the areas of functional, logic, and collection-oriented languages. These improvements have sought to change the view of programming altogether. They can be viewed more as revolutionary changes than the more characteristic evolutionary changes just described.

A programming language provides the fundamental level of abstraction for problem solving with a computer. It demarcates the point where the human leaves off and the system takes over in the process of translating the problem solution into a set of actions to be performed by the computer. Language compilers, or interpreters, perform all subsequent translation.

The fundamental level of abstraction is very important. It defines the basis for the way we organize our activities to solve problems; that is, the fundamental level of abstraction is the basis for the software process model.

FEATURES OF A GOOD LANGUAGE

As a theory for problem solving, a language should satisfy certain objective requirements. The degree to which these requirements are met determines the significance of a language as a theory. Before a community invests time and money in designing and performing experiments related to a proposed language, it should ensure that the following features are present in that language.

First the language must be *unambiguous*. To satisfy this requirement there must be a mathematical definition of the syntax *and* semantics of the language. The *syntax* of a language provides a precise definition of the rules employed in order to construct grammatically correct (i.e., valid) sentences in the language. *Backus-Naur Form (BNF)* is commonly used for syntax definitions. *Attribute grammars* are another form used in syntax definition, permitting the description of semantic constraints such as data typing constraints.

The *semantics* of a language provide a precise definition of the meaning of a sentence stated in the language. Semantics can be stated using the denotational, axiomatic, or operational approaches, or through the use of other formal languages. Consider, as an example, a syntactic definition of the natural numbers,

$$T = \{zero, succ(zero), succ(succ(zero)), \ldots\}$$

The Backus-Naur Form allows for the construction of a finite set of rules that define how any element of the infinite set, T, is constructed. In other words, the finite set of recursive rules defines an infinite set of elements:

$$T ::= zero \mid succ(T)$$

Now consider the set of natural numbers:

$$N = \{0,1,2,3, \ldots\}$$

Formal semantics are given in a function definition. The function maps from the syntactic set T, to the semantic set, N, that is, $m{:}T \rightarrow N$. Equations define the function m. For example, consider the equations that perform the simple mapping from elements of T to elements of N:

$$
\begin{aligned}
m(zero) &= 0 &\quad(1)\\
m(succ(T)) &= +(m(T),1) &\quad(2)
\end{aligned}
$$

Using Equations 1 and 2, we can map precisely (i.e., unambiguously) from a syntactic to a semantic object:

$$
\begin{aligned}
m(succ(succ(zero))) &= ^{(2)}\\
+(m(succ(zero)),1) &= ^{(2)}\\
+(+(m(zero),1),1) &= ^{(1)}\\
+(+(0,1),1) &= 2
\end{aligned}
$$

Notice that the left-hand side (LHS) of Rules 1 and 2 refers to syntactic structures, while the right-hand side (RHS) indicates the semantics of the syntactic structure. Once the rules have been developed they can be analyzed to determine if ambiguity exists in the language definition. For example, if there are two rules with the same LHS but differing RHSs, then there are two meanings for one syntactic structure. Whenever multiple interpretations exist for the same syntactic structure, ambiguity exists in the language.

With the following modification to the Backus-Naur Form rule,

$$T ::= zero \mid succ(T) \mid T + T$$

together with additional semantic equations,

$$m(zero + zero) \qquad = 0 \qquad\qquad (3)$$
$$m(succ(T) + zero) \qquad = m(succ(T)) \qquad (4)$$
$$m(zero + succ(T)) \qquad = m(succ(T)) \qquad (5)$$
$$m(succ(T1) + succ(T2)) = +(m(T1 + T2),2) \ (6)$$

one can provide for more sophisticated, yet equally precise mappings that specify the addition of natural numbers. Consider the expression *succ(succ(zero))* + *succ(succ(zero))*:

$$m(succ(succ(zero)) + succ(succ(zero))) =^{(6)}$$
$$+(m(succ(zero) + succ(zero)),2) \qquad =^{(6)}$$
$$+(+(m(zero + zero),2),2) \qquad =^{(3)}$$
$$+(+(0,2),2) \qquad\qquad = \quad 4$$

Now consider the expression *succ(zero)* + *succ(succ(zero))*:

$$m(succ(zero) + succ(succ(zero))) =^{(6)}$$
$$+(m(zero + succ(zero)),2) \qquad =^{(5)}$$
$$+(m(\ succ(zero)),2) \qquad\qquad =^{(2)}$$
$$+(+(m(zero),1),2) \qquad\qquad =^{(1)}$$
$$+(+(0,1),2) \qquad\qquad = \quad 3$$

The formal (i.e., unambiguous) syntax and semantic definitions of a language are objective requirements that a new language should satisfy.

Another requirement for a good computer language has to do with its size. It must possess a small number of features that are easy to combine in any number of ways in order to produce complex problem solutions. Such languages are called *orthogonal*. They allow one to design complex problem solutions through the interaction of a small set of language features. The syntax of a language provides important insight into the extent to which one can claim that the language is orthogonal. Consider the following grammar definitions:

```
FOR      ::= for id := E to E do ?;
WHILE    ::= while C do ?;
IF       ::= if C then ? else ?;
ASSIGN   ::= id := E;
READ     ::= readln(id);
WRITE    ::= writeln(E);
STATE    ::= FOR | WHILE | IF | ASSIGN | READ |
             WRITE | STATE; STATE
```

If one replaces all the question marks in the preceding definitions with the nonterminal STATE, the language has a good degree of orthogonality. The goodness is due to the fact that one is able to nest any control structure inside any other control structure.

The *writability* of a language has to do with how difficult it is to encode a problem solution. In general, an orthogonal language is arguably more writable than a nonorthogonal language. For the same reason, the *readability* of the orthogonal language—the ability to decipher the problem solution—is an improvement over nonorthogonal languages.

The *conciseness of the problem solutions* that can be developed in a language is often considered a requirement for a good language; however, conciseness must be considered within the context of a language's readability and writability. For example, suppose a language has a unique one-character symbol for each problem solution known to humankind—obviously requiring an infinite supply of one-character symbols. Now assume that in this language the pound symbol (#) represents a heap-sort program. The solution to the sort and any other problem in this language is definitely as concise as can be envisioned, but a problem exists in regard to its readability and writability. To be an effective problem solver, the programmer who writes or reads the program must recall that the pound symbol represents the heap-sort program and must remember this fact as distinguished from the potentially infinite number of other pairings between a single symbol and a problem solution.

The table-lookup quality to this hypothetical language would seem to go against the traditional efforts of computer scientists. Beginning with Alan Turing, computer scientists have focused on the identification of a small set of primitive elements that constitute problem solving. The design and choice of the primitives takes into consideration the degree to which they can be combined to "build up" complicated problem solutions. Thus, the conciseness of the language itself (rather than the size of the problem solutions written in the language), together with the degree to which the language constructs can be combined (i.e., the orthogonality of the language) would seem to be higher priority features. In a language with these higher priority features, however, the conciseness of solutions becomes a reasonable metric.

A good programming language is capable of representing the Universal Turing Machine. Such *Turing-computable languages* can solve any problem that can be stated as an algorithm. Simply put, an *algorithm* is a set of easy-to-follow instructions that, given an input, will produce a result. [Cohen86] Implied by the previous statement is the requirement that the algorithm will "halt." Given an arbitrary input, an algorithm must produce an answer (or result) in a finite amount of time. Thus, a language that can state any possible algorithm is Turing-computable and is capable of solving any solvable problem (i.e., one for which there is an algorithmic solution).

Coherence is another necessary feature of a good language. [Zave] Coherence requires that language features be drawn from the same abstraction level. Recall the quote given earlier (under the head "Theoretical Language Research") from Wirth: "One of the most crucial steps in the design of a language is the choice of abstraction upon which programs are to base." Two sentences later, in the same text, Wirth says, "[The language designer] should restrict his selection [of language features] from the same level which are in some sense compatible with each other." [Wirth74]

Coherence of a language is important because it avoids the problem of a programmer having to understand a given program on two differing levels of abstraction. Suppose there is a version of a procedural language like Pascal that allows the programmer to *dip* into the assembler level of representation. If a change is made to a program in this language, the programmer must understand the change at both the Pascal and the assembler level. In other words, it is necessary to understand the interaction of the machine code generated by the compiler and the assembler code embedded in the source program. A coherent language will not present this problem.

Good languages also have *regularity*, meaning that language features operate in a consistent and uniform manner independent of context. Put another way, regularity requires similar actions to have similar consequences. One way to view regularity is from the standpoint of a human interface. A computer system that has a mouse ought to have the mouse button(s) perform in a uniform manner at all times. Suppose a mouse has two buttons. If button X opens any available pop-up windows at the operating system level, it should do the same for any application program one might enter from the operating-system level. If button X performs function A in one application program and function B in another, the overall interface design is not consistent, not regular, and not particularly good.

Now we begin to migrate away from objective requirements into the realm of nonobjective requirements. A qualitative measure of a language is that it be *intuitive*, meaning that it allows the problem solver to follow instinct and intuition in solving the problem. Since intuitiveness is a qualitative measure, one can determine whether one language is more intuitive than another only through experimentation. Experimental computer science is costly and rarely done for language comparisons. However, if languages can be shown to meet most of the objective requirements discussed thus far, it would be ideal if they could be compared experimentally for the more qualitative characteristics.

EXPERIMENTAL SCIENCE: COMMENTARY

At least two approaches to empirical language studies are possible. The first approach involves careful evaluation of a language leading to a value judgment on the part of the researcher. This approach is not unlike the one Wirth took in the Oberon project. [See Wirth92]

The formalisms developed to describe languages are analogous to the differential equations employed in describing and modeling physical phenomena. Just as the study of the models of physical phenomena has led to breakthroughs in physics, so the study of mathematical models describing language approaches will likely advance our understanding of problem solving.

The second approach to empirical language studies involves the development of controlled experiments, in which case measurements must be devised and controls established for variables. To some extent, computer scientists are like physicists attempting to study thermodynamics without a thermometer. Nonetheless, controlled experiments need to be undertaken.

If software advances are to keep pace with hardware advances, languages and other software tools must improve the productivity of software engineers. The more intuitive those languages and other tools are, the better they will facilitate productivity in problem solving. The degree of intuitiveness of a language is a nonobjective consideration that requires controlled experimentation of at least two major forms:

1. To determine which languages are best suited for a given type of problem solver.
2. To determine which languages are best suited for a given type or domain of problems.

Ideally, computer language research should be based upon a framework similar to that found in the physical sciences, wherein there is a healthy interaction between theory and experiment, each driving the other.

Suppose one viewed a new language as a theory about how to best approach a certain type of problem solving. The language would be expected to meet certain criteria, like those discussed earlier. Once the theory was accepted, the language would be subjected to experimental research, comparing it empirically with competing language approaches. The experimental activity might require sociological and psychological testing to determine which language provided the most intuitive approach.

Unfortunately, there is no pervasive and well-organized experimental arm of computer language research. When languages are introduced, some are adopted by industry for use and others are not, more or less arbitrarily. This, combined with the tendency of some language designers to rush their languages to application before they are carefully studied (like Wirth accomplished in the Oberon project) culminates in a situation where neither approach to empirical study is accomplished for most new languages. Those languages adopted for use are employed in industry to develop software with few if any empirical studies being done beforehand. For a particular company, it may be the case that a poor language choice is made. Typically the company has invested a sizable amount of money in software written in the undesirable language before realizing what a poor choice it is and therefore must continue to use it. Indeed, some poorly designed languages become *stuck* in industry.

The industrial situation described here is the closest approximation computer language research has to an experimental community. But it is not a true experimental community, because there are no controlled experiments, and the falsification of a theory is not always possible. *Falsification* refers to the demonstration that another language theory provides a more suitable model of problem solving for a given domain. Regrettably, industry cannot afford to engage in the falsification of language theories. Yet, falsification is critical to language design if the goal of keeping pace with hardware advances is to be realized. Nonintuitive and poorly designed languages that become stuck in industrial practice are counterproductive to software advances.

The problem is threefold. First, people using the poor languages are certainly not as productive as they would be if they were using better designed, more intuitive languages. Second, when poor languages are used, research resources are expended on efforts to determine practices and tools to improve the productivity of those who work, at a disadvantage, with the poor languages. Third, the lack of falsification subverts the feedback from the experimental to the theoretical communities.

Based upon the interaction between the theoretical and experimental communities of the physical sciences, Thomas Kuhn, in his now classic text *The Structure of Scientific Revolutions*, identified two types of theoretical science. The first, called *ordinary science*, attempts to modify, extend, or refine theories so that they do a better job explaining empirical results that are not explained by the unrefined theories. The second, called *extraordinary science*, takes place when a radically new view (or theory) is proposed that explains empirical evidence, subsuming the old theory and all of its subsequent refinements. Extraordinary science results in paradigm shifts and in scientific revolutions.

A good example of a scientific revolution is the shift from Ptolemaic to Copernican astronomy. In the Ptolemaic theory (or abstraction) the planets and stars were viewed as orbiting the earth. The Copernican view radically changed our understanding of literally the ground we stand upon since it views the earth and the other planets as orbiting the sun.

One can argue that there have been examples of extraordinary science in language research, beginning with the Von Neumann architecture, then FORTRAN, Lisp, Algol/Pascal (to a lesser degree), and Prolog. The revolutionary approaches of greatest impact were the Von Neumann architecture and FORTRAN. Many will argue that the object-oriented approach is revolutionary as well. However, one can also argue the other side—that the object-oriented approach is a refinement (and improvement) to the procedural approach and manifests an evolutionary rather than revolutionary impact.

DESIGN OF THE TEXT

In this book the reader will study the methods and mathematical tools employed to design a language. The first section presents the methods to define a language syntactically and semantically and then explains how to develop a simple interpreter for a small language. The second section shows how to learn a new language. This section will be based upon the "constructs" for procedural languages by means of which the reader will explore each of the paradigms: the imperative (or procedural), object oriented, functional, logical, and collection-oriented languages.

REFERENCES

Jeremy Bernstein. *The Analytical Engine: Computers—Past, Present + Future*. Toronto: Vintage Books, 1963.

Wojciech Cellary. "Knowledge and Software Engineering in the Global Information Society," Keynote Address, *International Conference on Software Engineering and Knowledge Engineering 2000*. Chicago: July, 2000.

Daniel I.A. Cohen. *Introduction to Computing Theory.* New York: John Wiley and Sons, 1986.

Jacques Cohen. "A View of the Origins and Development of Prolog." *CACM* 31, no. 1 (January 1988):26–36.

Kenneth Ford. "Cognitive Prostheses," Keynote Address, *Ninth International Conference on Tools with Artificial Intelligence.* Newport Beach, CA: November, 1997.

Murray Gell-Mann. *The Quark and the Jaguar.* New York: W. H. Freeman & Company, 1995.

Thomas Kuhn. *The Structure of Scientific Revolutions.* Chicago: Chicago University Press, 1962.

David Parnas. "On Criteria to Be Used in Decomposing Systems into Modules." *CACM* 14, no. 1 (April 1972):221–227.

N. Wirth. "On the Design of Programming Languages." *Proc. IFIP Congress 74.* Amsterdam-New York: North-Holland Publishing Co., 1974, 386–393.

N. Wirth and J. Gutknecht. *Project OBERON: The Design of an Operating System and Compiler.* Reading, MA: Addison-Wesley, 1992.

P. Zave. "An Insider's Evaluation of PAISLey." *IEEE Transactions on Software Engineering* 17, no.3 (March 1991):212–225.

QUESTIONS AND EXERCISES

1. Write a program to read in an arbitrary set of digits one at a time. As you do, convert the set of digits from ASCII to an integer upon which you can do arithmetic. Do not use any built-in language features (or objects) that, for example, convert a character string to an integer. The program is meant to demonstrate the concept of mapping from a syntactic object (i.e., ASCII digits) to a semantic object (i.e., the type integer).

2. Modify the program developed for Question 1 to convert from an ASCII set of digits and the decimal point to the type real (or floating-point).

3. Modify the semantic equations for adding natural numbers:

$$
\begin{array}{lll}
m(zero) & = 0 & (1) \\
m(succ(T)) & = +(m(T),1) & (2) \\
m(zero + zero) & = 0 & (3) \\
m(succ(T) + zero) & = m(succ(T)) & (4) \\
m(zero + succ(T)) & = m(succ(T)) & (5) \\
m(succ(T1) + succ(T2)) & = +(m(T1 + T2),2) & (6)
\end{array}
$$

to provide for multiplication:

$$T ::= zero \mid succ(T) \mid T + T \mid T*T$$

SECTION ONE

LANGUAGE DESIGN
AND INTERPRETATION

2

LANGUAGE SYNTAX DESIGN

The goal of syntax design is to establish a finite definition that can be used to construct a valid sentence from a potentially infinite language. A syntax definition is required in any language to lend predictability, protocol, and efficiency to communication. Imagine a world with a vocabulary but without syntax. Consider the sentence, "I like you." In the absence of a grammar that provides predictability as to where the subject, verb, and object of a sentence appears, I can choose to express this thought in any of the following ways:

I like you.
You like I.
Like I you.
Like you I.
I you like.
You I like.

Some of the preceding sentences could easily be interpreted as expressing the idea that you like me rather than I like you, or that I think you are *like* me. Without grammatical rules, the simple idea I want to express may never be communicated. The same principle holds true for computer languages.

This chapter introduces formal *metalanguages*, which are used to discuss and describe *target languages*, meaning languages that are being designed. These metalanguages are called *formal languages* because they have a precise, mathematical semantic definition. In Chapter 1, the reader was introduced to the semantics of positive integer addition. The metalanguage[1] employed to describe these semantics was a simple functional language. Computer languages are more complicated and require more powerful metalanguages for their definition.

BACKGROUND FOR LANGUAGE SYNTAX DESIGN

Let us adopt the following notational conventions from *set theory* and *automata theory*. Let S, $S1$, and $S2$ be arbitrary sets of elements. Assume the standard meaning for the set operators: union ($\cup$), intersection ($\cap$), Cartesian product ($\times$), membership (ϵ), containment ($\supseteq$ and $\supset$), and $|S|$ as giving the number of elements in (or the cardinality of) S. Let ϕ = the null set, and $S1 + S2 \in S1 \cup S2$. The expression $S1 + S2$ designates an arbitrary element from either set, $S1$ or $S2$. Also needed is an expression to denote all strings of $n > 0$ characters from set S. To denote an arbitrary string formed using n elements of S, we shall employ $S^1 = S$ and if $n > 1$ then $S^n = S \times S^{n-1}$. The expression $S^* = S^0 \cup S^1 \cup \cdots \cup S^n \cup \cdots$, where S^0 is the empty string, denotes all strings of words producible from the elements of set S. This last set is necessarily an infinite one.

The first step in designing a target language is to establish an initial syntax. It is an "initial" syntax because language design typically requires an iterative activity. One may have to redesign the language syntax at a later date.

The syntax of a language revolves around its *vocabulary*, which is the exhaustive set of words and symbols one can use when constructing sentences in the language. A *sentence* in a programming language is a program. The vocabulary of a programming language is the full set of reserved words and symbols of the language together with the complete sets of legal constants and identifiers. The vocabulary of Pascal, for example, includes the reserved words *readln, read, writeln, write, while, do, for,* and *to* and the symbols $+$, $-$, $*$, and *div*, among other symbols and reserved words.

Syntax is concerned with how one combines elements of the vocabulary to produce understandable sentences in the language. In other words, the first step in deciphering the meaning of a sentence is to make certain that the sentence is in a form conducive to understanding—recall the "I like you" example, which demonstrates the need for a protocol for communication. Rarely does a language consist of all possible strings producible from its vocabulary. Stated differently, a language is rarely a set of Cartesian products on its vocabulary; that is, rarely is it true that a language equals the closure of its vocabulary, or $L = V^*$. The syntax of a language, L, constrains it to be some subset of V^*, that is, $V^* \supset L$, where L is the set of all sentences that belong to the language, and V^* is the set of all possible strings that can be formed with the language vocabulary.

---

[1]Some metalanguages may themselves be implemented as computer languages.

SET NOTATION AS METALANGUAGE
FOR SYNTAX DESCRIPTION

A simple approach to syntax design is to enumerate all valid sentences in the target language. This approach requires two constraints on the language:

1. Finite vocabulary.
2. Limit (or upper bound) on the length of a sentence.

Consider a simple language, L, where vocabulary $L(V) = \{me, you, like\}$, and no sentence in L can contain more than two words from $L(V)$.

    Therefore,

$L = L(V) \cup$
{<me,me>, <me,you>, <me,like>, <you,me>, <you,you>, <you,like>, <like,me>, <like,you>, <like,like>}

or, stated more succinctly:

$L = L(V) \cup (L(V) \times L(V))$.

Tuples are given in the preceding equations (e.g., <me,you>) in order to provide for a collection produced as a Cartesian product. An alternative to this notation is to simply concatenate the strings combined through the Cartesian product:

$L = L(V) \cup$
{meme, meyou, melike, youme, youyou, youlike, likeme, likeyou, likelike}

    Given L as before and an arbitrary sentence, s, it is possible to determine if s is valid by checking to see if it is an element of L with $s \in L$. If we refer to $L(V)$ by V, and we adopt the previous conventions—where V^n indicates all strings of length, n, that you can form from V (i.e., $V^n = V \times V^{n-1}$), and V^* denotes the infinite set of all finite strings of any length that you can form from V (i.e., $V^* = V^0 \cup V^1 \cup \cdots \cup V^n \cup \cdots$ where V^0 is the empty string)— then it becomes possible to restate L with $\{s \mid s \in V^0 \cup V^1 \cup V^2\}$. If we relax either restriction on the language (i.e., that either V or the length of sentences be limited to some finite size), the set L becomes infinite. Therefore, it is impossible to check membership by comparing with all elements of L, because you must store an infinite set to check for membership. What we need is another metalanguage that is capable of expressing, in a precise way, how one can construct a valid element of L.

    Using the conventions from automata theory and set-builder notation, it is possible to define infinite sets such as

    Evens $= \{x \mid x \in$ INTEGERS $\& x \bmod 2 = 0\}$

There is profound power in a definition like the preceding. In fact, set theory is a "metalanguage" that allows one to give finite definitions of infinite sets.

NOTATIONAL CONVENTION 1

Before we continue, we need to review some additional notational conventions. To review the conventions already introduced, assume $S1$ and $S2$ are sets. $S1^*$ is the set of all finite strings one may build using the elements of $S1$, including the empty string. $S1 + S2$ is an element of $S1 \cup S2$. Therefore, $(S1 \cup S2)^*$ is the set containing any string one can build using elements of $S1$ or $S2$. For example, if $S1 = \{a,b\}$ and $S2 = \{c,d\}$, then

$S1 \cup S2 \quad = \{a,b,c,d\}$
$(S1 \cup S2)^2 = \{aa,ab,ac,ad,ba,bb,bc,bd,ca,cb,cc,cd,da,db,dc,dd\}$
$(S1 \cup S2)^* = \{a,b,c,d,aa,ab,ac,ad,ba,bb,bc,bd,ca,cb,cc,cd,da,db,dc,dd,$
$\qquad\qquad aaa,aab,aac,aad, . . .\}$

Additionally, there is need for conventions allowing α and β to serve as any possible string of vocabulary or category symbols[1]:

$\alpha \in (C \cup V)^*$

and

$\beta \in (C \cup V)^*$

Recall that this definition allows α and β to be empty strings.

[1]Category symbols will be introduced in the next section.

In Chapter 1 the *Backus-Naur Form* (BNF) was used to provide the rules for sentences representing counting numbers. BNF is also used to state the rules for a grammar, typically referred to as *productions*. Following is an example of two sets of productions, one in the left column and another in the right column.

D	$::= 0$		D	$::= 0$
	$::= 1$		D	$::= 1$
	$::= 2$		D	$::= 2$
	$::= 3$		D	$::= 3$
	$::= 4$		D	$::= 4$
	$::= 5$		D	$::= 5$
	$::= 6$		D	$::= 6$
	$::= 7$		D	$::= 7$
	$::= 8$		D	$::= 8$
	$::= 9$		D	$::= 9$
I	$::= ID$		I	$::= ID$
	$::= D$		I	$::= D$

Both of these sets are equivalent. The one in the left column follows a more commonly used approach, where left-hand-side (LHS) symbols are not repeated for right-hand-side (RHS) alternatives.

Recall that a language, L, can be an infinite set of sentences that are valid combinations of the language's vocabulary, that is, $L(V)$. A language's grammar, $L(G)$, is a finite set of rules governing the construction of the legal sentences of L. More formally stated, given $L(G)$, and an arbitrary sentence, s, if one can derive s from the starting point $L(S)$ for $L(G)$, then s must be an element of L. This last sentence, stated formally, is $(L(S) \overset{*}{\Rightarrow} s)$ *iff* $(s \in L)$. This statement says that s is derivable, in zero-to-many steps $\overset{*}{\Rightarrow}$ using the starting point and productions of $L(G)$ *iff* s is an element of L. Consider the following simple derivation for the sentence $s = 123$:

$$I \Rightarrow ID \Rightarrow I3 \Rightarrow ID3 \Rightarrow I23 \Rightarrow D23 \Rightarrow 123$$

Thus, the production rules, P, of a programming language are typically given in a formal specification language, BNF, that is based upon predicate calculus. The most primitive form of BNF is indeed small, but extremely powerful. In the next section we will elaborate on the basics of BNF.

NOTATIONAL CONVENTION 2

We can now introduce additional notational conventions. Uppercase A and B are used as metasymbols to denote arbitrary elements of the category set (i.e., $A \in C$, and $B \in C$). Likewise, lowercase a and b are employed as metasymbols to denote arbitrary elements of the vocabulary set (i.e., $a \in V$, and $b \in V$).

BACKUS-NAUR FORM (BNF)

John Backus was the leader of the team that designed FORTRAN. He introduced the beginnings of the notation that we now call BNF in the late 1950s. In the early 1960s he and Peter Naur worked on a predecessor of Pascal called Algol and thereby made the modifications in the notation for syntax description that resulted in BNF.

The basic components of BNF are a *vocabulary set*, denoted by V, a *syntactic category set*, denoted by C, and the rewrite symbol (::=). Vocabulary symbols are often called *terminals*, and syntactic categories are often called *nonterminals*. Recall that $C \cap V = \phi$.

The basic form of a syntax rule is

LEFTHANDSIDE ::= RIGHTHANDSIDE

The left-hand-side (LHS) of a rule is an element of a syntactic category. The right-hand-side (RHS) can be any combination of elements from either V or C:

LHS ::= RHS
where LHS $\in C$, and RHS $\in \{V \cup C\}^*$

Consider, in the way of an example, LI, the language of integers. There is a mistake in the first attempt at defining the grammar, but it will be corrected in a later version and is placed here to show that one's first attempt at a grammar definition is not always successful.

In defining the language of integers, one first identifies the vocabulary $LI(V)$ = {0,1,2,3,4,5, 6,7,8,9,−} and the syntactic categories $LI(C)$= {D,I}, where D stands for a syntactic category, digits, and I stands for the category of integers and serves as the start symbol for derivations. Now it is possible to elaborate the BNF, or $LI(P)$:

$$
\begin{array}{ll}
D & ::= 0 \\
  & ::= 1 \\
  & ::= 2 \\
  & ::= 3 \\
  & ::= 4 \\
  & ::= 5 \\
  & ::= 6 \\
  & ::= 7 \\
  & ::= 8 \\
  & ::= 9 \\
I & ::= ID \\
  & ::= -ID \\
  & ::= D \\
  & ::= -D
\end{array}
$$

Notice that the grammar can be organized formally:

$LI(G) = (LI(V),LI(C),LI(P),LI(S))$

where

$LI(V) = \{0,1,2,3,4,5,6,7,8,9,-\}$
$LI(C) = \{D,I\}$
$LI(P) = \{D::=0,\cdots,D::=9,I::=ID,I::=-ID,I::=D,I::=-D\}$
$LI(S) = I$

These rules indicate that a digit is a zero (0), a one (1), . . . , or a nine (9). Now it is possible to determine whether some sentence, s, is an element of the language of integers, LI (i.e., $s \in L$). Rather than checking for set membership, we will see whether we can derive s using the grammar $LI(G)$—a computable approach to language recognition. Each step in the derivation is denoted by $\Rightarrow$. In *LI* the start symbol is *I*. Consider the derivation when *s* is -47653:

$$I \Rightarrow I\underline{D} \Rightarrow \underline{I}3 \Rightarrow I\underline{D}3 \Rightarrow \underline{I}53 \Rightarrow I\underline{D}53 \Rightarrow \cdots \Rightarrow \underline{I}7653 \Rightarrow -\underline{D}7653 \Rightarrow -47653$$

Each derivation step replaces an LHS category symbol with an appropriate RHS option. Each step must indicate a legal replacement based on the language productions. The goal is to remove all category symbols and have remaining only the exact string that was to be derived. If this goal is met, the string is valid; it is an element of the language, since it can be derived using the language's grammar. That is, $L(S) \overset{+}{\Rightarrow} s$ *iff* $s \in L$.

In this derivation, some steps are indicated by ellipses. As a rule, we will not employ the ellipses to summarize derivation steps. Instead, we will employ a special symbol to indicate one-to-many derivation steps:

$$\overset{+}{\Rightarrow}$$

or zero-to-many steps:

$$\overset{*}{\Rightarrow}$$

Now we can see the meaning of the formal definition, $LI(S) \overset{*}{\Rightarrow} s$ *iff* $s \in LI$, more clearly.

Consider now the derivation (or the attempted derivation) of $s = 45\#3$

$$I \Rightarrow I\underline{D} \Rightarrow \underline{I}3 \Rightarrow I\underline{D}3 \Rightarrow \underline{\text{error}}$$

After attempting all other possible derivations, we can conclude that 45#3 is not a valid sentence in the language generated by this grammar.

Consider the example $s = -43$. There are two possible derivations, even when we restrict the derivation to be rightmost or leftmost derivations. A rightmost derivation always derives the rightmost nonterminal in the current string next, as the underlined elements indicate in the following example:

$$I \Rightarrow I\underline{D} \Rightarrow \underline{I}3 \Rightarrow -\underline{D}3 \Rightarrow -43$$

or

$$I \Rightarrow -I\underline{D} \Rightarrow -\underline{I}3 \Rightarrow -\underline{D}3 \Rightarrow -43$$

The grammar must be corrected to disallow *ambiguous derivations*. A grammar is ambiguous if there is more than one left- or right-most derivation of the same string. While correcting the grammar, it is also possible to improve its readability by means of the following technique, which is often used in BNF: In the set *P* there are ten rules, with *D* serving as the LHS category symbol. These ten alternative definitions of *D* are rightly viewed as disjunctive. Through the use of the '|' symbol, one is able to represent a logical OR and abbreviate the original syntax description:

$D ::= 0 \mid 1 \mid 2 \mid 3 \mid 4 \mid 5 \mid 6 \mid 7 \mid 9$
$N ::= DN \mid D$
$I ::= N \mid -N$

With this grammar, it is no longer possible to derive -43 ambiguously. There is exactly one rightmost derivation, and there is exactly one leftmost derivation:

RIGHTMOST

$$\underline{I} \Rightarrow -\underline{N} \Rightarrow -D\underline{N} \Rightarrow -D\underline{D} \Rightarrow -\underline{D}3 \Rightarrow -43$$

LEFTMOST

$$\underline{I} \Rightarrow -\underline{N} \Rightarrow -\underline{D}N \Rightarrow -4\underline{N} \Rightarrow -4\underline{D} \Rightarrow -43$$

Consider this rule, which is said to be *right-recursive:*

$$N ::= DN \mid D$$

The *left-recursive* form of this rule turns out to have an equivalent meaning:

$$N ::= ND \mid D$$

From the standpoint of language translation, there are two fundamental approaches to syntax analysis. One of these approaches cannot be based on a grammar containing left-recursive rules. Given an arbitrary left-recursive grammar rule, there will be an algorithm to produce its right-recursive equivalent. You will see how to eliminate left recursion in Chapter 4.

The ability to construct a language of an infinite size is provided in the recursive rules of the language. Recursion can be *direct*, as exemplified in the rule $N ::= DN \mid D$, where the rule's LHS is referenced in a RHS alternative. Recursion can also be *indirect*, where a rule, $R1$, leads to some rule, Ri (derivable in some later step, $R1 \overset{*}{\Rightarrow} Ri$), and LHS$(R1)$ appears as a RHS alternative in Ri; that is, LHS$(R1) \in$ RHS(Ri).

Assume α and β are metasymbols that can represent any possible string (including the empty string) that one could construct from the sets C or V (i.e., $\alpha \in \{C \cup V\}^*$, and $\beta \in \{C \cup V\}^*$). A rule $A ::= \gamma A\Psi$ (where $\Psi \in \{C \cup V\}^*$, and $\gamma \in \{C \cup V\}^*$) is directly recursive when its LHS symbol, A, can satisfy the derivation step,

$$\alpha A\beta \Rightarrow \alpha\gamma A\Psi\beta$$

A rule is indirectly recursive if it is not directly recursive but can satisfy the derivation,

$$\alpha A\beta \overset{+}{\Rightarrow} \alpha'A\beta'$$

EXTENDED VERSIONS OF BNF

Additional symbols, like the $\mid$, have been introduced over the years to extend the BNF. All of these symbols reduce to the primitive BNF. In this book, assume that A and B are arbitrary nonterminal symbols (i.e., elements of C), and that a and b are arbitrary terminal symbols (i.e., elements of V):

$$A ::= a \mid b \qquad \text{is the same as} \qquad \begin{aligned} A &::= a \\ &::= b \end{aligned}$$

$A ::= B^+$ is the same as $A ::= B$
$B ::= a \mid b$ $B ::= aB \mid bB \mid a \mid b$

$A ::= B^*$ is the same as $A ::= B$
$B ::= a \mid b$ $B ::= aB \mid bB \mid \epsilon$

where epsilon (ϵ) represents the empty string:

$A ::= [a]b$ is the same as $A ::= b \mid ab$
$B ::= a \mid \cdots \mid e$ $B ::= a \mid b \mid c \mid d \mid e$

Now let's look at a more significant grammar—one for the construction of post-fix arithmetic expressions (where $x + y$ in infix is given as $xy+$ in postfix):

$V = \{*, /, +, -, a, \cdots, z\}$
$C = \{I, E\}$

$I ::= aE \mid \cdots \mid zE \mid a \mid \cdots \mid z$
$E ::= I{+}E \mid I{-}E \mid I{*}E \mid I/E \mid + \mid - \mid * \mid / \mid \epsilon$

EXAMPLE DERIVATION
$s = ab+cd+/$

$I \Rightarrow a\underline{E} \Rightarrow a\underline{I}{+}E \Rightarrow ab{+}\underline{E} \Rightarrow ab{+}\underline{I}/E \Rightarrow ab{+}c\underline{E}/E \Rightarrow ab{+}c\underline{I}{+}E/E$
$\Rightarrow ab{+}cd{+}E/\underline{E} \Rightarrow ab{+}cd{+}\epsilon/E \Rightarrow ab{+}cd{+}/\epsilon \Rightarrow ab{+}cd{+}/$

The linear derivation steps can be graphically depicted in a *derivation tree*. In the derivation tree shown in Figure 2.1, the root is the start symbol of the grammar. Recall that $s \in L$ *iff* $S \overset{*}{\Rightarrow} s$.

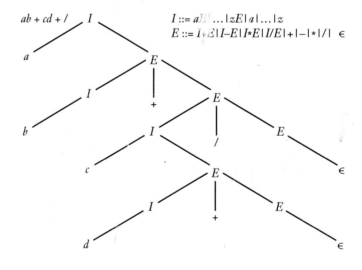

FIGURE 2.1

Consider an improvement wherein we add I as a RHS option of E:

$$I ::= aE \mid \cdots \mid zE \mid a \mid \cdots \mid z$$
$$E ::= I{+}E \mid I{-}E \mid I{*}E \mid I/E \mid + \mid - \mid * \mid / \mid I \mid \epsilon$$

With this change, has ϵ become superfluous?

EXAMPLE DERIVATION

$s = ab{+}cd{+}/$

$$I \Rightarrow a\underline{E} \Rightarrow a\underline{I}{+}E \Rightarrow ab{+}\underline{E} \Rightarrow ab{+}\underline{I}{+}E \Rightarrow ab{+}c\underline{E}{+}E \Rightarrow ab{+}c\underline{I}{+}E \Rightarrow ab{+}cd{+}\underline{E}$$
$$\Rightarrow ab{+}cd{+}/$$

In the next derivation tree shown in Figure 2.2 one can observe the origin of the terms *terminal* and *nonterminal*. All the leaves (terminating nodes in the tree) are labeled with vocabulary symbols. All of the interior nodes (nonterminating nodes) are labeled by syntactic category symbols. The left-to-right concatenation of the leaf (or terminal) elements forms the derived string.

A WHILE LANGUAGE

Now consider the syntax for the infix arithmetic expression:

$$E ::= T \mid E + T \mid E - T$$
$$T ::= F \mid T * F \mid T / F$$
$$F ::= (E) \mid \text{id} \mid \text{cons}$$

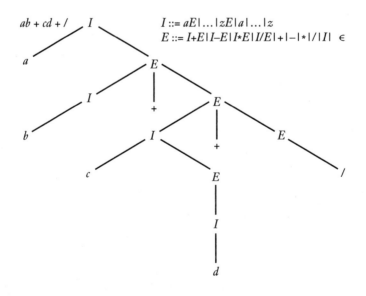

FIGURE 2.2

In this section the BNF for an entire language will be given, making use of the infix arithmetic expressions. The example language is called a WHILE language (i.e., *LW*). It is of interest in language design because, to some extent, it is the smallest procedural language that is Turing computable.

Recall from Chapter 1 that a Turing-computable language is a language that you can use to solve any solvable problem. In the mid 1960s Böhm and Jacopini proved that in terms of control structures, the only requirements for computability are (1) the ability to state a sequence of statements and (2) the WHILE-LOOP construct. With the WHILE it is possible to produce any other control structure. A WHILE loop can be a counting loop, and it can also be an IF-THEN-ELSE structure. Consider the following examples:

PASCAL

$f := 1;$
read$(n);$
for $i := 1$ to n do $f := f^*i;$

WHILE LANGUAGE

$f := 1;$
$i := 1;$
read$(n);$
while $i <= n$ do
$\quad\quad f := f^*i;$
$\quad\quad i := i + 1$
od;

PASCAL

if $x <> 0$ then
$\quad\quad q := n$ DIV x
else
$\quad\quad q := -$maxint;

WHILE LANGUAGE

$t := x;$
while $x <> 0$ do
$\quad\quad q := n$ DIV $x;$
$\quad\quad x := 0$
od;
$x := t;$
while $x = 0$ do
$\quad\quad q := -$maxint;
$\quad\quad x := 1$
od;
$x := t;$

It is possible to build any conceivable control structure using the WHILE language. The resulting structures are not always as expressive or straightforward as the equivalent Pascal structures, but they can indeed be built!

The motivation for the Böhm proof was meant to show that the GOTO statement was not necessary for programming. Bear in mind that the context of Böhm's effort was a programming-language environment dominated by FOR-TRAN and COBOL programming: both languages promoted the use of the GOTO. Practitioners and others had difficulty letting go of the GOTO statement, and a debate about the need for a GOTO continued for almost a decade after the Böhm and Jacopini effort.

Here is the BNF for a very simple WHILE language, *LW(G)*:

$P ::= S$
$S ::= V:=E$ | read(*V*) | write(*V*) | while *C* do *S* od | *S;S*
$C ::= E < E$ | $E > E$ | $E = E$ | $E <> E$ | $E <= E$ | $E >= E$
$E ::= T$ | $E + T$ | $E - T$
$T ::= F$ | $T * F$ | T / F
$F ::= (E)$ | I | V
$V ::= a$ | b | $\cdots$ | z | aV | bV | $\cdots$ | zV
$I ::= 0$ | 1 | $\cdots$ | 9 | $0I$ | $1I$ | $\cdots$ | $9I$

Productions like *V* and *I* are not always elaborated as they are here, since they construct well-known lexemes of the language. A *lexeme* is considered to be a minimal lexical unit of a language. A *lexical unit* represents some subset of a language's vocabulary (or lexicon). Using this grammar, let us attempt to demonstrate that the following program is a valid sentence with respect to *LW(G)*:

```
s:=0;
i:=1;
while i<=10 do
    read(a);
    s:=s+a;
    i:=1+i
od
write(s)
```

In the derivation that follows, some obvious steps are summarized by the $\overset{*}{\Rightarrow}$ symbol—in particular, where a similar derivation has already been elaborated. Prior to each derivation step, the next category symbol to be replaced is underlined. In the derivation of the conditional portion of the WHILE statement, the expressions being compared are derived in parallel because of the symmetry of the given condition:

$\underline{P} \Rightarrow S$
$\Rightarrow \underline{S};S$
$\Rightarrow \underline{V}:=E \; ;S$
$\Rightarrow s:=\underline{E} \; ;S$
$\Rightarrow s:=\underline{T} \; ;S$
$\Rightarrow s:=\underline{F} \; ;S$
$\Rightarrow s:=\underline{I} \; ;S$
$\Rightarrow s:=0;\underline{S}$

$\Rightarrow s:=0;\underline{S};S$

$\Rightarrow s:=0;\ \underline{V:=E};S$

$\overset{+}{\Rightarrow} s:=0;\ i:=1;\underline{S}$

$\Rightarrow s:=0;\ i:=1;\underline{S};S$

$\Rightarrow s:=0;\ i:=1;$ while $\underline{C}$ do S od;$S \Rightarrow s:=0;\ i:=1;$ while $\underline{E1\ <=\ E2}$ do S od;S

$\Rightarrow s:=0;\ :=1;$ while $\underline{T1\ <=\ T2}$ do S od;$S \Rightarrow s:=0;\ i:=1;$ while $\underline{F1\ <=\ F2}$ do S od;S

$\Rightarrow s:=0;\ i:=1;$ while $\underline{V\ <=\ I}$ do S od;S

$\Rightarrow s:=0;\ i:=1;$ while $i <= 10$ do $\underline{S}$ od;$S \Rightarrow s:=0;\ i:=1;$ while $i <= 10$ do $\underline{S};S$ od;S

$\Rightarrow s:=0;\ i:=1;$ while $i <= 10$ do read$\underline{(V)};S$ od; S

$\Rightarrow s:=0;\ i:=1;$ while $i <= 10$ do read$\underline{(a)};S$ od; S

$\Rightarrow s:=0;\ i:=1;$ while $i <= 10$ do read$(a);\underline{S};S$ od; S

$\Rightarrow s:=0;\ i:=1;$ while $i <= 10$ do read$(a);\ \underline{V:=E};S$ od; S

$\Rightarrow s:=0;\ i:=1;$ while $i <= 10$ do read$(a);\ s:=\underline{E + T};\ S$ od;S

$\Rightarrow s:=0;\ i:=1;$ while $i <= 10$ do read$(a);\ s:=\underline{T + F};\ S$ od;S

$\Rightarrow s:=0;\ i:=1;$ while $i <= 10$ do read$(a);\ s:=\underline{F + V};\ S$ od;S

$\Rightarrow s:=0;\ :=1;$ while $i <= 10$ do read $(a);\ s:=\underline{V} + a;\ S$ od;S

$\Rightarrow s:=0;\ i:=1;$ while $i <= 10$ do read$(a);\ s:=s + a;\ \underline{S}$ od;S

$\overset{+}{\Rightarrow} s:=0;\ i:=1;$ while $i <= 10$ do read$(a);\ s:=s + a;\ i:=i+1$ od;$\underline{S}$

$\overset{+}{\Rightarrow} s:=0;\ i:=1;$ while $i <= 10$ do read$(a);\ s:=s + a;\ i:=i+1$ od;write(s)

A HIERARCHY OF LANGUAGES

The *hierarchy of languages* (defined by Noam Chomsky) [1956; 1959] is based on an ever increasing set of restrictions on the grammar rules of a language. In this discussion, we will assign the following meanings to the symbols:

C	A set of syntactic categories
V	A set of vocabulary symbols
A,B	Single elements of C
a,b	Single elements of V
α	A string of zero-to-many elements of $(C \cup V)$
β	A string of zero-to-many elements of $(C \cup V)$
$\alpha \mid \beta$	String α or string β
α^*	Zero-to-many occurrences of α
α^+	One-to-many occurrences of α

Now consider a general form for a syntax rule:

$\alpha ::= \beta$

A level in the hierarchy inherits the restrictions placed on previous levels. At the top level of the hierarchy are Type 0 languages. There are no restrictions on the grammar rules for Type 0 languages. They are called *recursively enumerable* languages and are equivalent to Turing machines.

Type 1 languages place the following restriction on grammar rules: Given $\alpha := \beta$, then $|\alpha| <= |\beta|$, where $|\alpha|$ is the number of symbols from either C or V that appear in α. This type of language is termed *context-sensitive*. Spoken languages are all context-sensitive.

Type 2 languages inherit all previous restrictions and furthermore require that $\alpha \in C$. Note the complete meaning of this restriction: the LHS contains exactly one nonterminal and nothing more. Languages at this level are termed *context-free*. A context-free language provides the necessary flexibility for describing a programming language.

Type 3 languages inherit all previous restrictions and furthermore require that all productions for a given language be either *right-linear* or *left-linear*, where right-linear is $\beta = aA \mid a$, and left-linear is $\beta = Aa \mid a$. This type of language is termed *regular*. It corresponds to the regular expressions recognizable by finite state automata.

In terms of programming language design, languages of Type 2 and 3 are of great interest in that we can construct tractable machines to recognize these types of languages. Consider first the Type 3 language. It allows us to read strings of characters and recognize vocabulary symbols of a computer language, $L(V)$. For example, consider the following Type 3 grammar:

$$L(V) = \{a, \cdots ,z, 0, \cdots ,9\}$$
$$L(C) = \{D, N, V\}$$

$$L(P) = \{$$
$$D ::= 0D \mid 1D \mid \cdots \mid 9 \mid 0 \mid 1 \mid \cdots \mid 9$$
$$N ::= -D \mid D$$
$$V ::= aV \mid bV \mid \cdots \mid zV \mid a \mid b \mid \cdots \mid z \}$$

The rules given satisfy the Type 3 restrictions. The vocabulary of this language is the set of characters that, when grouped according to the language rules $L(P)$, form constants or variables. Notice that the sentences of this Type 3 grammar form some of the vocabulary symbols (V and I) of the WHILE language, $LW(G)$, described earlier.

The Type 3 language is not powerful enough to describe nested structures. For that, we must allow for β with a size of 3 or more. Type 2 languages suffice:

$$S ::= (E)$$

Type 3 languages are not powerful enough to describe nested structures, because languages at level 3 (i.e., regular expressions) are equivalent to and recognized by a *finite state automata* (FSA). One cannot match or count symbols with an FSA. Assume the following general view of a sentence:

Leading_symbols S Trailing symbols

To match symbols one must be able to stack the leading symbols as they are encountered. Once S is recognized, one can match the trailing symbols with the leading symbols using successive *top/pop* stack operations.[2] Therefore, it is possible to check for the correctness of sentences such as

$$((9-8)/3)+4$$

To accomplish this, we add a stack to the FSA to form the *pushdown automata* (PDA). The PDA, which is capable of recognizing a context-free language, corresponds to the syntax-analysis portion of a language compiler. The lexical analysis of the compiler (which precedes syntax analysis) is accomplished by the FSA. The basic design of the front end of a compiler is depicted in Figure 2.3. Notice that the syntax and semantic analysis are accomplished in the same step. As each statement is found to be syntactically correct, the meaning of the statement is determined.

In the next chapter the denotational and axiomatic semantics are introduced as a means of formally defining the semantics of a programming language. Chapter 4 will focus on the basic design of a language translator (like that depicted in Figure 2.1).

---

[2]The discussion hints at the significance of the *palindrome*. FSAs cannot recognize palindromes at all. The pushdown automata (PDA), which recognizes context-free grammars, can recognize palindromes with a sentinel (like S above). A nondeterministic PDA can recognize a palindrome without a sentinel. To recognize palindromes without sentinels in a deterministic manner, one must have a 2PDA (i.e., an FSA with two stacks), which is equivalent to a Turing machine.

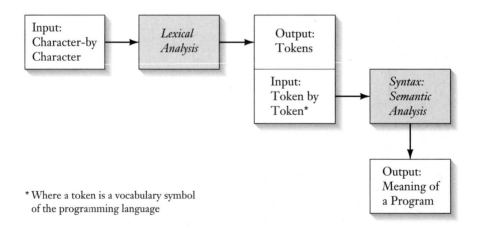

* Where a token is a vocabulary symbol
  of the programming language

FIGURE 2.3   Language translation.

REFERENCES

C. Böhm and G. Jacopini. "Flow Diagrams, Turing Machines, and Languages with Only Two Formation Rules." *Communications of the ACM* (May 1966: 366–371).

Noam Chomsky. "Three Models for the Description of Language." *IRE Transactions on Information Theory* 2, no. 3: 113–124.

Noam Chomsky. "On Certain Formal Properties of Grammars." *Information and Control* 2, no. 2: 137–167.

QUESTIONS AND EXERCISES

1. Given $L = \{s \mid s \in V^0 \cup V^1 \cup \ldots \cup V^n\}$ and the size of V is obtained with $\mid V \mid$, write an equation that will indicate the size of L—that is, $\mid L \mid$ is what?

2. Based upon the general form $\alpha A\beta \Rightarrow \alpha\gamma A\Psi\beta$ of a derivation involving direct recursion, modify the formula to characterize direct left recursion.

3. Ambiguity exists in the following grammar:

   D ::= 0
   ::= 1
   ::= 2
   ::= 3
   ::= 4
   ::= 5
   ::= 6
   ::= 7
   ::= 8
   ::= 9
   I ::= ID
   ::= $-ID$
   ::= D
   ::= $-D$

   To remove the ambiguity, we modified the grammar this way:

   $D ::= 0 \mid 1 \mid 2 \mid 3 \mid 4 \mid 5 \mid 6 \mid 7 \mid 9$
   $N ::= DN \mid D$
   $I ::= N \mid -N$

   What is a simpler modification that will also result in an unambiguous grammar?

4. Show the derivation tree that results from parsing the expression $(a+c)/d\$$ according to the following grammar, given start symbol S:

   S ::= $E\ \$$
   E ::= $T\ E1$
   $E1$ ::= $+T\ E1$

$$::= -T\ E1$$
$$::=$$

T $::= F\ T1$
$T1$ $::= *\ F\ T1$
      $::= /\ F\ T1$
$$::=$$
F $::= \text{id}$

5. Assume a WHILE language that enables you to write strings, connect relations with logical connectives (AND, OR, NOT), and write the result of an arithmetic expression. Write a WHILE language program segment that is equivalent to the following Java segment:

```
if (n==0)
        {write("error")}
else
        {write(n/d)}
```

6. Notice that the following grammar is ambiguous:

$P ::= S\$$
$S ::= V:=E \mid read(V) \mid write(V) \mid while\ C\ do\ S\ od \mid S;S$
$C ::= E1 < E2 \mid E1 > E2 \mid E1 = E2 \mid E1 <> E2 \mid E1 <= E2 \mid E1 >= E2$
$E ::= T \mid E + T \mid E - T$
$T ::= F \mid T * F \mid T / F$
$F ::= (E) \mid I \mid V$
$V ::= a \mid b \mid \cdots \mid z \mid aV \mid bV \mid \cdots \mid zV$
$I ::= 0 \mid 1 \mid \cdots \mid 9 \mid 0I \mid 1I \mid \cdots \mid 9I$

The ambiguity is demonstrated in the rightmost derivations of the program:

read(*a*);
read(*b*);
t:=*a*;
while*a*>*b* do $\cdots$ od
a:=*t*;
while*b*>*a* do $\cdots$ od$

$\underline{P} \Rightarrow \underline{S}\$ \Rightarrow \underline{S};S\$ \Rightarrow S;\underline{S};S\$ \Rightarrow S;S;\underline{S};S\$ \Rightarrow S;S;S;\underline{S};S\$ \Rightarrow S;S;S;S;\underline{S};S\$ \Rightarrow \cdots \Rightarrow$
$S;S;S;S;\underline{S};$ while*b*>*a* do $\cdots$ od$\Rightarrow \cdots \Rightarrow$
$S;S;S;\underline{S};$ *a*:=*t*;while*b*>*a* do $\cdots$ od$\Rightarrow \cdots \Rightarrow$
$S;S;\underline{S};$ while*a*>*b* do $\cdots$ od; *a*:=*t*;while*b*>*a* do $\cdots$ od$\Rightarrow \cdots \Rightarrow$
$S;\underline{S};$ *t*:=*a*; while*a*>*b* do $\cdots$ od; *a*:=*t*;while*b*>*a* do $\cdots$ od$\Rightarrow \cdots \Rightarrow$
$S;$ read(*b*); *t*:=*a*; while*a*>*b* do $\cdots$ od; *a*:=*t*;while*b*>*a* do $\cdots$ od$ \Rightarrow \cdots \Rightarrow$
read(*a*); read(*b*); *t*:=*a*; while*a*>*b* do $\cdots$ od; *a*:=*t*;while*b*>*a* do $\cdots$ od$

$\underline{P} \Rightarrow \underline{S}\$ \Rightarrow \underline{S};S\$ \Rightarrow \cdots \Rightarrow$
$\underline{S};$while*b*>*a* do $\cdots$ od$\Rightarrow$
$S;\underline{S};$while*b*>*a* do $\cdots$ od$\Rightarrow \cdots \Rightarrow$

$\underline{S};a:=t;\text{while}b>a \text{ do } \cdots \text{ od}\$\Rightarrow$
$\underline{S};\underline{S};a:=t;\text{while}b>a \text{ do } \cdots \text{ od}\$\Rightarrow \cdots \Rightarrow$
$\underline{S}; \text{while}a>b \text{ do } \cdots \text{ od};a:=t;\text{while}b>a \text{ do } \cdots \text{ od}\$\Rightarrow$
$\underline{S};\underline{S}; \text{while}a>b \text{ do } \cdots \text{ od};a:=t;\text{while}b>a \text{ do } \cdots \text{ od}\$\Rightarrow \cdots \Rightarrow$
$\underline{S}; t:=a; \text{while}a>b \text{ do } \cdots \text{ od};a:=t;\text{while}b>a \text{ do } \cdots \text{ od}\$\Rightarrow$
$\underline{S};\underline{S}; t:=a; \text{while}a>b \text{ do } \cdots \text{ od};a:=t;\text{while}b>a \text{ do } \cdots \text{ od}\$\Rightarrow \cdots \Rightarrow$
$\underline{S}; \text{read}(b); t:=a; \text{while}a>b \text{ do } \cdots \text{ od};a:=t;\text{while}b>a \text{ do } \cdots \text{ od}\$\Rightarrow \cdots \Rightarrow$
$\text{read}(a); \text{read}(b); t:=a; \text{while}a>b \text{ do } \cdots \text{ od}; a:=t;\text{while}b>a \text{ do } \cdots \text{ od}\$$

Correct the grammar to remove the ambiguity.

7. Construct the grammar(s) from which the following sentences are derived:

$A \Rightarrow c$

$A \Rightarrow aAa \Rightarrow aaAaa \Rightarrow aabAbaa \Rightarrow aabcbaa$

$A \Rightarrow bAb \Rightarrow bbAbb \Rightarrow bbaAabb \Rightarrow bbacabb$

3

LANGUAGE SEMANTICS DESIGN

Whereas the *syntax* of a target language defines the valid ways in which one can combine elements of the language vocabulary to form grammatically correct sentences, the *semantics* define the ways in which one can determine the meaning of a grammatically correct sentence. Chapter 2 presented a metalanguage for precisely defining the syntax of a target language. This chapter presents two metalanguages that are often used to provide precise definitions of the semantics of a language.

Just as there is an abstract definition for the syntax of a language, so there is an abstract definition for its semantics. Recall that the abstract syntax of a language is a set of rules that, with reference to the language vocabulary, define how to produce valid sentences in the language. Likewise, the semantic definitions of a language reference its abstract syntax rules to define precisely the meaning of the syntactic structure.

Languages with precise syntactic and semantic definitions are called *formal languages*. Those without these important attributes are likely to be syntactically and semantically *ambiguous*. For example, natural (or spoken) languages are not defined precisely and therefore have a lot of ambiguity. Consider the English word "nurse." The word is syntactically ambiguous because it can be a noun or a verb. Without clues from the context, the statement "Nurse!" could be viewed as a command to nurse (given the implied subject "you") or as a call for a nurse's attention (given the implied verb "come").

The purpose of a programming language is to provide instructions to a computer. Computers work as automatons. If a programmer tells the computer to perform Task A, the computer does not have the wherewithal to stop and ask the programmer what is meant by performing Task A. An automaton must carry out its work without clarification. Therefore, the meaning of the computer instructions must be absolutely clear. Precise semantics are required.

Once the syntax of a target language is defined formally, one can develop the target language's semantic description. In this chapter, two approaches to semantic definition are presented. First is the *denotational approach*, which is based on lattice theory and a lambda calculus–based metalanguage. Next is the *axiomatic approach*, which is based on a logiclike language.

DENOTATIONAL SEMANTICS

The denotational approach to language definition, developed by Scott-Strachey [Stoy], is based on *lattice theory*. A *lattice* is a partially ordered set, S, that has a least upper bound, called the *supremum* of S, and a greatest lower bound, called the *infimum* of S. The supremum is where elements of S join, and the infinum is where they meet. Consider the example in Figure 3.1, which depicts in a *Hasse diagram* the partial ordering of the subset relation on the power set of $\{a,b,c\}$, that is, $P\{a,b,c\}$:

Assume that the node containing $\{a,b,c\}$ is at level 0 of the diagram and that the null set, $\{\}$, is at level 3. One can see that the subsets of a level i set are found in level $i + 1$. The edges of the diagram connect a set with its corresponding subsets. In other words, the subset relation is the basis of the ordering. The elements of $P\{a,b,c\}$ join in the least upper bound, which is the set $\{a,b,c\}$, and meet in the greatest lower bound, which is the null set.

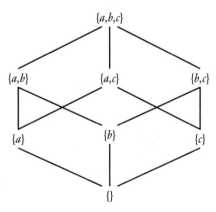

FIGURE 3.1   Hasse diagram.

The notion of *containment* is essential in the lattice. Whenever information is ordered by the subset relation, the ordering implies the amount of information contained in an element. For example, since {*a,b,c*} ⊇ {*b,c*}, the set {*a,b,c*} contains more information. The integers are ordered as shown in Figure 3.2. Note the integers are ordered as a "flat" set. The numerical ordering relation, ≤, does not convey the notion of containment (⊇). For example, the integer 3 does not "contain" the information of the integer 2. The special elements top and bottom, ⊤ and ⊥, respectively, indicate all values (a contradictory situation) and no values, respectively. These elements form the least upper bound and greatest lower bound of the integer lattice.

The goal of the denotational approach is to identify functions that *map* from a *syntactic domain* to a *semantic domain* (where domains may be infinite or finite). The semantic domains are based on the mathematical notion of the lattice—that is, semantic domains are not sets, they are lattices. Before mappings can be defined, we must first build up the domains involved in the mappings. We must also develop an understanding of another metalanguage that can precisely define how the functions perform their mappings.

To demonstrate, we will develop a small example language, *LE*, for arithmetic expressions:

$E ::= E + E \mid E - E \mid E * E \mid E / E \mid (E) \mid C$
$C ::= CD \mid D$
$D ::= 0 \mid 1 \mid 2 \mid \cdots \mid 9$

This grammatical definition corresponds with the BNF definitions from the previous chapter. Notice that there are no variables in this language; assume only integer constants. The syntactic domains of this language are:

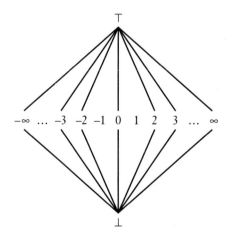

FIGURE 3.2   Integer lattice.

SYNTACTIC DOMAINS

C: Cons
E: Exp
D: Digits

The syntactic domains correspond to the LHSs of the productions. This is always the case. For every LHS of a production there is a syntactic domain. It seems clear that the mapping from one of *LE*'s syntactic objects (either *C, E,* or *D*), yields a semantic object from the domain of integers:

$$v:N = \{\cdots,-2,-1,0,1,2,\cdots\}$$

The complete semantic domain is referred to by *N*, while *v* is a metavariable that can take on any possible integer value. Semantic domains require two additional elements to denote the possibility of erroneous and undefined values. These values are represented by two special symbols: the top and bottom of a lattice, respectively:

Top: $\top$
Bottom: $\bot$

It is now possible to denote the semantic domain:

SEMANTIC DOMAIN

$$v:N = \{\top,\cdots,-2,-1,0,1,2,\cdots,\bot\}$$

This latter definition often appears as $\{\cdots,-2,-1,0,1,2,\cdots\}^{\circ}$, where the degree symbol ($^{\circ}$) denotes inclusion of $\bot$ and $\top$.

The next step involves the declaration of a *function*, which will map from a syntactic to a semantic domain. The general form of a function declaration is

$$\Sigma : \text{LHS} \rightarrow \text{semantic\_domain}$$

where Σ is a semantic function name, "LHS" in this function declaration is an LHS of a BNF rule, and "semantic_domain" is a previously defined semantic domain.

Now the semantic functions that will map from the syntactic domain of Exp to the semantic domain of *N*, and from Cons to *N* are declared:

SEMANTIC FUNCTION DECLARATION

$\varepsilon : \text{Exp} \rightarrow N$
$\iota : \text{Cons} \rightarrow N$
$\delta : \text{Digits} \rightarrow N$

Given an expression or a constant based on this BNF, a meaning is construed in terms of integers:

$$\varepsilon : \text{Exp} \rightarrow N$$

The preceding expression declares which syntactic domain is mapped to which semantic domain. The expression indicates that there is a function, ε, that maps from the syntactic Exp to the semantic *N*. It is now necessary for semantic equations to be elaborated for each semantic function so as to describe precisely *how* the mapping will take place.

Recall that for every LHS of the BNF there is a syntactic domain. It is also true that for every RHS option of the BNF there is a *semantic equation*. Semantic equations are of the general form,

$$f \ll \text{RHS} \gg = \text{semantic\_definition}$$

The symbol f is a semantic function previously declared. The RHS is a syntactic object as defined by a RHS option for the BNF. The equal (=) sign is a replacement operator. In determining the meaning of an instruction, see if you can match $f \ll \text{RHS} \gg$ precisely. If so, you can replace $f \ll \text{RHS} \gg$ with the corresponding "semantic_definition." The relationships among BNF, domains, semantic function declaration, and semantic equations are given in Figure 3.3.

A semantic equation states precisely how the mapping is to be performed. The operators, $\ll \gg$, are employed to enclose and isolate syntactic objects on the LHS of the semantic equations. The equations should be read as follows: the syntactic object in the operators, $\ll \gg$, on the LHS of the equal sign, =, is defined and replaced by the expression on the RHS of the equal sign.

SEMANTIC FUNCTION EQUATIONS

a.	$\varepsilon \ll E1+E2 \gg$	=	$\varepsilon \ll E1 \gg$	+	$\varepsilon \ll E2 \gg$
b.	$\varepsilon \ll E1-E2 \gg$	=	$\varepsilon \ll E1 \gg$	−	$\varepsilon \ll E2 \gg$
c.	$\varepsilon \ll E1*E2 \gg$	=	$\varepsilon \ll E1 \gg$	*	$\varepsilon \ll E2 \gg$
d.	$\varepsilon \ll E1/E2 \gg$	=	$\varepsilon \ll E1 \gg$	/	$\varepsilon \ll E2 \gg$

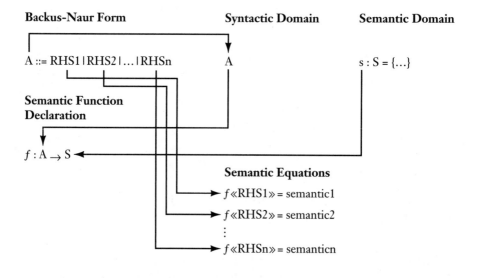

FIGURE 3.3 Relationships among syntax and semantics.

e.	$\varepsilon \ll (E) \gg$	$=$	$\varepsilon \ll E \gg$
f.	$\varepsilon \ll C \gg$	$=$	$\iota \ll C \gg$
g.	$\iota \ll CD \gg$	$=$	$((10 \times \iota \ll C \gg) + \delta \ll D \gg)$
h.	$\iota \ll D \gg$	$=$	$\delta \ll D \gg$
i.	$\delta \ll 0 \gg$	$=$	0
j.	$\delta \ll 1 \gg$	$=$	1
k.	$\delta \ll 2 \gg$	$=$	2
	$\vdots$		$\vdots$
r.	$\delta \ll 9 \gg$	$=$	9

The semantic equations define how to map from a syntactic specification of integer arithmetic to integers and integer arithmetic. For example, Equations "i" through "r" map from a syntactic integer digit to an integer. Equations "f" through "h" define how to map from multidigit syntactic integers to multidigit semantic integers. Equations "a" through "f" map from a specification of integer operations to the actual integer operations.

Consider the derivation of an integer. The mapping that follows is from a syntactic representation of a number to a semantic representation. Intuitively, the mapping can be viewed as analogous to a program—one that you may have written yourself—that converts an ASCII character representation of an integer to an integer representation—that is, a representation upon which you can perform numerical computations.

In the first step, you find the meaning of the syntactic characters 2345.

$$\iota \ll 2345 \gg \;=\; ((10 \times \iota \ll 234 \gg) + \delta \ll 5 \gg)$$

The function reference matches the LHS of semantic equation g. The reference $\iota \ll 2345 \gg$ is replaced by an appropriate instantiation equation "g" 's RHS, as seen on the right in the preceding displayed example. The resulting expression includes two references to semantic functions, $\iota \ll 234 \gg$ and $\delta \ll 5 \gg$. These references form the LHS of Equations "g" and "n," respectively. The references result in the following substitutions:

$$= ((10 \times ((10 \times \iota \ll 23 \gg) + \delta \ll 4 \gg)) + 5)$$

The references $\iota \ll 23 \gg$ and $\delta \ll 4 \gg$ result in appropriate replacements from Equations "g" and "m":

$$= ((10 \times ((10 \times ((10 \times \ll 2 \gg) + \delta \ll 3 \gg)) + 4)) + 5)$$

The references to $\iota \ll 2 \gg$ and $\delta \ll 3 \gg$ result in the following replacements according to Equations "h" and "l," respectively.

$$= ((10 \times ((10 \times ((10 \times \delta \ll 2 \gg) + 3)) + 4)) + 5)$$

Now the final substitution is made according to Equation "k." Since there are no further references to semantic functions, the expressions are evaluated according to the standard definitions of integer arithmetic:

$$= ((10 \times ((10 \times ((10 \times 2) + 3)) + 4)) + 5)$$
$$= ((10 \times ((10 \times (20 + 3)) + 4)) + 5)$$
$$= ((10 \times ((10 \times 23) + 4)) + 5)$$
$$= ((10 \times (230 + 4)) + 5)$$
$$= ((10 \times 234) + 5)$$
$$= (2340 + 5)$$
$$= 2345$$

Before we introduce more complicated definitions, some general notational conventions should be explained. An equal sign ($=$) will have as a superscript the letter of the semantic equation that specifies the transformation step, that is, the equation governing the transformation from the equal sign's left-hand to right-hand side. Consider this string of equalities:

$$e_1 =^a e_2 =^b e_3 =^c \cdots =^d e_{n-1} =^e e_n$$

The expression e_1 matches the LHS of Equation "a" and is replaced by e_2, which matches the LHS of Equation "b" and is replaced by e_3, which matches the LHS of Equation "c", and so on. Each e_i where $i > 1$ will include a right-hand side from the governing semantic equation. For brevity, when equations may apply in parallel, an ampersand (&) is used. When the same equation may apply to several terms, a factor is assigned the equation. Consider the evaluation of this arithmetic expression:

$\varepsilon \ll (3+2) / (4-2) \gg$			$=^d$
$\varepsilon \ll (3+2) \gg$	/	$\varepsilon \ll (4-2) \gg$	$=^{2 \bullet e}$
$\varepsilon \ll 3+2 \gg$	/	$\varepsilon \ll 4-2 \gg$	$=^{a \& b}$
$\varepsilon \ll 3 \gg + \varepsilon \ll 2 \gg$	/	$\varepsilon \ll 4 \gg - \varepsilon \ll 2 \gg$	$=^{4 \bullet f}$
$\iota \ll 3 \gg + \iota \ll 2 \gg$	/	$\iota \ll 4 \gg - \iota \ll 2 \gg$	$=^{4 \bullet h}$
$\delta \ll 3 \gg + \delta \ll 2 \gg$	/	$\delta \ll 4 \gg - \delta \ll 2 \gg$	$=^{l,k,m,k}$
$3+2 / 4-2$			

Even with the formal definitions there is ambiguity in the result: $3 + 2 / 4 - 2$. Precise definitions can lead to ambiguity if not developed properly. The question arises: is 2.5 (or 2, since we are dealing with integers) the answer, or is it 1.5 (or 1)? This ambiguity frustrates our goal of obtaining a precise definition of infix integer arithmetic. To solve the problem of ambiguity, we will alter the BNF for expressions, the semantic equations, and we will adopt two conventions for evaluating the equations. Instead of a breadth-first application of semantic equations, we will choose a depth-first application and adopt the additional convention that integer expressions and subexpressions are to be evaluated at the earliest possible point in the derivation.

As the semantics of integer data are now well understood, future examples will refer to integers simply as *cons*—and we will assume the syntactic construction and semantic derivation of integers. Specifically, this abbreviation is meant to summarize the earlier syntax, which describes how to syntactically construct an integer. Likewise, the semantics will summarize Equations "g" through "r," which state how to interpret the syntactic representation of the integer. Consider the BNF as altered to separate additive and multiplicative operations:

$E ::= T \mid E + T \mid E - T$
$T ::= F \mid T * F \mid T / F$
$F ::= (E) \mid \text{cons}$

This set of equations results in the following domains:

SYNTACTIC DOMAINS
  E: Exp
  T: Ter
  F: Fac

We will continue to map to the semantic domain of integers:

SEMANTIC DOMAIN
  $v : N = \{\bot, \cdots, -2, -1, 0, 1, 2, \cdots, \top\}$

As we now have three syntactic categories from the BNF LHSs, we need to declare three semantic functions:

SEMANTIC FUNCTION DECLARATION
  ε : $\text{Exp} \to N$
  α : $\text{Ter} \to N$
  β : $\text{Fac} \to N$

Next we elaborate the semantic equations for all RHSs for a given BNF syntax rule. In Equation "g" the RHS is altered by placing parentheses around the semantic expression, thus increasing its precedence for evaluation. In Equation "h" the integer corresponding to the syntactic integer is selected, summarizing informally Equations "g" through "r" from the original semantics.

SEMANTIC EQUATIONS
  a. $\varepsilon \ll E + T \gg$ $=$ $\varepsilon \ll E \gg$ $+$ $\varepsilon \ll T \gg$
  b. $\varepsilon \ll E - T \gg$ $=$ $\varepsilon \ll E \gg$ $-$ $\varepsilon \ll T \gg$
  c. $\varepsilon \ll T \gg$ $=$ $\alpha \ll T \gg$
  d. $\alpha \ll T * F \gg$ $=$ $\alpha \ll T \gg$ $*$ $\alpha \ll F \gg$
  e. $\alpha \ll T / F \gg$ $=$ $\alpha \ll T \gg$ $/$ $\alpha \ll F \gg$
  f. $\alpha \ll F \gg$ $=$ $\beta \ll F \gg$
  g. $\beta \ll (E) \gg$ $=$ $(\varepsilon \ll E \gg)$
  h. $\beta \ll \text{cons} \gg$ $=$ element of N corresponding to cons

Now consider the evaluation of an expression employing the two conventions mentioned earlier and the altered semantic equations. The equation letter over the equal sign indicates the pertinent LHS/RHS relationships.

$\varepsilon \ll (3 + 2) / (4 - 2) \gg$ $= c$

$\alpha \ll (3 + 2) / (4 - 2) \gg$ $= e$

$\alpha \ll (3 + 2) \gg / \alpha \ll (4 - 2) \gg$ $= f$

$\alpha \ll (3 + 2) \gg / \beta \ll (4 - 2) \gg$ $= g$

$\alpha \ll (3 + 2) \gg / (\varepsilon \ll 4 - 2 \gg)$ $= b$

$\alpha \ll (3 + 2) \gg / (\varepsilon \ll 4 \gg - \varepsilon \ll 2 \gg)$ $= 2 \bullet c$

$\alpha \ll (3 + 2) \gg / (\alpha \ll 4 \gg - \alpha \ll 2 \gg)$ $= 2 \bullet f$

$\alpha \ll (3 + 2) \gg / (\beta \ll 4 \gg - \beta \ll 2 \gg)$ $= 2 \bullet b$

$\alpha \ll (3 + 2) \gg$	/	$(4 - 2)$	$=$ math
$\alpha \ll (3 + 2) \gg$	/	2	$= f$
$\beta \ll (3 + 2) \gg$	/	2	$= g$
$(\varepsilon \ll 3 + 2 \gg)$	/	2	$= a$
$(\varepsilon \ll 3 \gg + \varepsilon \ll 2 \gg)$	/	2	$= 2 \bullet c$
$(\alpha \ll 3 \gg + \alpha \ll 2 \gg)$	/	2	$= 2 \bullet f$
$(\beta \ll 3 \gg + \beta \ll 2 \gg)$	/	2	$= 2 \bullet b$
$(3 + 2)$	/	2	$=$ math
$5/2$			$=$ math
2			

In the next section we develop the metalanguage employed for more complicated semantic equations.

DENOTATIONAL SEMANTIC METALANGUAGE

In this section, much of the metalanguage employed in denotational semantic defintions is presented. In the previous section we observed simple syntactic and semantic domains. It is possible to construct more complicated domains from existing domains with the product ($\times$) and sum ($+$) operators.

PRODUCT DOMAINS

Given domains $D_1, D_2, \cdots, D_n$, it is possible to form a new domain, $N = D_1 \times D_2 \times \cdots \times D_n$, which gives a set of ordered n-tuples: $<d_1, d_2, \cdots, d_n>$, where for each $i: d_i \in D_i$. This is a *product domain*. For example,

Given $B = \{t, f, \bot, \top\}$
and
$V = \{a, b, c\}°$
$B \times V = \{<t,a>, <t,b>, <t,c>, <f,a>, <f,b>, <f,c>\}°$

The *down arrow* is an operator that permits access to the components of a tuple formed by a product operation, $t \downarrow i$. In this operation, t is a tuple of a product domain, and i is an integer. Given $N = D_1 \times D_2 \times \cdots \times D_k$, $n \in N$, and $d_i \in D_i$, then $n \downarrow i = d_i$.

A special form of a product domain is denoted by D^n where $D^n = D_1 \times D_2 \times \cdots \times D_n$ *iff* $D_1 = D_2 = \cdots = D_n$. This set is to be distinguished from the asterisk (*) as a superscript. The set D^* is the set of all finite strings that can be formed using the elements of D. For example, assume $D = \{t,f\}°$:

$$D^* = \{t,f,tt,tf,ff,ft,\cdots\}°$$
$$D^n = \{<t,t,t>,<f,f,f>,<f,t,t>,<t,f,t>,<t,t,f>,<t,f,f>,<f,t,f>,<f,f,t>\}°$$

where $n = 3$.

Therefore, $D^* = D^0 \cup D^1 \cup D^2 \cup \cdots \cup D^i \cup \cdots$, where $D^0 = \epsilon$ (the empty string). D^* also includes all strings of lengths 1,2,3, and so on.

Consider the example in Figure 3.4, where $B = \{t,f\}°$, $L = \{a,b,c\}°$, and $P = B \times L$.

SUM DOMAINS

Given domains $D_1, D_2, \cdots, D_n$, it is possible to form a new domain, $S = D_1 + D_2 + \cdots + D_n$, which gives a set of elements in which, for any element, $x \in S$, there is some i such that $x \in D_i$. This is a *sum domain*. For example, suppose I is the set of integers, C the set of alphabetic characters, and R the set of real numbers. One possible use of these sets and the metalanguage operators is to specify the output domain of a programming language. The output specification, $(I + C^* + R)^*$, would indicate a metalanguage that can be used with programming languages that produce strings of integers, real numbers, and characters as output.

The example domain, $(I + C^* + R)^*$, warrants inspection. Inside the parentheses one may observe that an output can be an integer (I), a character string (C^*), or a real number (R). The quantity thus formed may itself allow for strings. In other words, we can obtain any string that can be formed from the sum domain itself. Thus, the output of a program can be any conceivable combination

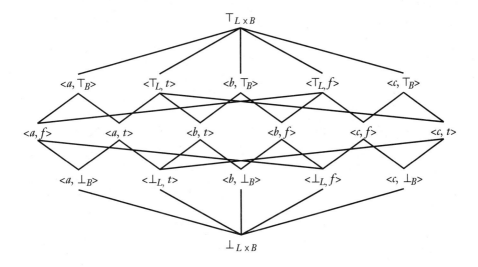

FIGURE 3.4 Example of a product domain.

of integer, character, or real strings. Included in the output domain are the following:

5

10.43

a

The value of *r* is 5, and the value of *s* is 8.95
Etc.

In Figure 3.5, $B = \{t,f\}°$, $L = \{a,b,c\}°$, and $P = B + L$.

FUNCTIONS

Because the goal of the semantic definitions is to map from a syntactic to a semantic domain, function definition is central to our concern. *Functions* are declared according to the general form,

$$F = D_1 \rightarrow D_2$$

This definition is akin to a type declaration stating the existence of a class of functions in which, given an element of D_1, the function will map to an element of D_2. It is possible to identify a specific function, *f*, that is an element of a function class:

$$f : F = D_1 \rightarrow D2$$

Therefore, $f(d_1) = d_2$, assuming $d_1 \in D_1$ and $d_2 \in D_2$—and assuming that mapping occurs between d_1 and d_2. Expressions for domains can be complicated:

$$D_1 \times D_2 \times \cdots \times D_n \rightarrow D_{n+1} + D_{n+2}$$

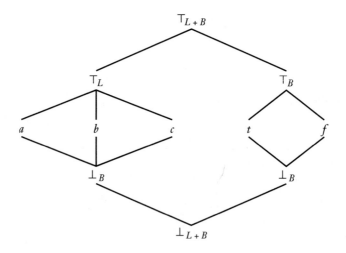

FIGURE 3.5   Example of a sum domain.

The precedence relationships in order of importance are $\times$, $+$, and $\rightarrow$. The mapping symbol, $\rightarrow$, is right-associative.

FUNCTION DOMAINS

Frequently it is necessary to define *function domains*, which map domain elements to functions:

$$D_1 \rightarrow (D_2 \rightarrow D_3)$$

Assume that C represents the syntactic representation of an integer and that N represents the semantic representation, or the set of integers. "Operators" in this example will refer to a set of arithmetic operators $\{*, /, +, -\}$. Now consider the following function domain definition:

$S = \text{Operators} \rightarrow (C \times C \rightarrow N)$
$s: S = \text{Operators} \rightarrow (C \times C \rightarrow N)$

Therefore, $s\,[+ (4,3)\,]$ selects the addition function, which in turn maps the pair 4,3 to 7.

LIST OPERATIONS

Recall that D^n denotes all lists of length n that can be formed using the elements of D. Furthermore recall that $D^* = \{\text{nil}\} + D^1 + D^2 + \cdots$ represents the infinite set of all possible finite lists of a domain, D. Special operators exist to manage lists serving as operands of the denotational semantic definitions:

hd*(L)*	$D^* \rightarrow D$
tl*(L)*	$D^* \rightarrow D^*$
append*(L,d)*	$D^* \times D \rightarrow D^*$
prefix*(d,L)*	$D \times D^* \rightarrow D^*$

Given $L = \text{nil}$, then both the hd and the tl function return top, $\top$, an erroneous condition. Notice that tl([20]) evaluates to nil, but one will never see a nil from the hd operation. Suppose $D = (N + C^*)$, where N is the domain of integers and C is the domain of characters. D^* could thus represent an output file, $O = D^*$. The process of writing to an output file could be represented by the append function. An input file, $I = (CN + CC^*)^*$ (where CN and CC are, respectively, syntactic representations of integers and characters) could be represented by two operations: the input value obtained with hd, and the subsequent input file obtained by the tl:

append*(O,d)*	For output
hd*(I)*	For an input value
tl*(I)*	For the input file resulting from an input operation

Consider the following examples, where $I = [7,8,9]$:

append(I,10)	=	[7,8,9,10]
prefix(6,I)	=	[6,7,8,9]

prefix(6,append(I,10))   =   [6,7,8,9,10]
hd(I)   =   7
tl(I)   =   [8,9]

DOMAIN OPERATIONS

It is common to have identifiers that map to memory locations or to procedures (i.e., subprograms). In order to represent identifiers as a domain, we can use this definition:

$$Id = L + P$$

where L is a set of locations, and P is a set of procedures.

Given an identifier, it is possible to map to locations or to procedures. Special operators exist to allow manipulation of the sum domains just exemplified. For these definitions, assume the general sum domain of $S = D_1 + \cdots + D_n$. Also assume that P is a set of named programmed segments, L is a set of named locations, and $Id = P + L$:

OPERATOR D IN S If d is an element of D_i, then d in S provides an element of S corresponding to d. This operation allows you to "inject" elements of the smaller domain into the larger, as, for example, during declarations of procedures and variables. Therefore, when a procedure, p, is declared, one would use the expression p in Id. The in operator is not to be confused with the membership relation: instead of testing for membership, the in operator forces membership. From a practical standpoint, this operation defines the use of an identifier after its use is declared.

OPERATOR $s \mid D$, If s is an element of S, then $s \mid D_i$ provides the element of D_i corresponding to s. This operation allows you to "project" elements of the smaller domain from the larger—for example, during references. When a variable, id, is referenced, the expression id in L is used to obtain the location of id. Projection on the name of a procedure would obtain an appropriate segment of code in the case of a procedure name.

OPERATOR s E D, If s is an element of S, then s E D_i iff s is squarely in D_i. This operation is used to guard actions of injection and projection and thus make certain that an object is where one thinks it is.

Assume again that $Id = P + L$ in considering the following example:

if id E P then id in $P + L$

In this example, an identifier representing some unit of code (presumably a subprogram) is being injected into the sum domain of procedures and locations. In the next example, a named segment of code is obtained in the presence of a reference to a procedure name:

if id E P then $id \mid P$

REPLACEMENT OPERATION

The operator that allows for the replacement of information in the context of a function is $f[a/b]$. It denotes function f', which is identical to f except for the fact that in f', b maps to a.

Given $f[a/b]$, one subsequently finds that $f[b]=a$. In denotational semantics one can define a mapping with $f[a/b]$ and then reference it with $f[b]$.

SEMANTIC EQUATIONS

The goal of the semantic definitions is to map from a syntactic object to a semantic object. Two important operators are found in a semantic equation. The first is a special set of brackets used only to encapsulate (and thus isolate) syntactic objects:

«   syntactic object   »   .

One can state conditional semantic equations using the operator IF-THEN. Consider the following semantic equation, which obtains the value of a variable:

μ « V » σ =   if V $\in$ L then σ [V|L] else $\top$

This equation states that the meaning of the variable can be evaluated in one of two ways: (1) if the variable is in the domain of locations, L, then the meaning of the variable is projected from the locations domain with respect to the current state, meaning that you will obtain the value mapped to the location to which the variable is mapped; otherwise (2), an erroneous condition exists. Notice that the semantic equation is similar to a lambda function. The fundamental notion is one of replacement. When the LHS of an equation is matched—as in the case of μ « V » σ, it is replaced by the RHS: IF V $\in$ L THEN σ[V|L] ELSE $\top$. The arguments of the function are V and σ. The general form of a semantic equation is

LHS = RHS
or
LHS = if CONDITION then RHS(true) else RHS(false)

MORE INTERESTING EXAMPLES

A syntactic metavariable, V, can take on the value of any legal variable in the target language, legality being based on the BNF syntax definitions. Suppose the following BNF rule exists:

$V ::= aV \mid bV \mid \cdots \mid zV \mid a \mid b \mid \cdots \mid z$

We can apply the knowledge we have gained so far by refining our language of arithmetic expressions to allow for variables. To do this, we will need a function that allows us to map from the syntactic variable domain to a semantic domain containing values to which the variable may be assigned. (We will not require the injection/projection operators, since no subprogram names will be involved in the language we will develop here.) The mapping from variables to values must be done with respect to a state, σ: σ[V] yields the value to which V is assigned in state σ. By augmenting the original syntax for arithmetic expressions, presented at the beginning of this chapter, we obtain arithmetic expressions that provide for the use of variables:

NEW SYNTAX

$S ::= V := E$
$E ::= T \mid E + T \mid E - T$
$T ::= F \mid T * F \mid T / F$
$F ::= (E) \mid \text{cons} \mid V$

As cons and V should both be viewed as syntactic categories, it can be claimed that each syntactic category is a *syntactic domain*, meaning a class of syntactic objects from which you can map to semantic objects. However, we will not declare them as syntactic domains, since the syntactic construction of variables and constants is well understood.

NEW SYNTACTIC DOMAIN

S: Stmt
E: Exp
T: Ter
F: Fac

From the syntactic domain, one maps to semantic domains. In this case the semantic domains are as follows:

NEW SEMANTIC DOMAIN

σ: $St = V \rightarrow N$
v: $N = \{\cdots, -2, -1, 0, 1, 2, \cdots\}°$

For each LHS in the BNF, we declare a semantic function. The semantic function declarations are as follows:

SEMANTIC FUNCTIONS

Σ: Stmt $\rightarrow St \rightarrow St$
ε: Exp $\rightarrow St \rightarrow N$
α: Ter $\rightarrow St \rightarrow N$
β: Fac $\rightarrow St \rightarrow N$

The semantic function symbol, Σ, is declared to take as input a statement from the syntactic domain and, based on that statement, map from an input state to some output state. In other words, statements, after they are interpreted, alter the state of the computation in which they execute. Each function declared maps from a syntactic domain to a semantic domain.

Considering these declarations, we can better understand the corresponding semantic equations. For example, given the function declaration of Σ : Stmt $\to$ St $\to$ St, there is one equation ("j" in the following list) corresponding to the single RHS option for a statement in the syntax. The LHS of the semantic equation contains (1) the syntactic RHS option used to select the equation and (2) the additional argument, σ, to be used as the current state. The RHS of the semantic equation describes how the mapping is to be accomplished and is used to replace the LHS of the semantic equation with, in the case of Equation "j," a new state:

SEMANTIC EQUATIONS

a. $\varepsilon \ll E + T \gg \sigma$	$=$	$\varepsilon \ll E \gg \sigma$	$+$	$\varepsilon \ll T \gg \sigma$
b. $\varepsilon \ll E - T \gg \sigma$	$=$	$\varepsilon \ll E \gg \sigma$	$-$	$\varepsilon \ll T \gg \sigma$
c. $\varepsilon \ll T \gg \sigma$	$=$	$\alpha \ll T \gg \sigma$		
d. $\alpha \ll T * F \gg \sigma$	$=$	$\alpha \ll T \gg \sigma$	$*$	$\alpha \ll F \gg \sigma$
e. $\alpha \ll T / F \gg \sigma$	$=$	$\alpha \ll T \gg \sigma$	$/$	$\alpha \ll F \gg \sigma$
f. $\alpha \ll F \gg \sigma$	$=$	$\beta \ll F \gg \sigma$		
g. $\beta \ll (E) \gg \sigma$	$=$	$(\varepsilon \ll E \gg \sigma)$		
h. $\beta \ll \text{cons} \gg \sigma$	$=$	element of N corresponding to cons		
i. $\beta \ll V \gg \sigma$	$=$	$\sigma[V]$		
j. $\Sigma \ll V{:=}E \gg \sigma$	$=$	$\sigma[\varepsilon \ll E \gg \sigma / V]$		

Equation "i" obtains the value associated with a variable. Given the full set of equations here, if a variable is undefined, a null value is obtained—not undefined, but null.

Equation "j" assigns the meaning of the expression E (on the RHS of the assignment operator in the syntactic structure) to the variable (on the LHS). For example, consider the meaning of the statement $e{:} = (a + 10)/d$ assuming "a" maps to 14 and "d" maps to 6 in Σ:

$\Sigma \ll e{:=}(a + 10)/d \gg \sigma$	$= j$
$\sigma[\varepsilon \ll (a + 10)/d \gg \sigma/ e]$	$= c$
$\sigma[\alpha \ll (a + 10)/d \gg \sigma/ e]$	$= e$
$\sigma[\alpha \ll (a + 10) \gg \sigma / \alpha \ll d \gg \sigma/ e]$	$= f$
$\sigma[\beta \ll (a + 10) \gg \sigma / \alpha \ll d \gg \sigma/ e]$	$= f$
$\sigma[\beta \ll (a + 10) \gg \sigma / \beta \ll d \gg \sigma/ e]$	$= i$
$\sigma[\beta \ll (a + 10) \gg \sigma / \sigma [d] / e]$	$= g$
$\sigma[(\varepsilon \ll a + 10 \gg \sigma) / 6 / e]$	$= a$
$\sigma[(\varepsilon \ll a \gg \sigma + \varepsilon \ll 10 \gg \sigma) / 6 / e]$	$= 2 \bullet c$
$\sigma[(\alpha \ll a \gg \sigma + \alpha \ll 10 \gg \sigma) / 6 / e]$	$= 2 \bullet f$
$\sigma[(\beta \ll a \gg \sigma + \beta \ll 10 \gg \sigma) / 6 / e]$	$= i$
$\sigma[(\sigma [a] + \beta \ll 10 \gg \sigma) / 6 / e]$	$= b$
$\sigma[(14 + 10) / 6 / e]$	$= \text{math}$
$\sigma[24 / 6 / e]$	$= \text{math}$
$\sigma[4 / e]$	

In two steps, translations were carried out concurrently, marked by $2 \bullet c$ and $2 \bullet f$. This marking is meant to denote that Equation "c" was applied to two references: $\varepsilon \ll a \gg \sigma$ and $\varepsilon \ll 10 \gg \sigma$, respectively; and Equation "f" was applied to $\alpha \ll a \gg \sigma$ and $\alpha \ll 10 \gg \sigma$, respectively.

EXAMPLES INVOLVING WHILE LANGUAGE

In this section, the grammar and semantics presented earlier are extended to specify the syntax and meaning of the WHILE language introduced in the previous chapter.

SYNTAX

$P ::= S$

$S ::= V := E \mid read(V) \mid write(V) \mid while\ C\ do\ S\ od \mid S;S$

$C ::= E1 < E2 \mid E1 > E2 \mid E1 = E2 \mid E1 < = E2 \mid E1 > = E2 \mid E1 \neq E2$

$E ::= T \mid E + T \mid E - T$

$T ::= F \mid T * F \mid T / F$

$F ::= (E) \mid cons \mid V$

SYNTACTIC DOMAINS

P: Prog

C: Cond

S: Stmt

E: Exp

T: Ter

F: Fac

SEMANTIC DOMAINS

$\tau: B = \{true, false\}^\circ$

$\phi: Fi = N^*$

$\gamma: CF = St \times Fi \times Fi$

$\sigma: St = V \rightarrow N$

$v: N = \{\cdots, -2, -1, 0, 1, 2, \cdots\}^\circ$

The most complicated semantic domain is the configuration $\gamma: CF = St \times Fi \times Fi$. The configuration is a *3-tuple*, in which the first component is the state of the computation, the second is the state of the input file, and the third is the state of the output file. The three components can be obtained by $\gamma \downarrow 1 = \sigma$, $\gamma \downarrow 2 = \phi 1$, and $\gamma \downarrow 3 = \phi 2$, respectively.

SEMANTIC FUNCTION DOMAINS

M: Prog $\rightarrow Fi \rightarrow Fi$

Σ: Stmt $\rightarrow CF \rightarrow CF$

ζ: Cond $\rightarrow St \rightarrow B$

ε: Exp $\rightarrow St \rightarrow N$

α: Ter $\rightarrow St \rightarrow N$

β: Fac $\rightarrow St \rightarrow N$

SEMANTIC EQUATIONS

a. $\varepsilon \ll E + T \gg \sigma$	$=$	$\varepsilon \ll E \gg \sigma$	$+$	$\varepsilon \ll T \gg \sigma$
b. $\varepsilon \ll E - T \gg \sigma$	$=$	$\varepsilon \ll E \gg \sigma$	$-$	$\varepsilon \ll T \gg \sigma$
c. $\varepsilon \ll T \gg \sigma$	$=$	$\alpha \ll T \gg \sigma$		
d. $\alpha \ll T * F \gg \sigma$	$=$	$\alpha \ll T \gg \sigma$	$*$	$\alpha \ll F \gg \sigma$

e. $\alpha \ll T / F \gg \sigma$ $=$ $\alpha \ll T \gg \sigma$ / $\alpha \ll F \gg \sigma$

f. $\alpha \ll F \gg \sigma$ $=$ $\beta \ll F \gg \sigma$

g. $\beta \ll (E) \gg \sigma$ $=$ $(\varepsilon \ll E \gg \sigma)$

h. $\beta \ll cons \gg \sigma$ $=$ element of N corresponding to cons

i. $\beta \ll V \gg \sigma$ $=$ $\sigma[V]$

j. $\zeta \ll E1 < E2 \gg \sigma$ $=$ if $\varepsilon \ll E1 \gg \sigma < \varepsilon \ll E2 \gg \sigma$
   then true else false

k. $\zeta \ll E1 > E2 \gg \sigma$ $=$ if $\varepsilon \ll E1 \gg \sigma > \varepsilon \ll E2 \gg \sigma$
   then true else false

l. $\zeta \ll E1 = E2 \gg \sigma$ $=$ if $\varepsilon \ll E1 \gg \sigma = \varepsilon \ll E2 \gg \sigma$
   then true else false

m. $\zeta \ll E1 <= E2 \gg \sigma$ $=$ if $\varepsilon \ll E1 \gg \sigma <= \varepsilon \ll E2 \gg \sigma$
   then true else false

n. $\zeta \ll E1 >= E2 \gg \sigma$ $=$ if $\varepsilon \ll E1 \gg \sigma >= \varepsilon \ll E2 \gg \sigma$
   then true else false

o. $\zeta \ll E1 \neq E2 \gg \sigma$ $=$ if $\varepsilon \ll E1 \gg \sigma \neq \varepsilon \ll E2 \gg \sigma$
   then true else false

Since $\varepsilon \ll E1 \gg \sigma\ \Phi\ \varepsilon \ll E2 \gg \sigma$ (where Φ can be $=,<,>,>=,<=,\neq$) evaluates to $B = \{true,false\}^\circ$, Equations "j" through "o" can be simplified. For example, Equation "o" can be simplified as follows:

o.' $\zeta \ll E1 \neq E2 \gg \sigma$ $=$ $\varepsilon \ll E1 \gg \sigma \neq \varepsilon \ll E2 \gg \sigma$

The other equations can be simplified in like manner. Now consider the assignment statement:

p. $\Sigma \ll V{:}{=}E \gg \gamma$ $=$ $<\sigma[\varepsilon \ll E \gg \gamma \downarrow 1 / V], \gamma \downarrow 2, \gamma \downarrow 3 >$

The assignment is a fairly sophisticated statement. The state of the machine is modified by assigning to the variable V on the LHS of the assignment operator, the result of determining the meaning of the expression on the RHS. The expression $\varepsilon \ll E \gg \gamma \downarrow 1$ invokes the evaluation of the arithmetic expression, which makes use of the state ($\gamma \downarrow 1$), and not the input or output files. Clearly, the assignment has no effect on the input or output files, since these components are copied from the input to the output configuration.

q. $\Sigma \ll read(V) \gg \gamma$ $=$ if $\phi 1 \neq$ nil
   then
      $<\sigma[hd(\phi 1) / V], tl(\phi 1), \phi 2>$
   else
      $\top$

where $\gamma \downarrow 1 = \sigma$ & $\gamma \downarrow 2 = \phi 1$ & $\gamma \downarrow 3 = \phi 2$.

As you will see, the ASSIGNMENT and the READ statements have quite a bit in common. They are the only statements that modify the contents of the state, that is, replace the value of a variable. The difference between the statements is twofold. The value to be *assigned* to a variable is obtained by evaluating an arithmetic instruction (see Equation "p"). The value to be *read* into a variable is obtained from the second component of the configuration—the input file. The second difference is that the ASSIGNMENT statement affects only the state of the machine whereas the READ statement affects the state of the machine and the input file. The head of the input file replaces the value of the referenced program variable, and the tail of the input file provides the new state of the input file as obtained by evaluating the READ statement.

r. $\Sigma \ll write(V) \gg \gamma \quad = \quad$ if $\quad \sigma[V] \neq \bot$
$\qquad\qquad$ then
$\qquad\qquad\qquad$ $<\sigma, \phi 1, append(\phi 2, \sigma[V])>$
$\qquad\qquad$ else
$\qquad\qquad\qquad$ $\top$

where $\gamma \downarrow 1 = \sigma$ & $\gamma \downarrow 2 = \phi 1$ & $\gamma \downarrow 3 = \phi 2$.

The WRITE statement will append to the output file the meaning of the referenced variable V if that variable is defined. If it is not defined, an erroneous condition is the result of the WRITE statement's interpretation.

s. $\Sigma \ll while\ C\ do\ S\ od \gg \gamma \quad = \quad$ if $\zeta \ll C \gg \gamma \downarrow 1$ then
$\qquad\qquad\qquad$ $\Sigma \ll while\ C\ do\ S\ od \gg \quad \circ \quad \Sigma \ll S \gg \gamma$ else γ

The WHILE statement's meaning is conditional. When the condition, C, evaluates to false, the WHILE statement, while C do S od, is not to be evaluated, so the configuration input is passed through (if $\cdots$ else γ). When the condition evaluates to true, the meaning of the statement(s), S, composing the body of the loop, is to be evaluated. The resulting configuration is appended by the degree symbol (°) to a recursive reference to the WHILE statement that served as the input.

t. $\Sigma \ll S1;S2 \gg \gamma \quad = \quad \Sigma \ll S2 \gg \quad \circ \quad \Sigma \ll S1 \gg \gamma$

Equation "t" reverses the order of the statements so that they can be evaluated in the proper sequence. Usually we would expect the evaluation to proceed from left to right. However, the equations are right-associative—they are evaluated from right to left. Therefore, the evaluation of the rightmost expression provides the arguments for the next-to-rightmost operation.

An interesting fact about Equation "t" is that any number of statements can be reversed by repeated applications. For example, consider three statements, a, b, and c:

$$\Sigma \ll a,b,c \gg \gamma =^t \Sigma \ll c \gg \circ \Sigma \ll a,b \gg \gamma =^t \Sigma \ll c \gg \circ \Sigma \ll b \gg \circ \Sigma \ll a \gg \gamma$$

Another order of applications is possible, but the end result is the same:

$$\Sigma \ll a,b,c \gg \gamma =^t \Sigma \ll b,c \gg \circ \Sigma \ll a \gg \gamma =^t \Sigma \ll c \gg \circ \Sigma \ll b \gg \circ \Sigma \ll a \gg \gamma$$

Equation "u" provides for the initial state of the machine:

u. $M \ll P \gg \phi 1 \quad = \quad (\Sigma \ll P \gg <\lambda\ \Xi.\bot, \phi 1, nil>) \downarrow 3$

This equation sets the output file to nil, copies the input file provided by the user to the second component of the configuration, and—through the use of a lambda function—sets all variables appearing in program P to undefined. Recall from our earlier language that the variables were null.

REVIEW OF EQUATIONS

Let's review the equations just presented. Notice, in particular, the equations for the READ, WRITE, and WHILE statements. The READ checks to see if the input file is not nil. If it is not, then the head of the file is assigned to the variable referenced in the READ, $\sigma[hd(\phi1)/V]$. Next, the remainder of the list is left for the input file, $tl(\phi1)$. The READ statement is much like an assignment in terms of its effect on the state of a computation. From the equations one can clearly see that the only statements altering the state of the machine are the READ and the assignment statements.

p. $\Sigma \ll V:=E \gg \gamma \quad = \quad < \sigma[\varepsilon \ll E \gg \gamma \downarrow 1 / V], \gamma \downarrow 2, \gamma \downarrow 3 >$

q. $\Sigma \ll read(V) \gg \gamma \quad = \quad$ if $\phi1 \neq$ nil

then

$\qquad <\sigma[hd(\phi1) / V], tl(\phi1), \phi2>$

else

$\qquad \top$

where $\gamma \downarrow 1 = \sigma$ & $\gamma \downarrow 2 = \phi1$ & $\gamma \downarrow 3 = \phi2$.

The WRITE statement appends the meaning of the referenced variable to the end of the output file, $append(\phi2, \sigma[V])$. As such it has no impact on the state of the machine.

r. $\Sigma \ll write(V) \gg \gamma \quad = \quad$ if $\quad \sigma[V] \neq \bot$

then

$\qquad <\sigma, \phi1, append(\phi2, \sigma[V])>$

else

$\qquad \top$

where $\gamma \downarrow 1 = \sigma$ & $\gamma \downarrow 2 = \phi1$ & $\gamma \downarrow 3 = \phi2$.

The WHILE statement is a complicated definition. It first checks the condition referenced:

$\Sigma \ll$ while C do S od $\gg \gamma \quad = \quad \cdots \zeta \ll C \gg \gamma \downarrow 1 \cdots$

Since ζ requires only the state, the first component of the configuration γ is obtained with $\gamma \downarrow 1$. If the condition is satisfied, the meaning of the statements of the WHILE (i.e., S in while C do S od) is obtained:

$\Sigma \ll S \gg \gamma$

The evaluated body of the WHILE forms a new configuration to be used when one reconsiders the WHILE loop. The totality of this semantic is denoted by

$\Sigma \ll$ while C do S od $\gg \quad \circ \quad \Sigma \ll S \gg \gamma$

When the condition, C, is not satisfied, the WHILE statements are bypassed. The bypass is effected by replacing the WHILE statement reference $\Sigma \ll$ while C do S od $\gg$ with the input configuration, γ. The accompanying box presents the entire definition of the WHILE language.

SYNTAX
$P ::= S$
$S ::= V := E \mid \text{read}(V) \mid \text{write}(V) \mid \text{while } C \text{ do } S \text{ od} \mid S;S$
$C ::= E1 < E2 \mid E1 > E2 \mid E1 = E2 \mid E1 <= E2 \mid E1 >= E2 \mid E1 \neq E2$
$E ::= T \mid E + T \mid E - T$
$T ::= F \mid T * F \mid T / F$
$F ::= (E) \mid \text{cons} \mid V$

SYNTACTIC DOMAINS
P: Prog
C: Cond
S: Stmt
E: Exp
T: Ter
F: Fac

SEMANTIC DOMAINS
τ: $B = \{\text{true,false}\}^\circ$
ϕ: $Fi = N^*$
γ: $CF = St \times Fi \times Fi$
σ: $St = V \to N$
ν: $N = \{\cdots, -2, -1, 0, 1, 2, \cdots\}^\circ$

SEMANTIC FUNCTION DOMAIN
M: Prog $\to Fi \to Fi$
Σ: Stmt $\to CF \to CF$
ζ: Cond $\to St \to B$
ε: Exp $\to St \to N$
α: Ter $\to St \to N$
β: Fac $\to St \to N$

SEMANTIC EQUATIONS

a. $\varepsilon \ll E + T \gg \sigma \qquad = \quad \varepsilon \ll E \gg \sigma \quad + \quad \varepsilon \ll T \gg \sigma$

b. $\varepsilon \ll E - T \sigma \qquad = \quad \varepsilon \ll E \gg \sigma \quad - \quad \varepsilon \ll T \gg \sigma$

c. $\varepsilon \ll T \gg \sigma \qquad = \quad \alpha \ll T \gg \sigma$

d. $\alpha \ll T * F \gg \sigma \qquad = \quad \alpha \ll T \gg \sigma \quad * \quad \alpha \ll F \gg \sigma$

e. $\alpha \ll T / F \gg \sigma \qquad = \quad \alpha \ll T \gg \sigma \quad / \quad \alpha \ll F \gg \sigma$

f. $\alpha \ll F \gg \sigma \qquad = \quad \beta \ll F \gg \sigma$

g. $\beta \ll (E) \gg \sigma \qquad = \quad (\varepsilon \ll E \gg \sigma)$

h. $\beta \ll \text{cons} \gg \sigma \qquad = \quad$ element of N corresponding to cons

i. $\beta \ll V \gg \sigma \qquad = \quad \sigma[V]$

j. $\zeta \ll E1 < E2 \gg \sigma \qquad = \quad$ if $\varepsilon \ll E1 \gg \sigma < \varepsilon \ll E2 \gg \sigma$
$\qquad\qquad\qquad\qquad\qquad\qquad$ then true else false

k. $\zeta \ll E1 > E2 \gg \sigma \qquad = \quad$ if $\varepsilon \ll E1 \gg \sigma > \varepsilon \ll E2 \gg \sigma$
$\qquad\qquad\qquad\qquad\qquad\qquad$ then true else false

l. $\zeta \ll E1 = E2 \gg \sigma$ $=$ if $\varepsilon \ll E1 \gg \sigma = \varepsilon \ll E2 \gg \sigma$
                                                    then true else false

m. $\zeta \ll E1 <= E2 \gg \sigma$ $=$ if $\varepsilon \ll E1 \gg \sigma <= \varepsilon \ll E2 \gg \sigma$
                                                    then true else false

n. $\zeta \ll E1 >= E2 \gg \sigma$ $=$ if $\varepsilon \ll E1 \gg \sigma >= \varepsilon \ll E2 \gg \sigma$
                                                    then true else false

o. $\zeta \ll E1 \neq E2 \gg \sigma$ $=$ if $\varepsilon \ll E1 \gg \sigma \neq \varepsilon \ll E2 \gg \sigma$
                                                    then true else false

p. $\Sigma \ll V{:}{=}E \gg \gamma$ $=$ $<\sigma[\varepsilon \ll E \gg \gamma \downarrow 1/V], \gamma \downarrow 2, \gamma \downarrow 3 >$

q. $\Sigma \ll \text{read}(V) \gg \gamma$ $=$ if $\phi 1 \neq$ nil
                                                    then
                                                            $<\sigma[hd(\phi 1)/V], tl(\phi 1), \phi 2>$
                                                    else
                                                            $\top$
                            Where $\gamma \downarrow 1 = \sigma$ & $\gamma \downarrow 2 = \phi 1$ & $\gamma \downarrow 3 = \phi 2$

r. $\Sigma \ll \text{write}(V) \gg \gamma$ $=$ if $\sigma[V] \neq \bot$
                                                    then
                                                            $<\sigma, \phi 1, \text{append}(\phi 2, \sigma[V])>$
                                                    else
                                                            $\top$
                            Where $\gamma \downarrow 1 = \sigma$ & $\gamma \downarrow 2 = \phi 1$ & $\gamma \downarrow 3 = \phi 2$

s. $\Sigma \ll \text{while } C \text{ do } S \text{ od } \gg \gamma$ $=$ if $\zeta \ll C \gg \gamma \downarrow 1$ then
                                                            $\Sigma \ll \text{while } C \text{ do } S \text{ od } \gg \circ \Sigma \ll S \gg \gamma$ else γ

t. $\Sigma \ll S1;S2 \gg \gamma$ $=$ $\Sigma \ll S2 \gg$ $\circ$ $\Sigma \ll S1 \gg \gamma$

u. $M \ll P \gg \phi 1$ $=$ $(\Sigma \ll P \gg <\lambda \; \Xi.\bot, \phi 1, \text{nil}>) \downarrow 3$

Consider the derivation of the following program:

$M \ll \text{read}(n); i{:}{=}1; \text{while } i<=n \text{ do } i{:}{=}i+1 \text{ od}; \text{write}(i) \gg [3]$ $=^u$

Equation "*u*" accomplishes several purposes. First, it establishes the initial configuration of the program. The initial configuration includes a state in which all program variables are declared to be undefined. The initial state is formed with a lambda function: $\lambda \; \Xi.\bot$. The second component of the configuration is the input list, in this case, [3]. The final component is the program output list, which is initially nil. The program's meaning will result from the meaning of the program's statements, Σ. The meaning of the statements will produce a final configuration, the third component of which ($\downarrow 3$, the output file) is the communicated meaning of the program:

$(\Sigma \ll \text{read}(n); i{:}{=}1; \text{while } i<=n \text{ do } i{:}{=}i+1 \text{ od}; \text{write}(i) \gg <\lambda \; \Xi.\bot, \phi, 1\text{nil}>)\downarrow 3$ $=^t$

Equation "t" rearranges statement pairs, since the program is evaluated as a lambda function, read from right to left, rather than left to right:

$(\Sigma \ll i{:}{=}1; \text{while } i<=n \text{ do } i{:}{=}i+1 \text{ od}; \text{write}(i) \gg \circ \Sigma \ll \text{read}(n) \gg <\lambda \; \Xi.\bot, \phi 1,$
      $\text{nil}>)$ $\downarrow 3$ $=^q$

The READ statement defines the reference variable with the head of the input list σ[hd([3]) /n] and adjusts the input list to remove the value just read tl([3]):

$$(\Sigma \ll i:=1; \text{ while } i<=n \text{ do } i:=i+1 \text{ od}; \text{write}(i) \gg \sigma[\ hd([3])\ /\ n], tl([3]), \text{nil}>) \downarrow$$
$$3 \quad =^t$$

Again, Equation "t" rearranges statement pairs:

$$(\Sigma \ll \text{while } i<=n \text{ do } i:=i+1 \text{ od}; \text{write}(i) \gg \circ \Sigma \ll i:=1 \gg <\sigma[3/n], \text{nil}, \text{nil}>) \downarrow 3 \quad =^p$$

The next three steps are followed to initialize program variable i:

$$(\Sigma \ll \text{while } i<=n \text{ do } i:=i+1 \text{ od}; \text{write}(i) \gg <\sigma[\varepsilon \ll 1 \gg \sigma /i], \text{nil}, \text{nil}>) \downarrow 3 \quad =^c$$
$$(\Sigma \ll \text{while } i<=n \text{ do } i:=i+1 \text{ od}; \text{write}(i) \gg <\sigma[\alpha \ll 1 \gg \sigma /i], \text{nil}, \text{nil}>) \downarrow 3 \quad =^f$$
$$(\Sigma \ll \text{while } i<=n \text{ do } i:=i+1 \text{ od}; \text{write}(i) \gg <\sigma[\beta \ll 1 \gg \sigma /i], \text{nil}, \text{nil}>) \downarrow 3 \quad =^b$$

Equation "t" rearranges statement pairs:

$$(\Sigma \ll \text{while } i<=n \text{ do } i:=i+1 \text{ od}; \text{write}(i) \gg <\sigma[1 /i], \text{nil}, \text{nil}>) \downarrow 3 \quad =^t$$

Now the loop semantics are entered for the first time:

$$(\Sigma \ll \text{write}(i) \gg \circ \Sigma \ll \text{while } i<=n \text{ do } i:=i+1 \text{ od} \gg <\sigma, \text{nil}, \text{nil}>) \downarrow 3 \quad =^s$$

The next several steps are followed to evaluate the loop condition:

$$(\Sigma \ll \text{write}(i) \gg \ \circ \ \text{if } \zeta \ll i<=n \gg \sigma \text{ then}$$
$$\Sigma \ll \text{while } i<=n \text{ do } i:=i+1 \text{ od} \gg \ \circ$$
$$\Sigma \ll i:=i+1 \gg <\sigma, \text{nil}, \text{nil}> \text{ else } <\sigma, \text{nil}, \text{nil}>) \downarrow 3 \quad =^m$$

The evaluation of $\zeta \ll i<=n \gg \sigma$ itself results in a conditional evaluation shown here as a nested conditional:

$$(\Sigma \ll \text{write}(i) \gg \ \circ \quad \text{if (if } \varepsilon \ll i \gg \sigma <= \varepsilon \ll n \gg \sigma \text{ then true else false) then}$$
$$\Sigma \ll \text{while } i<=n \text{ do } i:=i+1 \text{ od} \gg \ \circ$$
$$\Sigma \ll i:=i+1 \gg <\sigma, \text{nil}, \text{nil}> \text{ else } <\sigma, \text{nil}, \text{nil}>) \quad \downarrow 3 \quad =^{2 \bullet c}$$

$$(\Sigma \ll \text{write}(i) \gg \ \circ \quad \text{if (if } \alpha \ll i \gg \sigma <= \alpha \ll n \gg \sigma \text{ then true else false) then}$$
$$\Sigma \ll \text{while } i<=n \text{ do } i:=i+1 \text{ od} \gg \ \circ$$
$$\Sigma \ll i:=i+1 \gg <\sigma, \text{nil}, \text{nil}> \text{ else } <\sigma, \text{nil}, \text{nil}>) \quad \downarrow 3 \quad =^{2 \bullet f}$$

$$(\Sigma \ll \text{write}(i) \gg \ \circ \quad \text{if (if } \beta \ll i \gg \sigma <= \beta \ll n \gg \sigma \text{ then true else false) then}$$
$$\Sigma \ll \text{while } i<=n \text{ do } i:=i+1 \text{ od} \gg \ \circ$$
$$\Sigma \ll i:=i+1 \gg <\sigma, \text{nil}, \text{nil}> \text{ else } <\sigma, \text{nil}, \text{nil}>) \quad \downarrow 3 \quad =^{2 \bullet i}$$

$$(\Sigma \ll \text{write}(i) \gg \ \circ \quad \text{if (if } 1 <= \ 3 \text{ then true else false) then}$$
$$\Sigma \ll \text{while } i<=n \text{ do } i:=i+1 \text{ od} \gg \ \circ$$
$$\Sigma \ll i:=i+1 \gg <\sigma, \text{nil}, \text{nil}> \text{ else } <\sigma, \text{nil}, \text{nil}>) \quad \downarrow 3 \quad =^{\text{math}}$$

$$(\Sigma \ll \text{write}(i) \gg \ \circ \quad \text{if true then}$$
$$\Sigma \ll \text{while } i<=n \text{ do } i:=i+1 \text{ od} \gg \ \circ$$
$$\Sigma \ll i:=i+1 \gg <\sigma, \text{nil}, \text{nil}> \text{else } <\sigma, \text{nil}, \text{nil}>) \quad \downarrow 3 \quad =^{\text{math}}$$

Since the loop condition evaluates to true, the next several steps are followed to evaluate the loop body. The configuration obtained from the loop body will be used when the loop reference is to be reevaluated:

$$(\Sigma \ll \text{write}(i) \gg \ \circ \quad \Sigma \ll \text{ while } i<=n \text{ do } i:=i+1 \text{ od} \gg \ \circ \Sigma \ll i:=i+1 \gg$$
$$<\sigma, \text{nil}, \text{nil}>) \qquad \downarrow 3 \qquad =^p$$

$(\Sigma \ll \text{write}(i) \gg {}^{\circ}\quad \Sigma \ll \text{while } i{<=}n \text{ do } i{:=}i{+}1 \text{ od} \gg {<}\sigma[\varepsilon \ll i{+}1 \gg \sigma \;/i],$
$\qquad\qquad \text{nil,nil>}) \qquad\qquad \downarrow 3 \qquad\qquad =^{a}$

$(\Sigma \ll \text{write}(i) \gg {}^{\circ}\quad \Sigma \ll \text{while } i{<=}n \text{ do } i{:=}i{+}1 \text{ od} \gg {<}\sigma[\varepsilon \ll i \gg \sigma{+}\varepsilon \ll 1 \gg \sigma \;/i],$
$\qquad\qquad \text{nil,nil>})\downarrow 3 \qquad\qquad =^{2 \bullet c}$

$(\Sigma \ll \text{write}(i) \gg {}^{\circ}\quad \Sigma \ll \text{while } i{<=}n \text{ do } i{:=}i{+}1 \text{ od} \gg {<}\sigma[\alpha \ll i \gg \sigma{+}\alpha \ll 1 \gg$
$\qquad\qquad \sigma \;/i] \text{ ,nil,nil>}) \quad\downarrow 3 \qquad\qquad =^{2 \bullet f}$

$(\Sigma \ll \text{write}(i) \gg {}^{\circ}\quad \Sigma \ll \text{while } i{<=}n \text{ do } i{:=}i{+}1 \text{ od} \gg {<}\sigma[\beta \ll i \gg \sigma{+}\beta \ll 1 \gg \sigma \;/i],$
$\qquad\qquad \text{nil,nil>})\downarrow 3 \qquad\qquad =^{i+b}$

$(\Sigma \ll \text{write}(i) \gg {}^{\circ}\quad \Sigma \ll \text{while } i{<=}n \text{ do } i{:=}i{+}1 \text{ od} \gg {<}\sigma[1{+}1 \;/i] \text{ ,nil,nil>})$
$\qquad \downarrow 3 \qquad\qquad =^{\text{math}}$

The loop semantics are reentered:

$(\Sigma \ll \text{write}(i) \gg {}^{\circ} \Sigma \ll \text{while } i{<=}n \text{ do } i{:=}i{+}1 \text{ od} \gg {<}\sigma[2 \;/i],\text{nil,nil>})\downarrow 3 \qquad =^{s}$

The next several steps are followed to evaluate the loop condition:

$(\Sigma \ll \text{write}(i) \gg {}^{\circ} \text{ if } \zeta \ll i{<=}n \gg \sigma \text{ then}$
$\qquad\qquad\qquad \Sigma \ll \text{while } i{<=}n \text{ do } i{:=}i{+}1 \text{ od} \gg {}^{\circ}$
$\qquad\qquad\qquad \Sigma \ll i{:=}i{+}1 \gg {<}\sigma,\text{nil,nil> else} {<}\sigma,\text{nil,nil>}) \downarrow 3 \quad =^{m}$

$(\Sigma \ll \text{write}(i) \gg {}^{\circ} \text{ if } (\text{ if } \varepsilon \ll i \gg \sigma {<=} \varepsilon \ll n \gg \sigma \text{ then true else false }) \text{ then}$
$\qquad\qquad\qquad \Sigma \ll \text{while } i{<=}n \text{ do } i{:=}i{+}1 \text{ od} \gg {}^{\circ}$
$\qquad\qquad\qquad \Sigma \ll i{:=}i{+}1 \gg {<}\sigma,\text{nil,nil> else} {<}\sigma,\text{nil,nil>}) \downarrow 3 \quad =^{2 \bullet c}$

$(\Sigma \ll \text{write}(i) \gg {}^{\circ} \text{ if } (\text{ if } \alpha \ll i \gg \sigma {<=} \alpha \ll n \gg \sigma \text{ then true else false }) \text{ then}$
$\qquad\qquad\qquad \Sigma \ll \text{while } i{<=}n \text{ do } i{:=}i{+}1 \text{ od} \gg {}^{\circ}$
$\qquad\qquad\qquad \Sigma \ll i{:=}i{+}1 \gg {<}\sigma,\text{nil,nil> else} {<}\sigma,\text{nil,nil>}) \downarrow 3 \quad =^{2 \bullet f}$

$(\Sigma \ll \text{write}(i) \gg {}^{\circ} \text{ if } (\text{ if } \beta \ll i \gg \sigma {<=} \beta \ll n \gg \sigma \text{ then true else false }) \text{ then}$
$\qquad\qquad\qquad \Sigma \ll \text{while } i{<=}n \text{ do } i{:=}i{+}1 \text{ od} \gg {}^{\circ}$
$\qquad\qquad\qquad \Sigma \ll i{:=}i{+}1 \gg {<}\sigma,\text{nil,nil> else} {<}\sigma,\text{nil,nil>}) \downarrow 3 \quad =^{2 \bullet i}$

$(\Sigma \ll \text{write}(i) \gg {}^{\circ} \text{ if } (\text{ if } 2 {<=} 3 \text{ then true else false }) \text{ then}$
$\qquad\qquad\qquad \Sigma \ll \text{while } i{<=}n \text{ do } i{:=}i{+}1 \text{ od} \gg {}^{\circ}$
$\qquad\qquad\qquad \Sigma \ll i{:=}i{+}1 \gg {<}\sigma,\text{nil,nil> else} {<}\sigma,\text{nil,nil>}) \downarrow 3 \quad =^{\text{math}}$

$(\Sigma \ll \text{write}(i) \gg {}^{\circ} \text{ if true then}$
$\qquad\qquad\qquad \Sigma \ll \text{while } i{<=}n \text{ do } i{:=}i{+}1 \text{ od} \gg {}^{\circ}$
$\qquad\qquad\qquad \Sigma \ll i{:=}i{+}1 \gg {<}\sigma,\text{nil,nil>else} {<}\sigma,\text{nil,nil>}) \downarrow 3 \quad =^{\text{math}}$

Since the loop condition evaluates to true, the next several steps are followed to evaluate the loop body:

$(\Sigma \ll \text{write}(i) \gg {}^{\circ} \Sigma \ll \text{while } i{<=}n \text{ do } i{:=}i{+}1 \text{ od} \gg {}^{\circ} \Sigma \ll i{:=}i{+}1 \gg {<}\sigma,\text{nil,nil>})$
$\qquad \downarrow 3 \qquad\qquad =^{p}$

$(\Sigma \ll \text{write}(i) \gg {}^{\circ} \Sigma \ll \text{while } i{<=}n \text{ do } i{:=}i{+}1 \text{ od} \gg {<}\sigma[\varepsilon \ll i{+}1 \gg \sigma \;/i] \text{ ,nil,nil>})$
$\qquad \downarrow 3 \qquad\qquad =^{a}$

$(\Sigma \ll \text{write}(i) \gg {}^{\circ} \Sigma \ll \text{while } i{<=}n \text{ do } i{:=}i{+}1 \text{ od} \gg {<}\sigma[\varepsilon \ll i \gg \sigma{+} \varepsilon \ll 1 \gg \sigma \;/i],$
$\qquad \text{nil,nil>}) \quad\downarrow 3 \qquad =^{2 \bullet c}$

$(\Sigma \ll \text{write}(i) \gg {}^{\circ} \Sigma \ll \text{while } i{<=}n \text{ do } i{:=}i{+}1 \text{ od} \gg {<}\sigma[\alpha \ll i \gg \sigma{+} \alpha \ll 1 \gg \sigma \;/i],$
$\qquad \text{nil,nil>}) \quad\downarrow 3 \qquad =^{2 \bullet f}$

$(\Sigma \ll \text{write}(i) \gg {}^{\circ} \ll \text{while } i{<=}n \text{ do } i{:=}i{+}1 \text{ od} \gg {<}\sigma[\beta \ll i \gg \sigma {+} \beta \ll 1 \gg \sigma \;/i],$
$\qquad \text{nil,nil>}) \quad\downarrow 3 \qquad =^{i+b}$

$(\Sigma \ll \text{write}(i) \gg {}^{\circ} \Sigma \ll \text{while } i{<=}n \text{ do } i{:=}i{+}1 \text{ od} \gg {<}\sigma[2 {+}1 \;/i] \text{ ,nil,nil>})$
$\qquad \downarrow 3 \quad =^{\text{math}}$

Notice that the loop semantics are reentered for the third time:

$(\Sigma$ « write(i) » $\circ$ Σ « while $i<=n$ do $i:=i+1$ od » $<\sigma[3\ /i]$,nil,nil>) $\downarrow 3$ $=^s$

$(\Sigma$ « write(i) » $\circ$ if ζ « $i<=n$ » σ then
$\qquad\qquad\Sigma$ « while $i<=n$ do $i:=i+1$ od » $\circ$
$\qquad\qquad\Sigma$ « $i:=i+1$ » $<\sigma$,nil,nil> else $<\sigma$,nil,nil>) $\qquad$ $\downarrow 3$ $=^m$

$(\Sigma$ « write(i) » $\circ$ if (if ε « i » $\sigma<=\varepsilon$ « n » σ then true else false) then
$\qquad\qquad\Sigma$ « while $i<=n$ do $i:=i+1$ od » $\circ$
$\qquad\qquad\Sigma$ « $i:=i+1$ » $<\sigma$,nil,nil> else $<\sigma$,nil,nil>) $\qquad$ $\downarrow 3$ $=^{2\ \bullet\ c}$

$(\Sigma$ « write(i) » $\circ$ if (if α « i » $\sigma <=\alpha$ « n » σ then true else false) then
$\qquad\qquad\Sigma$ « while $i<=n$ do $i:=i+1$ od » $\circ$
$\qquad\qquad\Sigma$ « $i:=i+1$ » $<\sigma$,nil,nil> else $<\sigma$,nil,nil>) $\qquad$ $\downarrow 3$ $=^{2\ \bullet\ f}$

$(\Sigma$ « write(i) » $\circ$ if (if β « i » $\sigma <=\beta$ « n » σ then true else false) then
$\qquad\qquad\Sigma$ « while $i<=n$ do $i:=i+1$ od » $\circ$
$\qquad\qquad\Sigma$ « $i:=i+1$ » $<\sigma$,nil,nil> else $<\sigma$,nil,nil>) $\qquad$ $\downarrow 3$ $=^{2\ \bullet\ i}$

$(\Sigma$ « write(i) » $\circ$ if (if $3 <= 3$ then true else false) then
$\qquad\qquad\Sigma$ « while $i<=n$ do $i:=i+1$ od » $\circ$
$\qquad\qquad\Sigma$ « $i:=i+1$ » $<\sigma$,nil,nil> else $<\sigma$,nil,nil>) $\qquad$ $\downarrow 3$ $=^{\text{math}}$

$(\Sigma$ « write(i) » $\circ$ if true then
$\qquad\qquad\Sigma$ « while $i<=n$ do $i:=i+1$ od » $\circ$
$\qquad\qquad\Sigma$ « $i:=i+1$ » $<\sigma$,nil,nil>else $<\sigma$,nil,nil>) $\qquad$ $\downarrow 3$ $=^{\text{math}}$

Since the loop condition evaluates to true, the next several steps are followed to evaluate the loop body:

$(\Sigma$ « write(i) » $\circ$ Σ « while $i<=n$ do $i:=i+1$ od » $\circ$ Σ « $i:=i+1$ » $<\sigma$,nil,nil>)
$\qquad\downarrow 3$ $=^p$

$(\Sigma$ « write(i) » $\circ$ Σ « while $i<=n$ do $i:=i+1$ od » $<\sigma[\varepsilon$ « $i+1$ » $\sigma\ /i]$,nil,nil>)
$\qquad\downarrow 3$ $=^a$

$(\Sigma$ « write(i) » $\circ$ Σ « while $i<=n$ do $i:=i+1$ od » $<\sigma[\varepsilon$ « i » $\sigma+\varepsilon$ « 1 » $\sigma\ /i]$,
nil,nil>) $\downarrow 3$ $=^{2\ \bullet\ c}$

$(\Sigma$ « write(i) » $\circ$ Σ « while $i<=n$ do $i:=i+1$ od » $<\sigma[\alpha$ « i » $\sigma+\alpha$ « 1 » $\sigma\ /i]$, nil,nil>) $\downarrow 3$ $=^{2\ \bullet\ f}$

$(\Sigma$ « write(i) » $\circ$ Σ « while $i<=n$ do $i:=i+1$ od » $<\sigma[\beta$ « i » $\sigma+\beta$ « 1 » $\sigma\ /i]$, nil,nil>) $\downarrow 3$ $=^{i+b}$

$(\Sigma$ « write>(i) » $\circ$ Σ « while $i<=n$ do $i:=i+1$ od » $<\sigma[3\ +1\ /i]$,nil,nil>)
$\qquad\downarrow 3$ $=^{\text{math}}$

The loop semantics are evaluated for the final time:

$(\Sigma$ « write(i) » $\circ$ Σ « while $i<=n$ do $i:=i+1$ od » $<\sigma[4\ /i]$,nil,nil>) $\downarrow 3$ $=^s$

$(\Sigma$ « write(i) » $\circ$ if ζ « $i<=n$ » σ then
$\qquad\qquad\Sigma$ « while $i<=n$ do $i:=i+1$ od » $\circ$
$\qquad\qquad\Sigma$ « $i:=i+1$ » $<\sigma$,nil,nil> else $<\sigma$nil,nil>) $\qquad$ $\downarrow 3$ $=^m$

$(\Sigma$ « write(i) » $\circ$ if (if ε « i » $\sigma <=\varepsilon$ « n » σ then true else false) then
$\qquad\qquad\Sigma$ « while $i<=n$ do $i:=i+1$ od » $\circ$
$\qquad\qquad\Sigma$ « $i:=i+1$ » $<\sigma$,nil,nil> else $<\sigma$,nil,nil>) $\qquad$ $\downarrow 3$ $=^{2\ \bullet\ c}$

$(\Sigma$ « write(i) » $\circ$ if (if α « i » $\sigma <=\alpha$ « n » σ then true else false) then

Σ « while $i<=n$ do $i:=i+1$ od » $\circ$
Σ « $i:=i+1$ » <σ,nil,nil> else <σ,nil,nil>) $\downarrow$3 $=^{2 \cdot f}$
(Σ « write(i) » $\circ$ if (if β « i » $\sigma <= \beta$ « n » σ then true else false) then
Σ « while $i<=n$ do $i:=i+1$ od » $\circ$
Σ « $i:=i+1$ » <σ,nil,nil> else <σ,nil,nil>) $\downarrow$3 $=^{2 \cdot i}$
(Σ « write(i) » $\circ$ if (if $4 <= 3$ then true else false) then
Σ « while $i<=n$ do $i:=i+1$ od » $\circ$
Σ « $i:=i+1$ » <σ,nil,nil> else <σ,nil,nil>) $\downarrow$3 $=^{\mathrm{math}}$
(Σ « write(i) » $\circ$ if false then
Σ « while $i<=n$ do $i:=i+1$ od » $\circ$
Σ « $i:=i+1$ » <σ,nil,nil>else <σ,nil,nil>) $\downarrow$3 $=^{\mathrm{math}}$

Since the condition evaluates to false, the configuration is passed through to the WRITE statement:

(Σ « write(i) » <σ,nil,nil>) $\downarrow$ 3 $=^r$
(<σ,nil,append(nil, $\sigma[i]$)>) $\downarrow$ 3 $=$append
(<σ,nil,[4]>) $\downarrow$ 3 $=$extract
[4]

■ ■

AXIOMATIC SEMANTICS IN A NUTSHELL

Among the other methods for defining the semantics of a programming language is that of *axiomatic semantic definitions*, developed by C.A.R. Hoare. These definitions enable you to prove programs partially correct. That is, you can use the axiomatic semantic definitions of a target language (combined with axioms from the problem domain) to prove programs written in the target language to be correct with respect to the specification of the program. Total correctness bears the additional requirement that the program will halt—that it will not execute forever.

The symbol $\supset$ is used for logical implication, and the symbol $\vdash$ is used for the statement, "It is true that . . ."

Assume the problem domain of a program to be integer arithmetic. First you would develop axioms for various arithmetic rules. These axioms describe the problem domain and indicate known truths such as the commutative, associative, and distributive properties of addition and multiplication.

A1: $x + y = y + x$
A2: $x * y = y * x$
A3: $(x + y) + z = x + (y+z)$
A4: $(x * y) * z = x * (y * z)$
A5: $x * (y + z) = x * y + x * z$
A6: $y < = x \supset (x - y) + y = x$
A7: $x + 0 = x$
A8: $x * 0 = 0$
A9: $x * 1 = x$

A basic template for proof is *Hoare's Triples:*

$$P\{Q\}R$$

where P is a precondition, R is a postcondition, and Q is a program (a sequence of or a single statement).

Using the basic form, we now have a series of axioms that give the semantics of the language features. These axioms define the language to be applied to the problem domain.

AXIOM OF ASSIGNMENT
D0: $\vdash P_0\{V{:}{=}E\}P$

Where V is an identifier, and E is an expression.

Meaning: P_0 is obtained from P by substituting E for all occurrences of V in P.

AXIOM OF CONSEQUENCE
D1:   if $\vdash P\{Q\}R$ and $R \supset S$ then $\vdash P\{Q\}S$
   if $\vdash P\{Q\}R$ and $S \supset P$ then $\vdash S\{Q\}R$

There is an important difference for implications that reference a precondition as opposed to those that reference a postcondition. Notice that when the implication involves a postcondition, the postcondition serves as the implication's antecedent. When the implication involves a precondition, the precondition serves as the consequent. The reasoning behind these relationships is significant.

Because an implication, $S \supset P$, is equivalent to $\neg S \vee P$, one cannot logically justify

   if $\vdash P\{Q\}S$ and $R \supset S$ then $\vdash P\{Q\}R$

since R is not necessarily true. However, one can justify

   if $\vdash P\{Q\}R$ and $S \supset P$ then $\vdash S\{Q\}R$

since S can be true or false, but in either case P remains true.

AXIOM OF COMPOSITION
D2:   if $\vdash P\{Q_1\}R_1$ and $R_1\{Q_2\}R$ then $\vdash P\{Q_1; Q_2\}R$

The axiom of composition is applicable when the postcondition of one statement, Q_1, also describes the precondition of another statement, Q_2. Since pre- and postconditions are describing states, Q_2 must immediately follow Q_1.

AXIOM OF ITERATION
D3:   if $\vdash P\&B\{S\}P$ then $\vdash P\{\text{while } B \text{ do } S \text{ od}\}P\&\neg B$

The axiom of iteration is a safe rule. When the pattern $P\&B\{S\}P$ is matched, it is safe to say that P is a loop invariant for statements S, in which case a WHILE loop can be formed. A *loop invariant* is a condition that remains true throughout all iterations of the loop's execution.

Since READ statements are like assignments, and since a WRITE statement does not alter the state or otherwise influence a computation, there is no need to define them for our present purposes.

Now consider a problem specification, a WHILE program solution, and a proof to show the program to be correct.

SPECIFICATION

x and n are input—initial values for i and r are zero.

$\neg \, i < n \, \& \, x = x * (i + 1) - r$

The program specified will multiply two numbers together (i.e., $x \times n$). The specification is an invariant. Because this program multiplies $x \times n$, it is important to indicate how one may compute x at any point in the program.

PROGRAM

$r:=0;$
$i:=0;$
while $i < n$ do
    $r:=r + x;$
    $i:=i + 1$
    od

PROGRAM PROOF

1. true $\supset x = x * (0 + 1) - 0$ Lemma 1

Step 1 is proved by lemma 1 seen later. This is an important step because it sets the stage for the proof. It is based upon the specification, is mathematically true, and provides for an initial state of the invariant.

2. $x = x * (0 + 1) - 0 \, \{r:=0\} \, x = x * (0 + 1) - r$ D0

Step 2 is based upon the axiom of assignment wherein the precondition can be obtained from the postcondition by substituting zero (the RHS of the assignment) for all occurrences of r (the LHS of the assignment).

3. $x = x * (0 + 1) - r \, \{i: = 0\} \, x = x * (i + 1) - r$ D0

Step 3 is also based upon the axiom of assignment wherein the precondition can be obtained from the postcondition by substituting zero (the RHS of the assignment) for all occurrences of i (the LHS of the assignment).

4. true $\{r:=0\} \, x = x * (0 + 1) - r$ D1 (1,2)

Step 4 employs the axiom of consequence.

5. true $\{r:=0; \, i:=0\} \, x = x * (i +1) - r$ D2 (4,3)

Since Step 4's postcondition matches Step 3's precondition, the axiom of composition can be used to concatenate program statements.

6. $x = x * (i + 1) - r \, \& \, i < n \supset x = x * ((i + 1) + 1) - (r + x)$ Lemma 2

Step 6 is proved by lemma 2. This, again, is an important step, because it sets the stage for establishing the needed WHILE loop. It is indeed based on the specification, is mathematically true, and provides for a loop invariant that makes use of the defined variables.

7. $x = x * ((i + 1) + 1) - (r + x) \{i:=i+1\} \, x = x * (i + 1) - (r + x)$ D0

Step 7 is based upon the axiom of assignment wherein the precondition can be obtained from the postcondition by substituting $i + 1$ (the RHS of the assignment) for all occurrences of i (the LHS of the assignment) in the postcondition.

8. $x = x * (i + 1) - (r + x) \{r:=r + x\} \, x = x * (i + 1) - r$ D0

Likewise, Step 8 is based on the axiom of assignment wherein the precondition can be obtained from the postcondition by substituting $r + x$ (the RHS of the assignment) for all occurrences of r (the LHS of the assignment) in the postcondition.

9. $x = x * ((i + 1) + 1) - (r + x) \{i:=i + 1; \, r:=r + x\} \, x = x * (i + 1) - r$
   D2 (7,8)

As Step 7's postcondition matches Step 8's precondition, the axiom of composition can be used to concatenate program statements.

10. $i < n \, \& \, x = x * (i + 1) - r \, \{i:=i + 1; \, r:=r + x\} \, x = x * (i + 1) - r$
   D1 (6,9)

Step 10 employs the axiom of consequence on Steps 6 and 9. This results in exactly the pattern for a WHILE loop application where P is $x = x^* (i + 1) - r$, and B is $i < n$.

11. $x = x * (i + 1) - r \, \{\text{while } i < n \text{ do } i:=i + 1; \, r:=r + x \text{ od}\} \, \neg \, i < n \, \& \, x = x * (i + 1) - r$ D3

Step 11 employs the axiom of iteration.

12. true $\{r:=0; \, i:=0; \, \text{while } i < n \text{ do } i:=i + 1; \, r:=r + x \text{ od}\} \, \neg \, i < n \, \& \, x = x * (i + 1) - r$ D2(5,11)

In a final application of the axiom of composition, Step 12 pulls the two program segments together. Thus the program is proved partially correct.

Partial correctness is satisfied when a program (like this one) is shown to be correct with respect to its specification. Notice in the proof given, that the postcondition derived is the specification of the program. To be totally correct it must also be proved that the program will terminate or halt. Dijkstra's guarded commands were developed to extend the idea of Hoare's Triples to provide for total correctness.

The arithmetic axioms are employed as follows to prove the lemmas:

LEMMA 1

$x = x$	
$x = x * 1$	A9
$x = x * 1 + 0$	A7
$x = x * 1 + 0 * x$	A8
$x = x * (1 + 0)$	A5
$x = x * (0 + 1)$	A1
$x = x * (0 + 1) - 0$	A7

LEMMA 2

$x = x * (i + 1) - r$	
$x = x * (i + 1) + x - (r + x)$	A6
$x = x * ((i + 1) + 1) - (r + x)$	A5

REFERENCES

Joseph E. Stoy. *Denotational Semantics: The Scott-Strachey Approach to Programming Language Theory.* Cambridge, MA: The MIT Press, 1977.

E. W. Dijkstra, "Guarded Commands," *Communications of the ACM* 18, no. 8, (1975):453–457.

C.A.R. Hoare, "An Axiomatic Basis for Computer Programming," *Communications of the ACM* 12, no. 10, (1969):576–580.

QUESTIONS AND EXERCISES

1. Write a program to convert character representation of a number to an integer value without using the string-to-integer conversions available in some languages.

2. Repeat the code written for Question 1 to convert from characters to real numbers.

3. Using the semantic equations, derive the meaning of the following:

   M « read(n); $i:=1$; while $i<=n$ do $i:=i+1$ od; write(i) » [2]

4. Assume $D = \{t,f\}^\circ$. Give the result of each of the following denotational operations:

   a. $<1, 4, [1,2,3,4], [6,5]> \downarrow 2$
   b. hd(dcba)
   c. tl(dcba)
   d. D^2
   e. D^*

5. Write a WHILE language program segment that is equivalent to this Java segment:

   ```
   s = 0;
   for (i = 0; i < 9; i++)
        {s:=s 1 i}
   ```

6. Using the WHILE language definitions (with the additions shown next), complete the following definition to implement the repeat-until loop construct:

   Σ « repeat S until C » $\gamma =$

   which means repeat the statements of S until the condition C is true. S is executed at least one time, since the test of the condition occurs at the end, not the beginning of the loop body. Additions to the syntax and semantics of the WHILE language are

   $C ::= E1 < E2 \mid E1 > E2 \mid E1 = E2 \mid E1 <= E2 \mid E1 >= E2 \mid E1 \neq E2 \mid$ not C
   ζ « not C » σ $\qquad = \qquad$ if ζ « C » σ then false else true

7. Using the syntax and denotational semantics of the WHILE language, show the steps necessary to de termine the formal meaning of

Σ « while $i < 2$ do $i:=i + 1$; $s:=s^* i$ od » $<\sigma, \phi 1, \phi 2>$

Assume in σ, that $i = 1$, and $s = 1$.

8. Devise the syntax and semantics for a parentheses-free language for postfix arithmetic expressions.

9. Recall the semantic equation for the WHILE statement:

s. Σ « while C do S od » $\gamma =$ if ζ « C » $\gamma \downarrow 1$ then
$\qquad\qquad\qquad\qquad\qquad\qquad\Sigma$ « while C do S od » $\circ$ Σ « S » γ else γ

Explain whether the following rule is equivalent:

s. Σ « while C do S od » $\gamma =$ if ζ « C » $\gamma \downarrow 1$ then
$\qquad\qquad\qquad\qquad\qquad\qquad\Sigma$ « while C do S od; S » γ else γ

4

LANGUAGE TRANSLATION

■ ■

TRANSLATION IN A NUTSHELL

Translation is the process of converting a *source program*—which is a problem solution stated in a given target language—into a machine-executable form. There are two approaches to the automation of language translation: interpretation and compilation. An *interpreter* executes program statements as they are encountered during the translation process. At least two methods of program interpretation are possible:

1. As statements are deciphered, subprograms to carry out the functions specified are invoked.
2. As statements are deciphered, a machine-independent form of the program is generated and then executed by an emulator.

The latter approach is similar to that taken in the current approach to Java program translation. Both methods will be explored in this chapter. Each shares a great deal in common with program compilation.

A *compiler* builds a machine-code representation of the translated source program. Compilation comprises several phases. The *lexical-analysis* phase, which is repeated many times in the compilation of a program, entails a character-by-character scan of a program. It results in the identification of each lexical unit, or language vocabulary symbol. For example, suppose we have a simple language of arithmetic expressions consisting only of constants and operators, $+$, $-$, $*$, and $/$. Given the following input "program,"

> $45 + 67 * 3$

the lexical analyzer would be executed (or invoked) at least five times. The first time it would read two characters and recognize the constant of 45. It would know the extent of the constant because in modern languages, spaces and operators also serve as *delimiters*, providing the boundary points of lexical units. The next time the lexical analyzer was invoked, it would recognize the plus ($+$) operator. The space is ignored because it is not an operator—it is only a delimiter—and has already served its delimiting purpose. The lexical analyzer would be invoked three more times, recognizing, in order, the vocabulary symbols 67, $*$, and 3.

But what invokes the lexical analyzer? What is it that needs lexical units identified one at a time? The answer is, the *syntax analyzer*, which is based on the syntax definitions of the language and "drives" the next phase of compilation.

Suppose the language we are compiling consists of the following definition:

> $S ::=$ constant $+ S$ | constant

Notice that to determine whether an input program is a valid program (with respect to the grammar), the syntax-analysis routine will need to determine whether the next input symbol is a constant or the plus ($+$) operator. To make this determination, the syntax-analysis routines will invoke the lexical analyzer and then match the symbol with the next symbol expected.

For example, assuming a $ symbol marks the end-of-file, a routine to match the additive expression just specified would be:

```
Function S:Boolean;
Begin
            If Lex = constant then
                    Begin
                    Accept;
                    If Lex = "+" then
                            Begin
                            Accept;
                            If S then
                                    return true
                            Else
                                    return false
                            End
                    Else
                    If Lex = "$" then
                            return true
                    Else
                            return false
                    End
            Else
                    return false
End;
```

Notice that a slight change in Pascal is made here. Usually, one would indicate "s:=false" instead of "Return false." The same holds for returning "true." The returned value is considered to be an improvement over recursive structures (as will be seen later) such as

if e then e:=true else e:=false;

The function is named after the LHS symbol from the BNF rule that specifies the function. When a lexical term is matched with the expected symbol, the Accept function will produce the next token (or terminal symbol) and assign it to the variable Lex. Notice, in Figure 4.1, that there is an IF-THEN-ELSE structure for each RHS alternative in the BNF rule.

The fact that both RHS alternatives begin with "constant" requires us to effectively factor out the common prefix. If the constant matched is followed by the plus sign, then the first RHS alternative is followed. If a plus sign does not follow the constant matched, then an attempt to match end-of-file is made. If the attempt is successful, then the second alternative is satisfied.

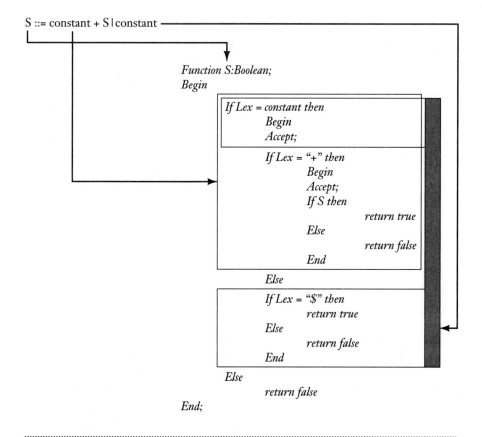

FIGURE 4.1   IF-THEN-ELSE structure.

Otherwise, or if a constant is not matched from the beginning, the function variable is set to false, indicating that the input sentence is not valid according to the grammar.

At this point one can address the semantics of the language. Both of the approaches discussed earlier for implementing the semantics require a *semantic action stack (SAS)*. In the SAS, we will capture information about operands and the results of operations. Then we will embed in the syntax routine the semantic actions to manipulate the SAS and to execute the specified operation, as shown in boldface in the following example:

```
Function S:Boolean;
Var Op1, Op2:integer;
Begin
        If Lex = constant then
                Begin
                Push(SAS,Lex);
                Accept;
                If Lex = "+" then
                        Begin
                        Accept;
                        If S then
                                Begin
                                Op2:=pop(SAS);
                                Op1:=pop(SAS);
                                Push(SAS,Op1 + Op2)
                                return true;
                                End
                        Else
                                return false
                        End
                Else
                If Lex = "$" then
                        return true
                Else
                        return false
                End
        Else
                return false
End;
```

It is assumed that a potentially intermediate result (i.e., Op2) has been pushed during a recursive call to *S*, and that the final result of the expression will remain at the top of the stack after the final return from *S*. Whereas this code executes the specified instruction as it translates the instruction, the second approach to interpretation generates a machine-independent version of the code—similar to the byte-code approach in Java. The machine-independent instruction set has the general format of

Operator, Operand1, Operand2, Result

This form of instruction is called a *quad*. The idea is that the operator is applied to operand 1 and, optionally, operand 2, leaving the result in the result field. The operands can be variables or constants from the program being translated, or temporary variables that can be generated as needed using a function such as *gentemp*. One set of operators follows:

rd, rdln, wr, wrln	Input-Output
+, −, *, /	Arithmetic
<, >, <=, >=, =, <>	Relational
jtrue, jfalse, jump	Conditional/unconditional jumps
:=	Assignment

Typically generated quads are placed in a *quad table*. Each entry has an index that can serve as the destination of a jump instruction. For the semantics of a program, a *genquad* procedure is usually used that accepts four arguments: operator, operand 1, operand 2, and result. Notice there is no notion of registers or memory management; the language is machine-independent. Now consider the original syntactic function with semantic actions embedded for the generation of quads:

```
Function S:Boolean;
Var Op1, Op2:integer;
        T:temp;
Begin
        If Lex = constant then
                Begin
                Push(SAS,Lex);
                Accept;
                If Lex = "+" then
                        Begin
                        Accept;
                        If S then
                                Begin
                                T:=gentemp;
                                Op2:=pop(SAS);
                                Op1:=pop(SAS);
                                Gen_quad(+,Op2,Op1,T);
                                Push(SAS,T)
                                return true;
                                End
                        Else
                                return false
                        End
                Else
                If Lex = "$" then
                        return true
```

> Else
>> return false
> End
Else
> return false
End;

Bear in mind that the person writing the interpreter must write the function *gentemp* and the procedure *gen_quad*. The language we are recognizing here is clearly very simple. The quad language is quite powerful and can represent the semantics of much more complicated programs:

PASCAL PROGRAM SEGMENT		REPRESENTATIVE QUADS			
$f:=1$;	1.	:=	1,	,	f
for $i:=1$ to n do	2.	:=	1,	,	i
$f:=f*i$;	3.	<=	i,	n,	t1
	4.	jfalse	t1,	,	8
	5.	*,	f,	i,	f
	6.	+,	i,	1,	i
	7.	jmp,	,	,	3
	8.				

In Figure 4.2, the relationships involved in interpretation (Figure 4.2a) and compilation (Figure 4.2b) are presented. The translation of a source program results in an execution of the program by the translator (in the case of an interpreter) or an executable version of the source program (in the case of a compiled translation). Compiler construction is the subject of entire books. We shall focus on the construction of an interpreter. One should realize, however, that there is a large intersection of functionality between a compiler and an interpreter. You can see the overlap by comparing parts "a" and "b" of Figure 4.2.

As the figure shows, the front end of an interpreter and a compiler (for the same language) can be identical in form and content. The lexical-analysis and the syntax-analysis phases are common to both. It is in the semantic-analysis and code-generation phases that the interpreter and compiler are typically most different.

LEXICAL ANALYSIS

The lexical analysis of a language translator precedes syntax analysis and is accomplished by means of a *finite state automata (FSA)*. The FSA, or lexical analyzer (LA) has as its vocabulary *LA(V)*, the set of ASCII characters, and itself has syntactic categories *LA(C)*. Its grammar, *LA(G)*, is a Type 3 grammar.

In general, the LA takes for its vocabulary the set of ASCII characters. It scans the input, character by character, until the collection assembled matches a

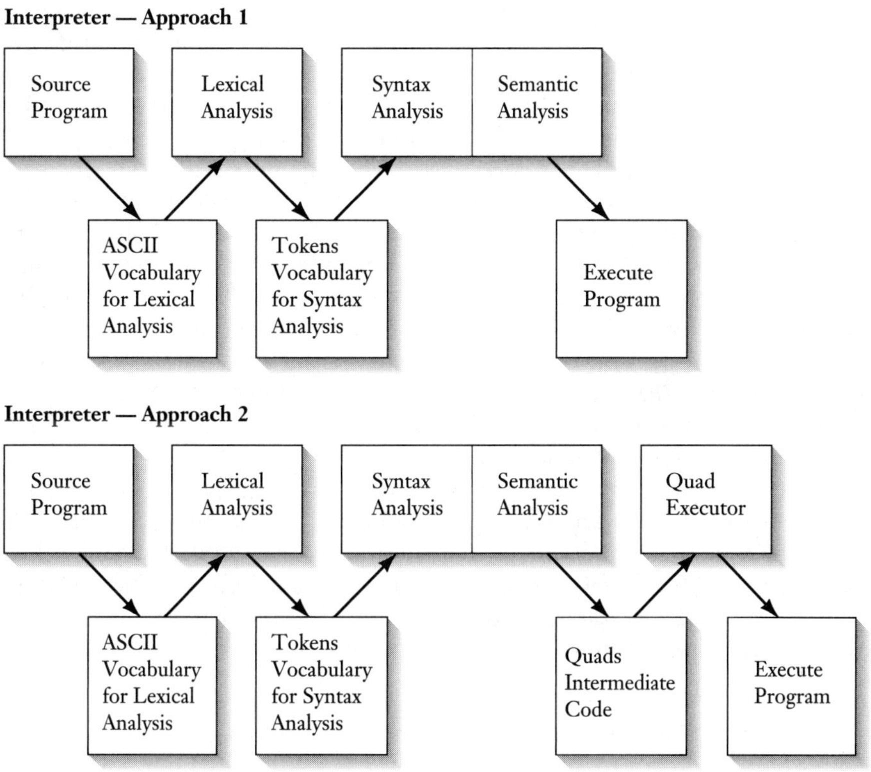

Interpreter — Approach 1

Interpreter — Approach 2

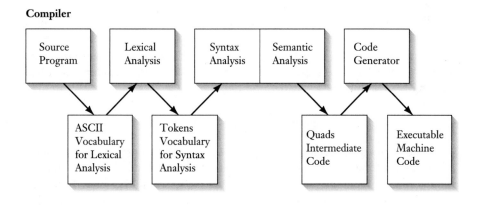

FIGURE 4.2A Language translation: interpretation.

Compiler

FIGURE 4.2B Language translation: compilation.

terminal symbol (called a *token*) of the target language. Therefore, the language recognized by the LA forms the vocabulary of a target computer language (see Figure 4.2 again). The syntax analyzer (SA) drives the LA and checks to see if the vocabulary elements recognized by the LA are combined correctly, forming legal sentences based on the syntax rules of the target language.

The LA also manages the symbol table. When an input symbol is recognized to be a legal identifier or constant, it is loaded into the symbol table (assuming it is not already there). When returning control to the SA, the LA indicates that a constant (or identifier) was recognized and also indicates the symbol-table entry of the symbol recognized. Alternatively, if a reserved word or symbol of the target language is recognized, the symbol or word itself is returned to the SA.

When the programmer violates a rule in entering a constant or identifier, a *lexical error* is issued. For example, embedding alphabetic characters in a numeric constant is typically erroneous and detectable as such by the LA (e.g., 34mm.23 is not a legal real number).

In scanning the input, the LA must know where a symbol begins and ends. Consequently, it must know the legal delimiters of the target language. As explained earlier, delimiters set the boundaries for input symbols. Many delimiters are symbols of the target language itself. For example, arithmetic operators, parentheses, square brackets, assignment operators, and relational operators are typically delimiters. Consider this input example:

```
sum:=sum+a[i];
     ^--- Next Character to be read
```

The LA recognizes one vocabulary symbol (of the target language) at a time. Assume the machine is in the state indicated and is now called by the SA to obtain the next symbol. The LA reads the "s" in "sum," and since it encounters no delimiter, reads the "u," and then the "m." The next symbol is an arithmetic operator (i.e., a delimiter), so the LA will halt, enter the identifier "sum" in the symbol table (if it is not already there), and return control to the SA, indicating that an *identifier* was recognized. These actions assume that sum is a legal identifier. When invoked next (by the SA) the LA will read the plus sign and stop, since it is a delimiter. It will return to the SA the fact that the plus sign token was encountered.

In most modern languages, the *space* character is a delimiter. If more than one space is entered, the extra spaces are ignored. For example, consider a modified version of our example:

```
sum :=      sum     +       a[i];
     ^--- Next Character to be read
```

Assume that the assignment operator was recognized during the last invocation of the LA, and that the SA is ready to receive the next symbol. Syntax analysis reinvokes lexical analysis. The spaces between the ":=" and the "s" of "sum" are scanned and ignored. The identifier "sum" is assembled as before, and the LA halts its reading when the space behind the "m" is encountered.

LEXICAL-ANALYSIS EXAMPLE

Let's consider an LA definition for the target grammar *AE(G)*:

$E ::= T \mid E + T \mid E - T$
$T ::= F \mid T * F \mid T / F$
$F ::= (E) \mid C \mid V$

In this grammar, C and V represent constants and variables, respectively. The LA's job is to recognize and build, from ASCII character input, the vocabulary of the grammar *AE(G)*. The vocabulary of the target grammar is

$\{+, -, *, /, (,), \text{constants, identifiers}\}$

To recognize this set, we will begin by identifying symbols:

$S ::= + \mid - \mid * \mid / \mid (\mid) \mid C \mid I$

As a symbol is recognized, the LA will encode it and return it to the SA. The SA functions drive the LA such that the SA invokes the LA to provide the next target-language vocabulary symbol. Now consider the definitions for the constants:

$C ::= 0 \mid 1 \mid \cdots \mid 9 \mid 0C \mid 1C \mid \cdots \mid 9C$

When a constant is identified, the LA will usually place it in the source program's symbol table and provide to the SA the information that a constant was recognized, together with the constant's location in the symbol table. When an identifier is recognized, the actions taken are identical to those taken for a constant. In both cases, symbols already loaded into the symbol table are not duplicated.

$V ::= a \mid b \mid \cdots \mid z \mid aV \mid bV \mid \cdots \mid zV$

Recalling Chomsky's hierarchy of grammars, the reader should ascertain that the productions S, V, and C are indeed regular (i.e., a Type 3 grammar). The full LAE definition for the expression grammar *AE(G)* is

$LAE(V) = \{\text{ASCII Character Set}\}$
$LAE(C) = \{S, C, V\}$
$LAE(P) = \{$
$S ::= + \mid - \mid * \mid / \mid (\mid) \mid V \mid C$
$V ::= a \mid b \mid \cdots \mid z \mid aV \mid bV \mid \cdots \mid zV$
$C ::= 0C \mid 1C \mid \cdots \mid 9C \mid 0 \mid 1 \mid \cdots \mid 9 \}$
$LAE(\text{start}) = S$

We will now begin building an interpreter for the simplified grammar:

$E ::= T \mid E + T \mid E - T$
$T ::= F \mid T * F \mid T / F$
$F ::= V$

The grammar is further simplified by eliminating constants and restricting identifiers to a single character:

$V ::= a \mid b \mid \cdots \mid z$

The lexical-analysis activity now requires only that the single symbol in input be provided to the syntax analysis. To do this, the LA will be the only subprogram to define a global variable we will call lex. In lex the SA will always find the *next* symbol in the input. From the interpreter's standpoint, this symbol is not *consumed* in input until the LA is reinvoked to provide the subsequent next symbol to be placed in lex. Once the SA has matched the current token (the value of lex) it invokes the LA to construct the next token, which results in the overwriting of or *consuming* of the current token. Following is a very simple LA routine for the arithmetic expressions given earlier:

```
program zwhile(prog,dat,output);
var
   :
   lex:char;
   prog,dat:text;
   :

function get:char;
var lex1:char;
begin
   read(prog,lex1);
   while lex1 = ' ' do
      read(prog,lex1);
   write(lex1);
   return lex1
end;
   :
begin
   :
   lex:=get;
   if syntax_analysis then writeln('ok');
   :
end.
```

The function get establishes the current value of the global variable lex. The main work of get is to ignore spaces until the next symbol to occupy lex is found. No symbol table will be required for this simple grammar. Thus, no symbol table actions are required by the lexical-analysis function.

In the main program one can observe that the first "next" symbol is obtained prior to invoking the SA (which is invoked by reference to a Boolean function, *syntax_analysis*, in the IF-statement in the main program). The SA will only reference lex, not define it (the LA defines it) and will determine when to consume lex by invoking the get function to obtain the next value of lex. The next section explains how the SA for this target language is developed.

SYNTAX ANALYSIS

After the lexical-analysis phase, you develop the SA. The SA takes as input the language's vocabulary, which is the output of lexical analysis. Consider again the grammar for a small language for arithmetic expressions, *AE(G):*

$AE(V) = \{+, -, *, /, a, b, \cdots, z\}$
$AE(C) = \{E, T, F\}$
$AE(P) = \{$
$E ::= T \mid E + T \mid E - T$
$T ::= F \mid T * F \mid T / F$
$F ::= V$ $\}$
$AE(\text{start}) = E$

The vocabulary of this language is $AE(V) = \{+, -, *, /, a, \cdots, z\}$. If we allowed multiple character identifiers, parenthesis, and constants, then it would be true that $AE(V) = $ LA. Assuming that we have no constants in the vocabulary and allow only single-character identifiers, we can conclude that all symbols of the target language are single characters. The syntactic categories of this language are $AE(C) = \{E, T, F\}$.

It turns out that the language defined by $AE(P)$ is not suitable for one type of syntactic parsing—namely, the recursive descent. *Recursive-descent compilers* are built according to the grammar rules of the language, just like the Boolean function *S* presented at the beginning of this chapter. Clearly, if we followed the same rules used in writing *S* to write a function for rule *E* in *AE(P)*, the result could be infinite recursive calls to *E* (see the second and third right-hand alternatives of *E*). Fortunately, there exist algorithms that can place the grammar in a form suitable for recursive-descent parsing and that remains equivalent to the original grammar. Several steps are involved, including

1. Elimination of left recursion.
2. Elimination of common prefixes.
3. Determination of selection sets.

In the following subsections we will perform these modifications.

ELIMINATE LEFT RECURSION

Given a grammar to be analyzed in recursive descent, one must ensure that there is no direct or indirect left recursion. *Direct left recursion* exists if and only if

$$A\beta \Rightarrow A\beta'$$

Notice that the following string, β, is not necessarily the same string after the derivation step. A rule is *indirectly left recursive* if and only if it is not directly left recursive but can satisfy the derivation of

$$A\beta \overset{+}{\Rightarrow} A\beta'$$

In eliminating left recursion, one first considers direct left recursion, which can be detected in the grammar itself:

$E ::= T \mid E + T \mid E - T$
$T ::= F \mid T * F \mid T / F$
$F ::= V$

Rules for E and T have left-recursive options. The following algorithm eliminates direct left recursion while preserving the meaning of the syntax description:

INPUT

Left recursive syntax Rule in a form wherein left recursive options precede non-left recursive options:

$B ::= B\alpha_1 \mid B\alpha_2 \mid \cdots \mid B\alpha_m \mid \alpha_{m+1} \mid \alpha_{m+2} \mid \cdots \mid \alpha_{m+n}$

OUTPUT

Two rules that are not directly left recursive but are equivalent to the input rule.

PROCEDURE

Replace B with two productions:

$$B ::= \alpha_{m+1}B1 \mid \alpha_{m+2} B1 \mid \cdots \mid \alpha_{m+n} B1$$
$$B1 ::= \alpha_1 B1 \mid \alpha_2 B1 \mid \cdots \mid \alpha_m B1 \mid \epsilon$$

The ϵ is an empty production that can be matched at any time with no consumption.
Applying this algorithm to the preceding grammar yields the following:

$E \quad ::= T \, E1$
$E1 \quad ::= + T \, E1$
$\quad\quad ::= - T \, E1$
$\quad\quad ::=$
$T \quad ::= F \, T1$
$T1 \quad ::= * F \, T1$
$\quad\quad ::= / F \, T1$
$\quad\quad ::=$
$F \quad ::= \text{id}$

Occasionally, the result of this algorithm includes obvious indirect recursion such as that found in

$E ::= EP \mid P$	$E ::= PE'$
$P ::= ET \mid T \mid (E) \mid ()$ Eliminate Left Recursion	$E' ::= PE' \mid \epsilon$
$T ::= [E] \mid []$	$P ::= ET \mid T \mid (E) \mid ()$
	$T ::= [E] \mid []$

In such cases, it is necessary to perform a *forward substitution* of the RHS options of the recursive symbol. These RHS options replace the recursive symbol in the subsequent production's RHS prefix. For example, in the modified grammar (i.e., the one on the right), E leads to PE', which can lead to ET. Therefore, the RHS options of E will replace E in the RHS option of P:

$E ::= PE'$
$E' ::= PE' \mid \epsilon$
$P ::= PE'T \mid T \mid (E) \mid ()$
$T ::= [E] \mid []$

Notice that the elimination of the indirect left recursion has led to direct left recursion. Therefore, we need to reapply the algorithm to eliminate direct left recursion:

$E ::= PE'$
$E' ::= PE' \mid \epsilon$
$P ::= TP' \mid (E)P' \mid ()P'$
$P' ::= E'TP' \mid \epsilon$
$T ::= [E] \mid []$

At this point there is no remaining left recursion (direct or indirect). However, there are common prefixes in two sets of RHS options. For example, the rule $P ::= TP' \mid (E)P' \mid ()P'$ has the common prefix of an open parenthesis, (, in the second and third RHS options.

ELIMINATE COMMON PREFIXES

The two grammar rules that require further improvement are boldfaced in the following display. The problem with these rules is that the choice of the RHS option to apply is not deterministic given a one-symbol look-ahead in the input (i.e., lex contains only the next input symbol):

$E ::= PE'$
$E' ::= PE' \mid \epsilon$
$\mathbf{P ::= TP' \mid (E)P' \mid ()P'}$
$P' ::= E'TP' \mid \epsilon$
$\mathbf{T ::= [E] \mid []}$

In P the last two RHS options begin with the symbol of an open parenthesis, (. In T both options begin with the symbol of an open bracket, [. The elimination of common prefixes is quite simple:

INPUT
Common prefix rule:

$$B ::= \alpha\beta_1 \mid \alpha\beta_2 \mid \cdots \mid \alpha\beta_m \mid \chi_{m+1} \mid \chi_{m+2} \mid \cdots \mid \chi_{m+n}$$

OUTPUT
Two rules that have no common prefixes.

PROCEDURE
Replace B with two productions:

$$B ::= \alpha B1 \mid \chi_{m+1} \mid \chi_{m+2} \mid \cdots \mid \chi_{m+n}$$
$$B1 ::= \beta_1 \mid \beta_2 \mid \cdots \mid \beta_m$$

Applying this algorithm to the rules *P* and *T* results in the following grammar:

$E ::= PE'$
$E' ::= PE' \mid \epsilon$
$P ::= TP' \mid (P''$
$P'' ::= E)P' \mid)P'$
$P' ::= E'TP' \mid \epsilon$
$T ::= [T''$
$T' ::= E] \mid]$

SELECTION-SET GENERATION

After the common prefixes are eliminated, you will need to generate *selection sets* for the grammar if the grammar possesses rules that have empty, or *epsilon, options*. For the grammar just presented, epsilon options exist for the rules *E'* and *P'*. *The selection sets are necessary to know when it is legal to apply an epsilon rule.*

Several steps are involved in generating selection sets. To illustrate these steps, we will use as an example the arithmetic expression grammar presented earlier, with the dollar sign, $, indicating an end-of-sentence. In the following grammar, integers are given where primes were used before:

$E \quad ::= T\ E1$
$E1 \quad ::= +\ T\ E1$
$\quad ::= -T\ E1$
$\quad ::=$
$T \quad ::= F\ T1$
$T1 \quad ::= *\ F\ T1$
$\quad ::= /\ F\ T1$
$\quad ::=$
$F \quad ::= \text{id}$

In order to generate the selection set, we must determine the grammar's *first* and *follow sets*. These sets lead to the selection set.

DETERMINE FIRST SET. A first set contains all vocabulary symbols that can be generated from the leftmost symbols of a rule's RHS options. For example, in performing a leftmost derivation beginning with symbol *E*, you can derive only the vocabulary symbol *id:*

$E \Rightarrow T\ E1 \Rightarrow F\ T1\ E1 \Rightarrow \text{id}\ T1\ E1$

Or, in the shorthand,

$E \overset{+}{\Rightarrow} \text{id}\ T1\ E1$

Thus, {*id*} is *E*'s first set. Therefore, if the leftmost symbol in an RHS option is a nonterminal, then one performs closure until all derivable terminals are found. The following sets are obtained in a similar fashion:

RULES   **FIRST SET**

E	::= *T E1*	{id}
E1	::= + *T E1*	{+}
	::= − *T E1*	{−}
	::=	
T	::= *F T1*	{id}
T1	::= * *F T1*	{*}
	::= / *F T1*	{/}
	::=	
F	::= id	{id}

DETERMINE FOLLOW SET.   There are three steps in generating the follow sets. The first is to set the follow set of the start symbol to {$}. Next, for each RHS $\alpha A \beta$, add non-ϵ elements of FIRST(β) to FOLLOW(*A*). The application of this second step results in the following intermediate follow sets:

RULES   **FIRST SET**   **FOLLOW SET**

E	::= *T E1*	{id}	{$}
E1	::= + *T E1*	{+}	{}
	::= −*T E1*	{−}	
	::=		
T	::= *F T1*	{id}	{+,−}
T1	::= * *F T1*	{*}	
	::= / *F T1*	{/}	
	::=		
F	::= id	{id}	{*,/}

The rule with LHS *T* obtains plus and minus because $\alpha A \beta$ corresponds to *T E1* so that the FIRST*(E1)* is added to the FOLLOW*(T)*. This substitution is based upon the following matches in the rule with LHS E : $\alpha = \epsilon$, $A = T$, and $\beta = E1$. The final step is an iterative step until no changes to follow sets occur.

The third step in generating follow sets is to repeat for each rule, $B ::= \alpha A \beta$, where $\beta \overset{*}{\Rightarrow} \epsilon$, add FOLLOW*(B)* to FOLLOW*(A)* until no changes. Notice that in the zero step of every production *(B)*, there is an epsilon. Therefore, if any RHS ends with a nonterminal symbol *A*, then *A*'s associated production will have added to its follow set the FOLLOW*(B)*:

RULES   **FIRST SET**   **FOLLOW SET**

E	::= *T E1*	{id}	{$}
E1	::= + *T E1*	{+}	{$}
	::= −*T E1*	{−}	
	::=		
T	::= *F T1*	{id}	{+,−}
T1	::= * *F T1*	{*}	{+,−}
	::= / *F T1*	{/}	
	::=		
F	::= id	{id}	{*,/}

Both *E1* and *T1* can produce epsilon. Therefore, FOLLOW*(E)* is added to
FOLLOW*(T)*, FOLLOW*(T)* is added to *(F)*, and FOLLOW*(T1)* is added to
FOLLOW*(F)*:

RULES		FIRST SET	FOLLOW SET
E	::= *T E1*	{id}	{$}
E1	::= + *T E1*	{+}	{$}
	::= − *T E1*	{−}	
	::=		
T	::= *F T1*	{id}	{+,−,$}
T1	::= * *F T1*	{*}	{+,−}
	::= / *F T1*	{/}	
	::=		
F	::= id	{id}	{*,/,+,−}

One more iteration of the rule is required before there are no further changes
to the follow sets. In this iteration the follow of *T* is added to the follow of T1
and the follow of *F*:

RULES		FIRST SET	FOLLOW SET
E	::= *T E1*	{id}	{$}
E1	::= + *T E1*	{+}	{$}
	::= − *T E1*	{−}	
	::=		
T	::= *F T1*	{id}	{+,−,$}
T1	::= * *F T1*	{*}	{+,−,$}
	::= / *F T1*	{/}	
	::=		
F	::= id	{id}	{*,/,+,−,$}

DETERMINE SELECTION SETS.   The selection set of a non-epsilon RHS
option is the option's first set. The selection set of an epsilon option is the rule's
follow set:

RULES		FIRST SET	FOLLOW SET	SELECTION SET
E	::= *T E1*	{id}	{$}	{id}
E1	::= + *T E1*	{+}	{$}	{+}
	::= − *T E1*	{−}		{−}
	::=			{$}
T	::= *F T1*	{id}	{+,−,$}	{id}
T1	::= * *F T1*	{*}	{+,−,$}	{*}
	::= / *F T1*	{/}		{/}
	::=			{+,−,$}
F	::= id	{id}	{*,/,+,−,$}	{id}

After the selection sets are generated, the full specification for a recursive-
descent SA exists. The selection sets provide the intelligence needed by syntax

analysis to apply an empty production correctly. If all other RHSs have been attempted and the next input symbol is an element of the empty production's selection set, then it is legal to apply the empty production. For a given production (e.g., *E1*) the intersection of selection sets is null (e.g., $\{+\} \cap \{-\} \cap \{\$\}$ = Θ). The null intersection of selection sets for a given rule provide for determinism in the application of RHSs. If the intersections are not null for even one rule, then the grammar is not suitable for a recursive-descent translation.

WRITING SYNTAX-ANALYSIS ROUTINES

In this section, the final version of grammar *AE*, shown in the following display, and its corresponding selection sets, will be used to develop a recursive-descent, syntax-directed interpreter.

```
AE(P) = {
E      ::= T E1
E1     ::= + T E1
       ::= − T E1
       ::=
T      ::= F T1
T1     ::= * F T1
       ::= / F T1
       ::=
F      ::= id          }
```

The start symbol for this grammar is *E*. Recall that for the two-epsilon productions, we have the selection sets $\{\$\}$ for *E1* and $\{+,-,\$\}$ for *T1*. Given the modified grammar in our example, the vocabulary remains as before. *AE(V)* = {identifiers, *, /, +, −}, and the syntactic categories become *AE(C)* = {*E, E1, T, T1, F*}. At this point we have the complete specification of the syntax-analysis routines. To complete the routines, one follows clearly defined rules for implementing the grammar specification:

For every LHS (or element of *C*)
    there is a Boolean function
        For every RHS option of a given LHS there will be an if-statement block, and if a given RHS option has multiple symbols, there will be, in that block, a nested if for each symbol. For a given RHS symbol there are three possible actions:
        1. In the case of matching an element of the vocabulary, *V*, i.e., if lex $\in$ *V*: consume the element (invoke the LA), and if it is the last item in the RHS option, set the LHS symbol to true. If you were supposed to match an element of *V* and did not, set LHS to false and output an error message.
        2. In the case where the RHS is an element of the syntactic category, *C* : invoke *C*'s function to see if it is true. If it is

true and is at the end of the RHS option, set the LHS symbol to true; otherwise, set the LHS to false.

3. In the case of an epsilon production, check to see if lex is an element of the selection set. If it is, set the LHS to true. Otherwise, set LHS to false and put out an error message.

Notice that error messages are written only when matching a vocabulary symbol or when applying an epsilon production. If you wrote error messages when elements of the syntactic categories failed, there would be a proliferation of spurious error messages. Some language compilers are notorious for their spurious messages. (The author once worked in a programming shop where there was an ongoing contest to find some single error that would result in the most error messages. The winner had more than a page of error messages resulting from a single error. Imagine having that error by accident! Think about how long it would take to wade through those messages in order to discover the offending piece of code.)

Taking one grammar rule of the *AE* language, and writing the syntax-analysis function according to the algorithm just presented, we would have the following:

$$E1 \quad ::= + \, T \, E1$$
$$::= -T \, E1$$
$$::=$$

This rule is a good example because it possesses all three of the actions mentioned in the algorithm to write the SA. According to the algorithm there will be a Boolean function for each LHS:

```
function e1:boolean;
begin

end;
```

Next, for each RHS option, there is an IF-statement block, which varies depending on the nature of the symbol under consideration. For the first RHS option there is, in the first symbol, the plus symbol (+), an element of the *AE(V)*. Therefore, if we match on this symbol, we must consume it:

```
function e1:boolean;
begin
  if lex = '+' then
    begin
    lex:=get;

end;
```

Following the plus symbol is the categorical symbol *T*. So a corresponding function, *t*, is invoked to see if it is satisfied:

```
function e1:boolean;
begin
      if lex = '+' then
        begin
        lex:=get;
        if t then


end;
```

Following *t* is the categorical symbol *E1*. So the function *e1* is recursively invoked to see if it is satisfied:

```
function e1:boolean;
begin
      if lex = '+' then
        begin
        lex:=get;
        if t then
            if e1 then


end;
```

Since the recursive reference to *e*1 is the last symbol of this RHS option, *e*1 is assigned the value of true if the reference to *e*1 returns true. Otherwise, if *e*1 is false, *e*1 is set to false (remember: no error messages here). If *t* has evaluated to false, we set *e*1 to false. If lex $\neq$ '+', we need to check for the next LHS option:

```
function e1:boolean;
begin
      if lex = '+' then
        begin
        lex:=get;
        if t then
            if e1 then
                return true
            else
                return false
        else
            return false
        end
      else
      if lex = '−' then


end;
```

The LHS option for minus is identical in structure, and most of its content is identical to the plus option. The only difference is that the initial symbol to match in lex is the minus sign, not the plus sign:

```
function e1:boolean;
begin
     if lex = '+' then
        begin
        lex:=get;
        if t then
           if e1 then
              return true
           else
              return false
        else
           return false
        end
     else
     if lex = '−' then
        begin
        lex:=get;
        if t then
           if e1 then
              return true
           else
              return false
        else
           return false
        end
     else

end;
```

The final LHS option applies the epsilon if the next symbol (in lex) is a member of the selection set:

```
else
if lex in ['$'] then
     return true
else
     begin
     writeln('ERROR: expecting a +, −, $, but
                 found: ', lex);
     return false
     end;
```

Application of the empty production requires only that the selection set contain the next item in input. If so, the function is set to true. Otherwise, an error message like the one just shown is appropriate. The entire function for the rule in question is as follows:

```
function e1:boolean;
begin
```

```
    if lex = '+' then
       begin
       lex:=get;
       if t then
          if e1 then
             return true
          else
             return false
       else
          return false
       end
    else
    if lex = '−' then
       begin
       lex:=get;
       if t then
          if e1 then
             return true
          else
             return false
       else
          return false
       end
    else
    if lex in ['$'] then
          return true
    else
       begin
       writeln('ERROR: expecting a +, −, $, but
                    found: ', lex);
       return false
       end
  end;
```

The function for *t1* is a symmetric case.

T1   ::= * *F T1*
       ::= / *F T1*
       ::=

All you need to do is alter the symbols being matched, the selection set, and the names of functions defined and referenced:

```
function t1:boolean;
begin
     if lex = '*' then
        begin
        lex:=get;
        if f then
```

```
            if t1 then
                return true
            else
                return false
        else
            return false
        end
    else
    if lex = '/' then
        begin
        lex:=get;
        if f then
            if t1 then
                return true
            else
                return false
        else
            return false
        end
    else
    if lex in ['+', '−', '$'] then
            return true
    else
            begin
            return false;
            writeln('ERROR: expecting a +, −, *, /, $, but
                        found: ', lex)
            end
end;
```

Similarly, functions *e* and *t* are symmetric cases of each other, except for the end-of-file marker, $.

$$E \quad ::= T \ E1$$
$$T \quad ::= F \ T1$$

They are very simple functions to write because they do not match on vocabulary symbols or selection sets:

```
function t: boolean;
begin
        if f then
            if t1 then
                return true
            else
                return false
        else
```

```
            return false

end;

function e:boolean;
begin
    if t then
       if e1 then
          if lex = '$' then
                return true
          else
                return false
       else
          return false
    else
       return false
end;
```

The only remaining rule to consider is

F   ::= id

This function will do a little bit of lexical analysis to make certain that the next character is a legitimate variable:

```
function f:boolean;
begin
    if lex in ['a' . . . 'z'] then
       begin
       lex:=get;
       return true
       end
    else
       begin
       writeln('expected id and found', lex)
       return false;
       end

end;
```

At this point, the SA is complete, and it is time to begin embedding semantic actions in it.

■ ■

SEMANTIC ANALYSIS

The syntax-analysis routine, as we have seen, parses arithmetic expressions that contain only variables. We must assume that all variables are predefined, since the grammar provides no means for assignment. In an interpreter, the state of the machine must be maintained. As the language under consideration contains only integer variables, the state of the machine will be predefined (prior to syntax analysis and interpretation) and will be kept in a linked list that pairs the single-character variables with their values. Given this arrangement, Figure 4.3 indicates the state and interpretation of the expression *a*b/c*. Notice that the results are obtained while performing the syntax analysis of the expression and stacked on a structure called *result*.

Our aim in the following subsections is to understand the semantic actions needed to support the full interpretation of the arithmetic expressions that can be formed with the grammar under consideration. We will consider the type of interpretation in which statements are executed as they are encountered. Figure 4.3 shows that modifications are needed to the syntax functions *f* and t1. Semantic actions will also be embedded in function e1 in order to provide for the evaluation of expressions containing additive symbols.

MODIFICATION OF FUNCTION *F*

Assume first that the following types are declared and that associated global variables exist.

```
type ptr = ^node;
     node = record
          right:ptr;
```

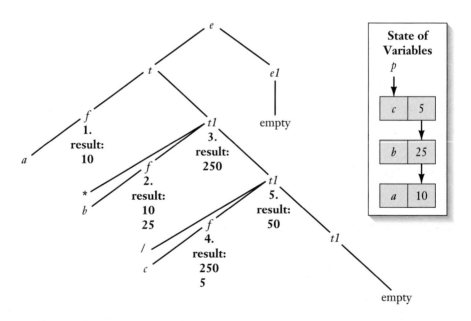

FIGURE 4.3   Syntax/semantic analysis of *a*b/c*.

```
          id:char;
          val:integer
          end;
  ptr2 = ^node2;
  node2 = record
          right:ptr2;
          val:integer
          end;

var p,q,r:ptr;
    result,p2:ptr2;
```

The structure called "node" contains the state of the machine, and the "node2" structure contains the result stack (called the *semantic action stack*). Assume for the node2 structure, the standard stack operations of push, pop, and so forth. Assume for the node structure, that variables are predefined. Therefore, the node structure must be predefined. All that is needed is the ability to find the value associated with a referenced variable, beginning with the first node pointed to by variable p. This task will be accomplished with a simple function to traverse the linked list. Its input will be a single-character identifier. Its output will be the value associated with the identifier in the linked list. For a serious attempt at this function, it would be appropriate to also have some erroneous value returned in the case where the identifier is not found in the linked list (i.e., the identifier is undefined).

Here is a function to find the value of a referenced identifier in the WHILE language:

```
function obtain(lex:char):integer;
var found:boolean;
begin
    q:=p;
    found:=false;
    while (q<>nil) and (not found) do
        if q^.id = lex then
            begin
            found:=true;
            return q^.val
            end
        else
            q:=q^.right;
    if not found then return error
end;
```

Notice that the undefined variable is a semantic, not a syntactic error. Recall that the syntax-analysis function to reference an identifier is called f. The semantic action for f in the interpreter is to push the value of the referenced identifier onto the semantic action stack.

```
push(obtain(lex));
```

It is important to perform this action prior to the consumption of the identifier:

```
function f:boolean;
begin
    if lex in ['a'. .'z'] then
        begin
        push(obtain(lex));
        lex:=get;
        return true
        end
    else
        begin
        writeln('expected id and found trash')
        return false;
        end
end;
```

Here one can observe a difference between a compiler and an interpreter. In the interpreter, one actually obtains the value associated with the identifier. In a compiler one obtains the semantic information associated with the identifier, which typically takes the form of the symbol-table address associated with the identifier. At a later stage of code generation, the symbol-table entry for the identifier will have a relative memory address associated with it. This address is used to help construct a machine-code statement that can reference the location associated with the identifier.

MODIFICATION OF FUNCTION $T1$

Recall the grammar that led to the syntax-analysis routines. In particular, focus on $t1$:

E	::= T E1
E1	::= + T E1
	::= − T E1
	::=
T	::= F T1
T1	**::= * F T1**
	::= / F T1
	::=
F	::= id

Notice that between the references to F and $T1$, there is an appropriate place to perform the semantic actions associated with the multiplication operation. This is particularly true if the operations are to be left-associative, that is, if we intend to perform operations by working from the left to right when we have multiple adjacent operations at the same level in the hierarchy. To perform the operation, after returning from F and prior to calling $T1$, one needs to pop the semantic action stack twice to obtain the operands, perform the operation, and then push the result of the operation on the stack:

```
function t1:boolean;
var i, op1, op2:integer;
begin
      if lex = '*' then
         begin
         lex:=get;
         if f then
            begin
            op1:=pop;
            op2:=pop;
            i:=op2*op1;
            push(i);
            if t1 then
               return true
            else
               return false
            end
         else
            return false
         end
      else
      if lex = '/' then
         begin
         lex:=get;
         if f then
            begin
            op1:=pop;
            op2:=pop;
            i:=op2 div op1;
            push(i);
            if t1 then
               return true
            else
               return false
            end
         else
            return false
         end
      else
      if lex in ['+','−','$'] then
         return true
      else
```

```
        return false
end;
```

Notice that the semantics are identical in the case of the division operation, the only difference being the operation performed. Likewise, the semantic actions added to the function *e1* are identical with the exception of the operations performed:

```
function e1:boolean;
var i, op1, op2:integer;
begin
        if lex = '+' then
          begin
          lex:=get;
          if t then
            begin
            op1:=pop;
            op2:=pop;
            i:=op2+op1;
            push(i);
            if e1 then
              return true
            else
              return false
            end
          else
            return false
          end
        else
        if lex = '−' then
          begin
          lex:=get;
          if t then
            begin
            op1:=pop;
            op2:=pop;
            i:=op2−op1;
            push(i);
            if e1 then
              return true
            else
              return false
            end
          else
            return false
          end
        else
```

```
        if lex in ['$'] then
            return true
        else
            return false
end;
```

As an exercise, determine the meaning that is obtained when one places the semantic actions shown in boldface after successful return from *e1* rather than before invoking *e1*. One should realize that in a compiler, the semantic action here would result in the generation of some intermediate code to represent the multiplication of the two operands popped from the semantic action stack. Recall that these operands would be represented by their respective symbol-table addresses rather than by their respective values.

THE INTERPRETER

Following is the listing of the entire interpreter for evaluating the arithmetic expressions:

```
program zwhile(prog,dat,output);
type ptr = ^node;
     node = record
              right:ptr;
              id:char;
              val:integer
              end;
     ptr2 = ^node2;
     node2 = record
              right:ptr2;
              val:integer
              end;
var  p,q,r:ptr;
     result,p2:ptr2;
     lex:char;
     prog,dat:text;
     op1,op2,i:integer;

function e: boolean; forward;
function e1: boolean; forward;
function t1: boolean; forward;
function t: boolean; forward;
function f: boolean; forward;

procedure push(i:integer);
begin
        new(p2);
        p2^.val:=i;
```

```
        p2^.right:=result;
        result:=p2
end;

function pop:integer;
begin
      if result <> nil then
         begin
         p2:=result;
         result:=result^.right;
         return p2^.val;
         dispose(p2)
         end
      else
         writeln('stack underflow')
end;

function obtain(lex:char):integer;
var found:boolean;
begin
      q:=p;
      found:=false;
      while (q<>nil) and (not found) do
            if q^.id = lex then
               begin
               found:=true;
               return q^.val
               end
            else
               q:=q^.right;
      if not found then return error
end;

function get:char;
var lex1:char;
begin
      read(prog,lex1);
      while lex1 = ' ' do
             read(prog,lex1);
      write(lex1);
      return lex1
end;

function t: boolean;
begin
```

```
        if f then
          if t1 then
            return true
          else
            return false
        else
          return false
end;

function t1:boolean;
var i, op1, op2:integer;
begin
        if lex = '*' then
          begin
          lex:=get;
          if f then
            begin
            op1:=pop;
            op2:=pop;
            i:=op2*op1;
            push(i);
            if t1 then
              return true
            else
              return false
            end
          else
            return false
          end
        else
        if lex = '/' then
          begin
          lex:=get;
          if f then
            begin
            op1:=pop;
            op2:=pop;
            i:=op2 div op1;
            push(i);
            if t1 then
              return true
            else
              return false
            end
          else
          return false
```

```
                end
        else
        if lex in ['+','−','$'] then
            return true
        else
            return false
end;

function e1:boolean;
var i, op1, op2:integer;
begin
        if lex = '+' then
            begin
            lex:=get;
            if t then
                begin
                op1:=pop;
                op2:=pop;
                i:=op2+op1;
                push(i);
                if e1 then
                    return true
                else
                    return false
                end
            else
                return false
            end
        else
        if lex = '−' then
            begin
            lex:=get;
            if t then
                begin
                op1:=pop;
                op2:=pop;
                i:=op2−op1;
                push(i);
                if e1 then
                    return true
                else
                    return false
                end
            else
                    return false
            end
        else
```

```
        if lex in ['$'] then
             return true
        else
             return false
end;

function e:boolean;
begin
      if t then
        if e1 then
           if lex = '$' then
                   return true
           else
                   return false
        else
             return false
      else
        return false
end;

function f:boolean;
begin
      if lex in ['a'. .'z'] then
         begin
         push(obtain(lex));
         lex:=get;
         return true
         end
      else
         begin
         return false;
         writeln(':expected id and found trash')
         end
      end;

      begin
            new(p);
            p^.id:='a';
            p^.val:=10;
            p^.right:=nil;
            new(q);
            q^.id:='b';
            q^.val:= 25;
            q^.right:=p;
            new(p);
            p^.id:='c';
            p^.val:=5;
```

```
            p^.right:=q;
            result:=nil;
            assign(dat,'inp.dat');
            assign(prog,'prog.dat');
            reset(prog);
            reset(dat);
            lex:=get;
            if e then writeln('ok');
                    writeln('result is ',pop)
    end.
```

QUESTIONS AND EXERCISES

1. Eliminate left recursion for the following grammar:

\<S>	::= \<S> \<S1>
	::=
\<S1>	::= \<LHS> if \<RHS>.
	::= \<LHS>.
\<RHS>	::= \<RHS> , \<LHS>
	::= \<RHS> ; \<LHS>
	::= \<LHS>
\<LHS>	::= p
	::= q
	::= r

2. Eliminate common prefixes for the grammar resulting from Exercise 1.

3. Produce the selection sets for the result of Exercise 2.

4. Write an emulator that can execute programs in the following quad language:

rd, rdln, wr, wrln	Input Output
$+, -, *, /$	Arithmetic
$<, >, <=, >=, =, <>$	Relational
jtrue, jfalse, jump	Conditional/unconditional jumps
:=	Assignment

5. Based on the grammar *AE(G)*, give an example of a lexical error.

6. Based on the grammar *AE(G)*, give an example of a syntax error.

7. Based on the grammar *AE(G)*, give an example of a semantic error.

8. Generate the selection sets for the following grammars:

```
E ::= PE'
E' ::= PE' | ∈
P ::= TP' | (P"
P" ::= E)P' | )P'
P' ::= E'TP' | ∈
T ::= [T"
T '::= E] | ]
```

SECTION TWO

PROGRAMMING LANGUAGE PARADIGMS

In this section the major language paradigms are presented: the procedural and its object-oriented extensions, the functional and the logical. Each paradigm is discussed in the context of the constructs of a programming paradigm and with the goal of understanding the motivation for the language-design effort.

While reading this section, keep in mind that some languages are better suited for certain problem domains, but some problem solvers are not adept with those particular languages. Thus, at times it is best to use a language that the problem solver is comfortable with, even though there are languages better suited to the problem. Of course, the old adage may apply here: "To the person with a hammer everything looks like a nail."

The remaining chapters will introduce new language structures for which the syntax and semantic definitions will be provided.

5

IMPERATIVE LANGUAGES

The *imperative paradigm* of programming (also called the *procedural paradigm*) is the oldest and certainly the most prevalent paradigm for problem solving. Examples of imperative languages include FORTRAN, COBOL, ALGOL, PLI, Pascal, C, Ada, and Modula. In the imperative paradigm one develops algorithms to specify problem solutions.

Since its inception in the mid 1950s, when it revolutionized problem solving, the imperative paradigm has been continuously evolving. In this chapter we will compare an early version of FORTRAN with Pascal. The contrast makes clear the evolution that has taken place. In the next chapter, we will discuss the continued evolution of imperative languages, exemplified by languages like Java.

As a prelude to this discussion, consider some of the attributes of a good language. First is the degree of *abstraction*, or symbolism. Niklaus Wirth, the inventor of Pascal, once stated that the most important decision one makes in designing a language is the determination of the abstraction upon which programs are to be based. Achieving a more intuitive and expressive language abstraction is the goal of most language designers. It is important that this goal be clear. The goal in Pascal was to provide a good interaction between control structures (i.e., algorithms) and data structures. The guiding insight was that the intelligent design of data structures often simplifies a problem solution.

Once the abstraction of a language is determined, it is necessary to have a *coherent* design of constructs. [Zave] Coherence means that all constructs are at a uniform level of abstraction. When some language constructs are at a high level and others are at a lower level, the language is incoherent. It is difficult for programmers to deal with an incoherent language, because they then are required to understand the process of problem solution from varying levels of abstraction.

The *size* of a language is important, too. The larger the language, the more the programmer must remember in order to use it. If the language is too complicated, just the challenges involved in using it will distract the problem solver from the task of problem solution. Therefore, a well-designed small language is ideal.

A language should also be *orthogonal*, meaning that the features of the language should interact well and, furthermore, interact in an intuitive manner. Additionally, there should be no capriciousness in the language design. That is, it is important that language features be *consistent* and that there be no arbitrary limits placed, for example, on levels of nesting.

Finally, the language translator should provide a small number of valid error messages and place safeguards in the run-time version of a program to prevent certain types of errors.

LANGUAGE CONSTRUCTS

Programming languages are composed of nonexecutable and executable commands. Modern languages vary from one another mostly in terms of their respective nonexecutable commands.

The executable commands are formed around categories, or *language constructs*, that are the building blocks of a computer language and are based upon the *Von Neumann computer architecture* depicted in Figure 5.1. Remember, a programming language is meant to provide instructions to a computer. Thus, a program is a precise specification of what a computer must do in order to solve some problem. From the study of computer architecture, we know that there is a limited number of actions the computer can perform. Consequently, there exists a correspondingly limited number of commands that can be issued to the computer.

A Von Neumann computer consists of a memory and a central processing unit (CPU). Both data and programs are stored in the memory. The programs provide a step-by-step algorithm for solving a problem. Instructions are executed in the order they are given unless there is an instruction that specifies an alternate order. In order to provide for this "control," the machine-code instructions of a program are stored in a *linear* fashion in memory—that is, one instruction follows another.

A *program counter* located in the CPU always contains a memory address that references the next instruction to be executed. The instruction to be executed is loaded from memory into the *instruction register*, also located in the CPU. The program counter is then updated to contain the address of the instruction that immediately follows—in memory—the one currently loaded in the instruction register.

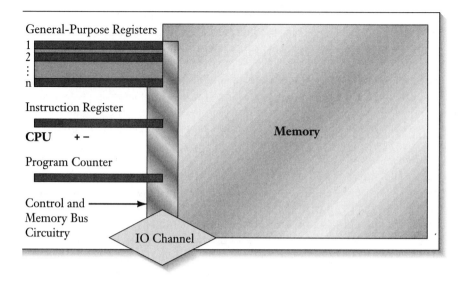

General-Purpose Registers
1
2
⋮
n

Instruction Register

CPU   + –

Program Counter

Control and
Memory Bus
Circuitry

IO Channel

Memory

FIGURE 5.1   Von Neumann architecture.

The currently loaded instruction is then executed. The binary pattern for a given instruction enables (and disables) electronic circuitry in a manner that causes the action specified in the instruction to be accomplished. The action specified in the instruction corresponds to the executable language constructs:

- Alter the flow of control in the program.
- Specify an input/output operation.
- Specify an arithmetic or comparison operation.

The sequence of events carried out by the Von Neumann architecture implements the sequencing of program statements and is called the *instruction cycle* (Figure 5.2). The first construct allows a program to modify its own flow of control. To do so, the architecture allows a program to modify the CPU's program counter ("Update program counter"). Therefore, a program can cause the CPU to fetch some instruction other than the one following the instruction currently being executed. The instruction cycle updates the program counter before, not after, the current instruction is executed ("Execute instruction"), making certain

Fetch ⟶ Update Program Counter ⟶ Execute Instruction

FIGURE 5.2   Instruction cycle.

that an instruction altering the flow of control does not have its effect altered by the machine.

The second type of instruction allows for input/output (I/O) transfers. These are accomplished through interactions between the I/O ports (or channels), the CPU, the memory bus, and the memory. Often channel processors exist to offload the I/O activities from the CPU. These specialized processors can transfer data from or to I/O devices and to or from memory, using *direct memory access*, which allows the channel processors to "steal" memory cycles from the CPU. When memory cycles are stolen, the channel processor has access to the memory bus to perform data transfers. Because many instructions executed by the CPU do not require memory access, the channel processor can use the memory bus in a way that does not interfere with continued progress by the CPU.

The third type of activity the computer can perform is arithmetic and comparative processing. The circuitry to perform arithmetic and comparisons exists between special memory locations located in the CPU called *general-purpose registers*. The only functionality that *must* be provided by the circuitry is an ability to add negative numbers and capture the sign of the result. If negative numbers can be added together, the computer can perform addition, subtraction, multiplication (multiple additions), division (multiple subtractions), and algebraic comparisons (to be discussed here in detail).

Since the circuitry to perform the arithmetic and comparative operations exists only among the general-purpose registers, at least one, if not all, operands involved in an operation must first be loaded into (a) register(s). The registers, the arithmetic circuitry, and *sign bit* (indicated by $+-$ in Figure 5.1) are often called the *arithmetic logic unit* (ALU) of the CPU. The sign bit is set whenever arithmetic is performed. This bit is used to represent the sign of a result and enables algebraic comparisons. In fact, the earliest form of an IF statement was the FORTRAN arithmetic IF, which referenced the sign of a result:

> if(arithmetic_expression)statement_number_1,statement_number_2,
> statement_number_3

The evaluation of the expression sets the sign bit. If the result is negative, control is transferred to "statement_number_1"; if zero, control is transferred to "statement_number_2"; if positive, control is transferred to "statement_number_3." To obtain an algebraic comparison of two expressions, A and B, one would form a statement such as

> if$(A-B)$10,20,30

The computer architecture's ability to subtract two numbers and capture the sign of the result serves as the basis for algebraic comparisons (i.e., the relational operators: $<$, $>$, $=$, $<=$, $>=$, and $<>$). Thus, the raw ability of the computer to compare the results of expressions is mirrored in the FORTRAN arithmetic-IF statement.

Assume that when an arbitrary relational expression is true, you want to transfer control to Statement 10. Otherwise, you want to transfer control to

Statement 20. Here is the way in which relational expressions are realized using the arithmetic IF:

if($A-B$)10,20,20	$A<B$
if($A-B$)10,10,20	$A<=B$
if($A-B$)20,10,20	$A=B$
if($A-B$)10,20,10	$A<>B$
if($A-B$)20,20,10	$A>B$
if($A-B$)20,10,10	$A>=B$

The *selective construct*, which allows the alternate flow of execution based on comparisons, has been much improved in modern languages and represents one form of the control construct. Through the use of the selective construct, one can obtain the *iterative construct*, yet another form of the control construct. We will later see that there are typically two types of iterative statements to implement definite and indefinite loops, respectively.

The *sequence* (i.e., the compound statement) is the final form of the control construct. Architecturally, the sequence is automatically implemented when the program counter is updated to point to the instruction following the one that is to execute next. If the current instruction modifies the program counter, control is transferred. Thus, transfer occurs as a result of a selective or iterative statement.

The complete list of language constructs follows:

- **Executable**
  Input-output
  Arithmetic
  Control, including sequence, selective, and iterative
- **Nonexecutable**
  Commands to the language translator

The final construct represents nonexecutable instructions. These instructions allow the programmer to establish program and data structures. The ability to specify procedures and functions allows for the definition of program structures; the ability to establish arrays, records, dynamic variables, and so forth, allows for the definition of data structures.

In the following sections, FORTRAN and Pascal will be compared with respect to these constructs. The reader should note that almost all features of a language will fall into one of the language categories in the preceding list. Therefore, these language constructs provide a sound foundation for learning a new language.

INPUT/OUTPUT (I/O)

In the following discussion, reference is made to an early version of FORTRAN. Consequently, the past tense will be used. Keep in mind, however, that early features remain available in current versions of FORTRAN.

Input and output were provided through the READ and WRITE statements of FORTRAN. These statements were augmented by the FORMAT statement, which was an instruction to the FORTRAN compiler.

The concept of *stream I/O* was not employed in FORTRAN. Stream I/O exists in Pascal, where input is viewed as a long stream of values that can occur virtually anywhere in terms of spacing. The main concern for input is that it be ordered so that the appropriate values show up for assignment to the corresponding input variables.

In FORTRAN input values had to be "formatted." To provide for formatting, a sublanguage was created. Some elements of this sublanguage follow:

nX
In
Fn.d
An

The uppercase letters X, I, F, and A are FORTRAN codes for spacing (X) and the data types of integer (I), reals (F), and alphabetic (A). The lowercase symbols n and d are user-specified integers. Thus, for spacing the user could specify 10X, which states that the reader should skip the next 10 characters in the input. Likewise, I4 indicates an integer of four digits is to be read. The "Fn.d" is particularly cryptic. The integer n indicates the entire size of the input field, including the decimal point. The d indicates the number of digits to occur to the *right* of the decimal point. The number of digits to the left of the decimal point is implied by the formula $n - (d+1)$, where the constant 1 represents the decimal point.

Consider the following example, where "5" in "READ(5,10)" indicates an input device, and "10" references a FORMAT statement:

        READ(5,10)A,I,B
   10   FORMAT(F5.3,2X,I3,F7.2)

This format specifies the following input line, shown with the *card column* positions to indicate the precise placement of input for you, the reader:

```
card columns:    12345678901234567890123456790
                 d.ddd   dddddd.dd
```

The d's are digits. Notice that the I3 field ends at the tenth input line column, and field F7.2 begins at the eleventh. Every time a READ statement is encountered, a new input line is read in.

This input process is particularly unforgiving. Both the programmer and the person setting up the input must be very careful. If an input item does not occur on the input line specified in the FORMAT statement, digits could be lost. For example, in the READ and FORMAT statements just given, suppose you read in the values 1.2, 5, and 32.34, respectively, into variables A, I, and B. The input line would appear as

```
card columns:    12345678901234567890123456790
                 1.2      5  32.34
```

If the digit 5 appeared in position 9 rather than 10, the value read into I would be 50.

The stream I/O concept varies dramatically from the FORTRAN approach to input. In stream I/O, there are only two constraints on the input: (1) the values must be ordered according to the program's ordering of input variables, and (2) input values must be separated by at least one space. To read the preceding input line, you could set up a number of different READ statement patterns in Pascal, as shown in Figure 5.3.

Furthermore, the person setting up the input file could place each value on a separate line, or use some other manner to maintain the order and have a space between each input value. Notice that the "readln" forces a new line of input.

Specifying output in FORTRAN is even more complicated than specifying input. In addition to the specifications one gives in a FORMAT statement associated with a READ statement, a FORMAT statement associated with a WRITE statement requires additional information. For example, any text that is to appear in the output must be enclosed in single quotes in the FORMAT statement, and one must specify codes for advancing the paper in the line printer.

Controlling the vertical position of the output page is called *carriage control*. The first character of each output line is stripped off, not written, and used for line printer carriage control. Carriage-control characters allow for single spacing (using a blank carriage-control character), advancing to the top of the next page (with the integer 1 for the carriage-control character), etc. Formatting of output in terms of horizontal spacing and the specification of output values is consistent with a READ statement's FORMAT.

Suppose you want to output the following information on the next line of output:

SUM = *ddddd*   AVERAGE = *ddd.dd*

To do so in FORTRAN, you will need these statements:

```
      WRITE(15,20)SUM, AVERAGE
20    FORMAT(' ','SUM = ', I5,6X,'AVERAGE = ',F6.2)
```

In Pascal, the output is achieved by

writeln('sum = ', sum,'   average = ',average)

One problem with the FORTRAN language is poor *locality of reference*. Since FORMAT statements are nonexecutable, they can appear anywhere in the

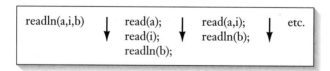

FIGURE 5.3   Stream I/O.

source program. Many FORTRAN programmers place all FORMAT statements in one section of the program. Therefore, when reading the code, you might have to dig through the listing in order to find how a particular input or output appears. This poor locality or reference affects FORTRAN's readability and writability, important issues for any language.

Readability has to do with the level of difficulty encountered in reading the listing of a program. For example, if it is possible to indent the body of a control structure, you should do this so that programs are easier to read. *Writability* has to do with the degree of difficulty encountered in writing a program in a given language. Readability and writability are often highly correlated.

Algol and Pascal improved greatly on FORTRAN's I/O statements. The improvements went far enough and were good enough so that most languages that have followed Pascal have not altered its approach to I/O in any significant way. If you understand I/O in Pascal, that understanding generalizes to most modern languages.

ARITHMETIC

Arithmetic in FORTRAN is very similar to arithmetic in Pascal. In fact, FORTRAN's arithmetic construct was designed so well that knowledge of it generalizes to other languages. The expressions are formed and evaluated in new languages just as they were in FORTRAN.

Since expressions are given in infix notation, a hierarchy of operations is specified. In general, an arbitrary expression is $a \theta b$. In the arbitrary expression, both a and b can be arithmetic expressions, which include constants, variables, and additional arithmetic expressions, and θ can be any arithmetic operator. In general, arithmetic expressions can be infix (i.e., $a \theta b$), prefix (i.e., $\theta a b$), or postfix (i.e., $a b \theta$).

In most (if not all) procedural languages, arithmetic expressions are written as *infix expressions*, expressions that result in ambiguity when operators are to be evaluated. Therefore, rules must be provided in order to eliminate the ambiguity.

First, a *hierarchy of operations* is given wherein subexpressions in parentheses are evaluated first. Next, *unary/function operations* are evaluated (e.g., signed numbers and functions such as absolute value are evaluated). Third, *multiplicative subexpressions* are evaluated (i.e., * and /). Finally, *additive operations* are evaluated (i.e., + and −). When two or more operations exist at the same level of the hierarchy, they are performed in a left-associative fashion. Therefore, the following infix expression would be evaluated as shown:

3+4*(6+3)*2*4	=	3+(((4*(6+3))*2)*4)	=
3+(((4*9)*2)*4)	=	3+((36*2)*4)	=
3+(72*4)	=	3+288	= 291

In FORTRAN, *mixed mode arithmetic*, in which real and integer data are combined in the same expressions, is accommodated in a fashion that is more liberal than in Pascal. Pascal disallows much of this type of processing. Along these same lines, Pascal has different operators to distinguish integer from real division. FORTRAN has one operator.

The assignment operator in FORTRAN is the equal sign (=), which of course, is problematic, since it is used in $x = x + 1$, which in terms of a relational expression, is always false. The assignment operator is the only mechanism for altering the state of the machine based upon computation. (Obviously, you can also alter the state through an input statement.) In Pascal, assignment is represented by the special operator :=.

Other than these differences, the same hierarchy of operations and the ability to override the hierarchy through the use of parentheses are the same in both languages.

CONTROL

At the heart of FORTRAN's control constructs is the GO TO statement, which allows for unconditional transfer of control. When paired with the IF statement, however, it allows for conditional transfer of control. The combination of conditional and unconditional GO TO statements provides for virtually limitless degrees of freedom in forming control structures and algorithms. With this unlimited freedom, programmers have shown themselves to be capable of extraordinary devilment. The GO TO statement has made possible control structures that are excellent approximations of the incomprehensible.

The design tool of the FORTRAN era was the *flowchart template*, an open and public confession that the focal point of complexity in FORTRAN programming was the control structure, or algorithm. One could transfer control beyond any number of FORTRAN statements and back again. As a result, serious problems could be created with virtual memory systems.

For example, when a statement transferred control beyond a page-frame boundary, the operating system had to read from disk the memory page of the program containing the target of the GO TO. If, in the target page, a GO TO transferred control back to the original page, the swapping of pages between memory and disk became very time-consuming. In fact, the notion of *thrashing* arose, in which more time was spent swapping pages than in executing statements on those pages. As with the FORMAT statement, the thrashing issue was also a matter of *locality of reference*. With the GO TO, however, there are performance implications beyond the problem of program readability and writability. The actual run-time efficiency (or performance) of the program is affected by the locality-of-reference problems that can result from poor use of the GO TO statement.

- -

SEMANTIC NOTE

The poor structure of all forms of the GO TO, the arithmetic IF, and the logical IF is also reflected by the fact that these statements do not lend themselves to simple semantic definitions. Locality of reference is a significant part of this difficulty. All of these statements can reference, via statement numbers, any statement in the program to which control can be transferred. For example, in order to produce the semantics for the GO TO, one would need to pair a set of statements with a statement label and then replace the statements being analyzed with the set of statements serving as the target of the GO TO. (The target of the GO TO is the statement with the same statement number as that referenced in the GO TO statement.)

* *

Pascal helped solve the locality-of-reference problem. With the exception of program modules, like procedures and functions, transfer of control in Pascal is most likely to take place within a small locus of program statements. (It should be noted that the GO TO does exist in Pascal but is unnecessary and should not be used— perhaps Wirth was hedging his bets).

There were three forms of the GO TO statement in FORTRAN: the unconditional, the computed, and the assigned. The computed and assigned GO TO statements looked very similar but acted very differently—an example of the inconsistency inherent in FORTRAN's design.

In the earliest version of FORTRAN, the unconditional GO TO statement was of the general form GO TO n, where n is a program-statement number to which control is to be transferred. The arithmetic-IF statement introduced earlier was the only selection statement. Suppose you are setting up a selective structure to print out the nature of a student's graduation based on grade point average (GPA). Assume the following:

If a student has a GPA > 3.5, he/she graduates with highest honors.
If a student has a GPA <= 3.5 and > 3.0, he/she graduates with honors.
If a student has a GPA <= 3.0 and > 2.5, he/she graduates in good standing.
If a student has a GPA <= 2.5 and > 2.0, he/she graduates.
If a student has a GPA <= 2.0, he/she is not allowed to graduate.

In the earliest version of FORTRAN, this algorithm would appear as

```
        IF(GPA-3.5)20,20,10
  10    WRITE(15,15)INUM
  15    FORMAT(' STUDENT',I9,' GRADUATES WITH HIGHEST
            HONORS')
        GO TO 100
  20    IF(GPA-3.0)40,40,30
  30    WRITE(15,35)INUM
  35    FORMAT(' STUDENT',I9,' GRADUATES WITH HONORS')
        GO TO 100
  40    IF(GPA-2.5)60,60,50
```

```
50      WRITE(15,55)INUM
55      FORMAT(' STUDENT',I9,' GRADUATES IN GOOD STANDING')
        GO TO 100
60      IF(GPA-2.0)80,80,70
70      WRITE(15,75)INUM
75      FORMAT(' STUDENT',I9,' GRADUATES')
        GO TO 100
80      WRITE(15,85)INUM
85      FORMAT(' STUDENT',I9,' CANNOT GRADUATE')
100     CONTINUE
```

This is a tough algorithm to decipher. There is no language support to help the programmer make the program readable. Consider the same algorithm in Pascal:

```
if gpa > 3.5 then
        writeln('student',student_number,
                'graduates with highest honors')
else
if gpa > 3.0 then
        writeln ('student',student_number,
                'graduates with honors')
else
if gpa > 2.5 then
        writeln('student',student_number,
                'graduates in good standing')
else
if gpa > 2.0 then
        writeln('student',student_number,
                'graduates')
else
        writeln('student',student_number,
                'cannot graduate')
```

Notice the greater simplicity of structure. Reconsider the FORTRAN segment with the FORMAT statements placed on a different page of the listing. The reader should be quickly gaining an appreciation for the advance Pascal represented in problem solving. The IF-THEN-ELSE of Pascal has not been improved since Pascal, and knowledge of Pascal's IF-THEN-ELSE generalizes to newer languages.

One should note the organization of the FORTRAN code. The statement numbers provided as the targets of GO TO statements and for FORMAT statements must be written in columns 1 through 5. The statement itself must begin in column 7. Statements had to fit on a single line—and if it was necessary to continue a statement on the next line, the next line would have a character in column 6 indicating that the line was a "continuation" of the previous line.

Moreover, indentation was not possible in the earliest versions of FORTRAN, and its absence negatively affected readability and writability. In Pascal, programs are written in a free form, so that instructions can be indented and can span several lines. A semicolon is used to indicate the termination of an instruction.

LOOPING Now consider the looping problem in an early version of FOR-TRAN. Let's redo our GPA problem in a loop that is reading an unspecified number of student number and GPA pairs:

```
1     READ(5,5,END=100)INUM,GPA
5     FORMAT(I9,F5.3)
      IF(GPA-3.5)20,20,10
10    WRITE(15,15)INUM
15    FORMAT(' STUDENT ',I9,' GRADUATES WITH HIGHEST
         HONORS')
      GO TO 1
20    IF(GPA-3.0)40,40,30
30    WRITE(15,35)INUM
35    FORMAT(' STUDENT ',I9,' GRADUATES WITH HONORS')
      GO TO 1
40    IF(GPA-2.5)60,60,50
50    WRITE(15,55)INUM
55    FORMAT(' STUDENT ',I9,' GRADUATES IN GOOD STANDING')
      GO TO 1
60    IF(GPA-2.0)80,80,70
70    WRITE(15,75)INUM
75    FORMAT(' STUDENT ',I9,' GRADUATES')
      GO TO 1
80    WRITE(15,85)INUM
85    FORMAT(' STUDENT ',I9,' CANNOT GRADUATE')
      GO TO 1
100   CONTINUE
```

The form of this algorithm gives no hint of the entry, exit, or condition for the loop. There is no loop construct at all. The parts of the loop are scattered throughout the loop structure as boldfaced and commented on in the following:

```
1     READ(5,5,END=100)INUM,GPA   /* ENTRY POINT
                                      AND LOOP CONDITION
5     FORMAT(I9,F5.3)
      IF(GPA-3.5)20,20,10
10    WRITE(15,15)INUM
15    FORMAT(' STUDENT ',I9,' GRADUATES WITH HIGHEST
         HONORS')
      GO TO 1                      /* CYCLE
20    IF(GPA-3.0)40,40,30
30    WRITE(15,35)INUM
35    FORMAT(' STUDENT ',I9,' GRADUATES WITH HONORS')
      GO TO 1                      /* CYCLE
40    IF(GPA-2.5)60,60,50
50    WRITE(15,55)INUM
55    FORMAT(' STUDENT ',I9,' GRADUATES IN GOOD STANDING')
      GO TO 1                      /* CYCLE
```

```
60    IF(GPA-2.0)80,80,70
70    WRITE(15,75)INUM
75    FORMAT(' STUDENT',I9,' GRADUATES')
      GO TO 1                              /* CYCLE
80    WRITE(15,85)INUM
65    FORMAT(' STUDENT',I9,' CANNOT GRADUATE')
      GO TO 1                              /* CYCLE
100   CONTINUE                             /* EXIT
```

The Pascal version of this code is much simpler and easier to understand:

```
readln(student_number,gpa);
while not (eof) do
        begin
        if gpa > 3.5 then
                writeln('student',student_number,
                        ' graduates with highest honors')
        else
        if gpa > 3.0 then
                writeln('student',student_number,
                        ' graduates with honors')
        else
        if gpa > 2.5 then
                writeln('student',student_number,
                        ' graduates')
        else
        if gpa > 2.0 then
                writeln('student',student_number,
                        ' graduates in good standing')
        else
                writeln('student',student_number,
                        ' cannot graduate');
        readln(student_number,gpa)
        end;
```

Later versions of FORTRAN offered this single automatic loop statement:

DO sn i=initial,test,increment

where "sn" is a statement number indicating the bottom boundary on the loop, i is a variable serving as the loop index, "initial" is the initial value of i, "test" is the limit on the loop index, and "increment" is an optional increment value for the loop index. This type of loop is strictly a *counting loop*. However, the basic design of the DO loop (with the exception of the statement number) generalizes to newer languages (i.e., FOR loops).

A counting loop is a loop to be executed a *predetermined* (or definite) number of times. In other words, prior to entering the loop, the number of iterations can be determined from the initial, test, and increment values. These values can be given as either constants or variables.

SPACES AND OTHER DESIGN PROBLEMS   The original FORTRAN compilers ignored spaces. That is, spaces were not considered to be delimiters. A delimiter is a way to isolate language objects such as reserved words, constants, and variables. (See Chapter 4 for more detail concerning delimiters.) FORTRAN also performed implicit typing of variables, meaning that variables did not have to be declared. If undeclared, a variable beginning with any letter between "I" and "N", inclusive, was an integer by default. Undeclared variables beginning with any other letter were real. It is computer science lore that because of the default declarations and the fact that spaces did not serve as delimiters, an important piece of software failed years ago. It seems that a programmer omitted the increment and the comma between the initial value and the test, resulting in something like the following:

DO 1000 I=1 200

This statement was taken to be an assignment to a real variable: DO1000I = 1200. Such a mistake could not happen in Pascal, which mandates that all variables be declared and in which spaces serve as delimiters.

FOR LOOP   Pascal provides for a counting loop with the FOR loop:

for i:=initial {to/downto} test [by increment] <statement>

where the items in {} represent a choice and items in [] indicate an optional structure. The <statement> can be a single statement or a compound statement. The boundaries of the loop are very clear in that compound statements are enclosed between the "begin-end."

CONDITIONAL LOOP   The other type of loop is the *conditional loop*. Conditional loops became easier to express with the introduction of the so-called *logical-IF statement*:

IF (ae.ro.ae)statement

In the FORTRAN logical IF-statement, "ae" is an arithmetic expression, "ro" is a relational operator (LT, LE, GT, GE, NE, EQ), and "statement" is any FORTRAN statement except another IF or a DO statement. Therefore, the language is not orthogonal (i.e., it is not possible to nest any structure inside any other structure). Now consider a short conditional loop in FORTRAN to compute the largest Fibonacci number less than 500:

```
      F1 = 0
      F2 = 1
10    F3 = F1 + F2
      IF(F3.GE.500)GO TO 20
      F1 = F2
      F2 = F3
      GO TO 10
20    WRITE(5,25)F3
25    FORMAT(' ', F5.1)
```

The equivalent Pascal code employs the REPEAT loop construct, which allows for one form of a conditional loop:

```
f1:=0;
f2:=1;
repeat
      f3:=f1 + f2;
      f1:=f2;
      f2:=f3
until f3 >= 500;
writeln( f3);
```

SEMANTIC NOTE

The REPEAT is easily incorporated into the WHILE language discussed in Chapter 3.

<u>Syntax change:</u>
$S ::= V:=E$ | read(V) | write(V) | while C do S od | $S;S$ | repeat S until C
$C ::=$ not (C) | $E1 < E2$ | $E1 > E2$ | $E1 = E2$ | $E1 <> E2$ | $E1 <= E2$ | $E1 >= E2$

<u>Semantic change:</u>
Σ « repeat S until C » γ $\quad = \quad$ Σ « S; while not C do S od » γ
ζ « not C » σ $\quad = \quad$ if ζ « C » σ then false else true

---

Notice that the Pascal loop construct is clear and easy to understand. In the FORTRAN code you must first determine that a loop exists and then figure out what it is doing, whereas all you have to do in Pascal is figure out what the loop is doing. Pascal allows for the WHILE loop and the IF-THEN-ELSE structures. Any structure can be nested in any other structure, so that the language is fully orthogonal.

LEARNING NEW LANGUAGES

The constructs of programming languages are general constructs. They are based upon the simple capabilities of computer architecture. They form categories in which every procedural programming language has statements. Therefore, the constructs form a solid basis from which to learn a new programming language. When faced with a new language, a programmer should say, for example, "I know it must have a selective structure, so how does the IF-THEN-ELSE or CASE statement exist in this language?" In other words, the constructs exist as knowledge of the basic semantic capabilities of any procedural language.

Another key to learning a language is to try out its features to make sure that you fully understand them. For example, in a FOR loop, one should know where the test is done—whether at the beginning of the loop body or at the end. If you do not know the answer, you should run a test program containing the following code segment:

```
flag:=false;
for i:=2 to 1 do
        flag:=true;
if flag then
        writeln('for-loop test done at the end of the loop')
else
        writeln('for-loop test done at the beginning of the loop');
```

COMMANDS TO LANGUAGE TRANSLATOR

Since the arithmetic constructs were fixed in FORTRAN, and most other executable constructs were fixed in Pascal, the greatest differences among other languages are found in their nonexecutable statements. The nonexecutable statements of a language allow the programmer to define program and data structures. Pascal will serve as the basis for the following discussion. Although one can define program structures and the array in FORTRAN, it is not a rich language when it comes to setting up program or data structures.

Pascal program structures are built using the following commands:

program—to identify the beginning of the program and its I/O files.
procedure—to identify the head of a procedure and its I/O parameters.
function—to identify the head of a function and its I/O parameters.
begin-end—to identify compound statements that serve as the body of a loop, a
    true or false sequence of an IF statement, a function body, a procedure body,
    a record layout, or the statements that compose a program.

Functions and procedures in Pascal may be recursive. They cannot be recursive in FORTRAN.

In terms of data structures, Pascal features the following commands:

cons—to define a constant value used throughout a program.
type—to identify user-defined data structures.
var—to declare program variables of predefined or user-defined types.

The predefined types of Pascal include

integer, real, char, Boolean—primitive types.

^type—a structured type; pointer to a structure of type *type*.

record—a structured type; allows for the definition of a structure composed of variables of various types.

array—a structured type that allows for a linear or tabular structure consisting of cells of some type.

In Pascal, you can nest any structure (be it a program or data structure) inside any other structure. Furthermore, you can use any program structure to process any data structure. For example, a WHILE loop can be used to traverse the elements of an array or a linked list. Consider this program, which first creates the elements of a linked list and then traverses the list:

```
program linkedlist(output);
type
        ptr = ^node;

        node = record
                next:ptr;
                info:integer;
        end;

var p,q,head:ptr;
        i:integer;

begin
        i:=10;
        new(p);
        head:=p;
        p^.info:=i;
        q:=p;
        while i <= 100 do
                begin
                new(p);
                i:=i+10;
                p^.info:=i;
                q^.next:=p;
                q:=p
                end;
        p:=head;
        while p <> nil do
                begin
                writeln(p^.info);
                p:=p^.next
                end
end.
```

THE PASCAL ABSTRACTION

Problem solutions in FORTRAN were almost purely algorithm-oriented. Consider an inorder traversal of a binary tree from a nonrecursive, more algorithmic standpoint. Although this solution will be given in Pascal (so as to help with readability), some of the limits of FORTRAN are imposed: no recursion and no pointer variables. All activities are accomplished, more or less, by brute force. Children of a node are computed arithmetically: a left child of node i is obtained by visiting $2 * i$; a right child is obtained with $2 * i + 1$. A parent is obtained by i div 2. After visiting a left or right node (via the left descent or right descent), code to return to a root (i.e., ascent to root) must be executed. Consequently, an interior node will be visited more than once via the descent and the ascent. In order to keep track of whether or not the node has been written out for the traversal, the node is marked in its second column $t[i,2]$.

```
program trees(output);
var
        done:boolean;
        c,i:integer;
        t:array[1..100,1..2] of integer;

begin
            :

        i:=1;
        done:=false;

        while not done do
                begin
                {left descent}
                while (t[i,1] <> 0) and (t[i,2]=0) do
                    i:=i*2;

                {ascent to root}
                i:=i div 2;
                while (t[i,2] > 0) and (i mod 2 > 1) do
                    i:=i div 2;

                {visit root}
                t[i,2]:=t[i,2]+1;
                if t[i,2] <=1 then
                    writeln('here: ',i,' ',t[i,1],' ',t[i,2])
                else
                if (i=1) and (t[i,2]>1) then
                    done:=true;
```

```
        {right descent}
        while (t[i,1] < > 0) and
             (t[i*2,2]< >0) and (t[i*2+1,2]=0) do
                 i:=i*2+1;

        {ascent to root}
        while (t[i,2] > 0) and (i mod 2 > 1) do
             i:=i div 2;
        end
end.
```

This algorithm is presented in contrast to the typical inorder traversal one learns in a CS2 or data structures class:

```
procedure inorder(root:ptr);
begin
        if root < > nil then
             begin
             inorder(root^.left);
             writeln(root^.info);
             inorder(root^.right)
             end
end;
```

The standard Pascal solution utilizes the pointer variables and recursive features not available in early versions of FORTRAN. One sees a conciseness and elegance in the solution—a level of elegance not attainable in FORTRAN. This elegance is obtainable only in an abstraction where data structures play a key role in the problem solution.

In the Pascal abstraction the choice of data structure employed in a problem solution is often key to the simplicity or complexity of the solution. Consider, as an exercise, the problem of converting a prefix arithmetic expression to an equivalent postfix expression. To solve this in a purely algorithmic manner requires a lot of effort from the problem solver. To solve this in an abstraction, which employs the data structure as an equal to the algorithm in a problem solution, one finds that the decision to employ a binary tree in the problem solution dictates a very simple algorithm. You simply construct a binary tree of the prefix expression in which parents are operations and children are constituent operands. Once the tree is constructed, a postorder traversal will yield the postfix expression.

▪ ▪

DATA TYPES

The nature and extent of data typing in a language are often significant distinguishing attributes. A language is *strongly typed* if all type checking is done when the program is translated to an executable form. Typing of data directs the language translator in determining architectural characteristics of a program. For example, most computers accommodate both integer and floating-point arithmetic. Thus, two different machine-level arithmetic instruction sets exist. One set accomplishes the floating-point arithmetic, and the other accommodates the integer arithmetic. Declaring a variable as integer or real also declares which instruction set applies if the location is involved in an arithmetic instruction. Consider the following example:

x:=y * z;

In Pascal this instruction will involve either an integer or a floating-point multiplication. The determination is based on the declaration of variables x, y, and z. If they are declared to be integer, integer arithmetic is performed. If they are declared to be real, floating-point arithmetic is performed. Mixed-mode instructions are not allowed in Pascal.

Mixed-mode instructions allow arithmetic to be performed between variables of different types. If, in the preceding example, y is integer and z is real, arithmetic is accomplished by *coercing* one variable to be the type of the other. FORTRAN allows mixed mode expressions. Therefore, $x = y * z$ is permitted as a mixed-mode statement. Suppose x and y are integer variables and z is real. In order to evaluate the expression, y is coerced to a real number and multiplied by z using the floating-point instruction set. Then the result of the instruction, a real number, is coerced to an integer to be stored in the integer location, x.

Obviously, information is often lost when data types are coerced. When one coerces a floating-point to an integer, fractions are typically truncated. When one coerces from integer to floating-point, approximation errors can occur. Suppose the floating-point 1 is approximated by 0.9999 in the XYZ computer. Also suppose that x is real and z and i are integers:

x = 1.0
i = x + z

After this sequence executes on XYZ, i would most likely equal z. Mixed-mode arithmetic can often lead to such subtle and potentially dangerous errors.

Most built-in data types, such as integer, Boolean, real, and character, are called *scalar structures*. Scalars hold exactly one occurrence of a data type.

Nonscalars are structures that can contain multiple scalars. Most languages allow for user-defined types and structured types. *Structured types* allow programmers to produce more complicated data structures. *Arrays* are available in most languages and allow programmers to produce homogeneous, nonscalar structures. For example, in Pascal one can declare

x : array [1..n] of integer;

The array is declared with two types. The *base type* declares the type of data the array is to hold. In the example declaration, x is declared to be an integer array. All data in an array must be of the same type. Hence, arrays are called *homogeneous* structures. The second type declared for an array is its *index type*, which determines its valid range of indices. In the array x, valid index or subscript values range from the integer 1 to some limit, *n*. To enforce the range of values for an index of *x*, you could declare the following *subrange type:*

```
const          n = 100
type           index = 1..n;
```

First *n* is declared as to be the constant 100. Next a data type is declared. Any variable subsequently declared of type "index" can hold only integer values from the subrange of 1 . . 100, inclusive.

Now suppose the following variable declarations are made:

```
var            x : array [index] of integer;
               i,j : index;
```

Presumably, *i* and *j* are to be used as subscripts to the array *x*. Any attempt to assign a value to *i* or *j* outside the range of integers from 1 to 100 will result in a run-time error. Thus, through data typing the programmer can ensure that array subscript limits are imposed.

RECORDS

Another structured-type capability found in most modern languages is the *record,* which is used for structuring *nonhomogeneous* data types. The internal structures formed by record definitions are often employed as the places in memory where the fields of a record are stored. For example, consider a simple record structure to hold student information:

```
type   students = record
               st_name   :   packed array[1..20]of char;
               st_id     :   packed array[1..9]of char;
               st_class  :   packed array[1..4]of char;
               st_major  :   packed array[1..4]of char;
               gpa       :   real;
               total_hrs :   integer;
       end;
```

One can envision many student records stored on disk. As a record is read, its data are placed into a variable declared to be of type "students":

```
var    x,y,z      :      students;
```

Once declared and defined through input instructions, individual fields of each record can be accessed in executable statements. For example:

```
x.st_gpa:=3.9;
writeln(x.st_gpa);
```

It is possible to have variant records in many languages. Variant records exist to allow for variations in data storage based on data stored in the records. The variant record in Pascal is achieved through a consistent application of the CASE statement. To store geometric point and line information, you could declare this record:

```
type   point = record
              x_coordinate, y_coordinate   :   real;
       end;

       line = record
              p1,p2                              :   point;
       end;
```

The variant record would allow for the storage of point or line data:

```
type   point = record
              x_coordinate, y_coordinate   :   real;
       end;

       line = record
              p1,p2                              : point;
       end;

       geometric_type = (pnt, lne);

       geom = record
              CASE flag:geometric_type OF
                     pnt : (dot:point);
                     lne : (edge:line)
              end;
```

The record, "geom," is a variant record that utilizes the enumerated type, "geometric_type," and the two record definitions, "point" and "line." If the first field of the record has a value of "pnt," the CASE statement causes the remainder of the record layout to be a *point record*. Alternatively, if the first field has a value of "lne," the remainder of the record is to be a *line record*.

Variables provide access to memory locations. When variables are declared, memory is allocated for the variable based on its type. Variables that are allocated memory at compile time are called *static variables*.

DYNAMIC DATA STRUCTURES

Many languages allow variables to be allocated while the program is executing. Variables allocated memory at run-time are called *dynamic variables*. Figure 5.4 shows one way a compiler might organize the memory segment of a compiled program. As static variables' declarations are encountered, memory locations are allocated by the compiler, beginning at the bottom of the memory segment and

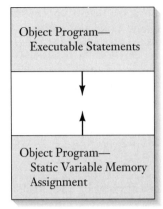

Object Program's Organization in a Memory Segment as Established by the Compiler at Compile Time

FIGURE 5.4   Object program organization.

proceeding upward. As executable statements are compiled into machine code, the machine-code instructions are placed in memory from the top of memory, working downward. The resulting executable program residing in a memory segment is called an *object program.*

Any unused area of memory (between the executable statements' section and the static variables' section) is used for activation records for functions and procedures and for the allocation of memory to be used by dynamic variables. Activation records will be discussed later.

In Pascal, dynamic variables are called *pointer variables.* A pointer variable serves as a means of access to areas of memory dynamically allocated. These variables are declared to be of type "pointer" and must be declared with reference to another type. The other type describes the memory structure to be allocated when the pointer variable is defined.

```
type   point = record
               x_coordinate, y_coordinate   :   real;
               end;
var    p, q : ^point;
```

Allocation of dynamic memory occurs while the program is executing. Therefore, once the preceding declarations exist, you can allocate a new area of memory of type "point" by referencing a built-in procedure that allocates memory and defines the pointer variable:

```
new(p);
new(q);
```

After these instructions are executed, two occurrences of the record "point" exist. The variables in the record are undefined. One record is pointed to by the variable *p*, the other by the variable *q*. Figure 5.5 pictorially represents what now exists in memory.

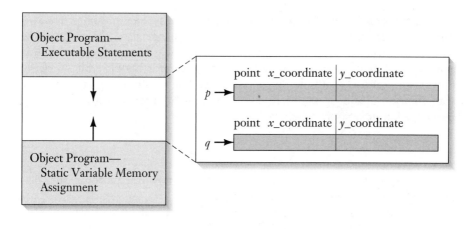

FIGURE 5.5   Pictorial of pointer variables after declaration.

Once allocated, the associated variables can be defined:

p^.x_coordinate:=14.5;
p^.y_coordinate:=9.0;
q^.x_coordinate:=16.5;
q^.y_coordinate:=3.2;

These instructions result in the dynamic-memory layout shown in Figure 5.6. Suppose, at this point, the following instruction is executed:

p:=q;

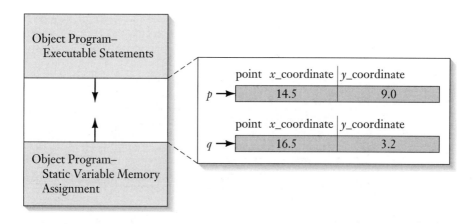

FIGURE 5.6   Dynamic memory layout, after assignment.

This instruction is permissible because of *name equivalence*, meaning that two variables declared to be of the same type can exchange data. (More on name equivalence will be presented later in this chapter.) The problem with this assignment is that *p*'s data are no longer accessible. Furthermore, the memory previously allocated to *p* is no longer available. The resulting dynamic memory configuration is shown in Figure 5.7. Assuming *p*'s information is no longer needed, a better set of instructions is

    dispose(p);
    p:=q;

In this case, the memory previously allocated to *p* is now freed through the "dispose(*p*)," so that it can be used for other purposes.

Some languages do not require explicit deallocation of memory. Instead, these languages perform *garbage collection* to free areas of dynamic memory that are no longer accessible (Figure 5.8). Garbage collection is an implicit, automatic approach to reclaim memory that is no longer needed. There are two phases of collection. The first phase identifies areas that are no longer needed because no active pointers point to them. The second phase makes these areas available for re-allocation. Some compilers may further *reorganize* dynamic memory by making the freed areas of memory contiguous. Thus, larger blocks of memory can be allocated as needed.

Name equivalence of types, mentioned earlier, exists when two variables are declared to be of the same type. For example, in the following declarations variables *p* and *q* are declared to be of type "point." Therefore, it is possible for these variables to be involved in the exchange of data so long as name equivalence is accommodated by the language translator.

    type   point = record
                    x_coordinate, y_coordinate   :   real;
                    end;
           var   p, q : point;

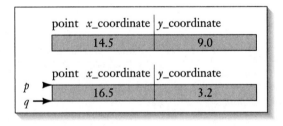

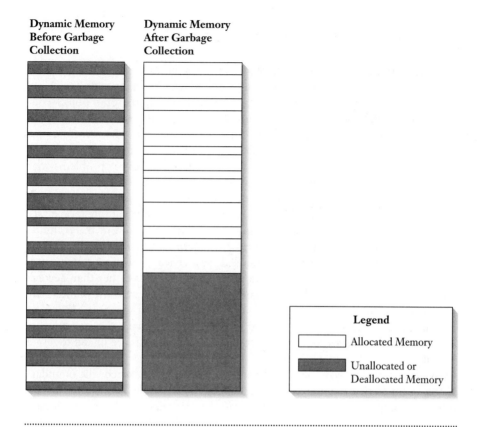

Dynamic Memory
Before Garbage
Collection

Dynamic Memory
After Garbage
Collection

Legend

Allocated Memory

Unallocated or
Deallocated Memory

FIGURE 5.8 Garbage collection.

Structure equivalence of types exists when two variables are declared to be of differently named types but turn out to be structured in the same way. For example, in the following declarations variables *r* and *s* are declared to be of type "point" and of type "position," respectively. These variables would not be considered to be equivalent by a compiler that accommodated only name equivalence. For these variables to be considered of the same type, the compiler must enforce structure equivalence.

```
type  point = record
            x_coordinate, y_coordinate   :    real;
            end;
      position = record
            x_position, y_position       :    real;
            end;
      var   r : point;
            s : position;
```

RUN-TIME ERROR MESSAGES

Refer again to Figure 5.4 to see the object-program boundaries above and below the dynamic-memory boundaries. These boundaries must be monitored and protected by the run-time portion of the compiler, which is a set of object-code instructions (including the subprograms "new" and "dispose," shown previously) inserted into the programmer's object-program area. The run-time portion handles, among other tasks, the allocation and deallocation of memory. The run-time portion also enforces memory boundaries to prevent problems with runaway pointers, array boundary violations, and runaway recursive functions.

Runaway pointer variables may occur when dynamic memory is allocated within a loop or recursive function. If infinite recursion or an infinite loop exists, dynamic memory will be exhausted, and the run-time portion of the compiler will issue an error. The error is often read as a *heap overflow* error rather than a *stack overflow*. Runaway pointers are called *heap errors* because the memory is allocated/deallocated according to the programmer's needs rather than according to a predefined order. There is no predefined order, because the pointers can be involved in the implementation of any conceivable data structure. As will be seen in the next section, a stack overflow is associated with the execution of functions or procedures, since the related activation records are linked together as a stack.

An *array boundary error* occurs whenever an array index exceeds the boundary of the array. When boundary violations occur, they should be reported by the language compiler's run-time facility. Some early languages did not (and do not) detect boundary and other errors. Instead, when the operating system catches the error, it unfortunately reports it as some seemingly unrelated problem.

For example, many versions of COBOL do not enforce array boundaries. The COBOL compiler organizes the object program by placing the data area of the program in front of the executable code. When an array index exceeds its limit within an infinite loop, the program can literally end up storing data on top of itself. This overlaying process continues until the program stores data—as a result of executing the current instruction—on top of the next executable instruction. When the computer attempts to execute the instruction that has been replaced by data, the operating system often reports "unrecognizable op-code." A programmer faced with this error might first react by saying, "How can this be? The compiler generated the executable instructions. Is there a bug in the compiler causing it to generate a bad instruction?" Only a fairly sophisticated programmer would be likely to determine that the program was storing data over the executable instructions.

The reporting of errors is an important concern. Misleading error messages are very costly in time wasted trying to figure out the actual problem. Error messages should be succinct and should accurately direct the programmer's attention to the true source of the problem. The importance of accurate error messages has led many modern compiler writers to develop excellent run-time facilities.

FUNCTIONS AND PROCEDURES

As pointed out earlier, all languages have commands to the compiler, or language translator. There are two categories of commands: those used to declare data types and structures (as seen in the previous section) and those used to establish program structures. Commands in this latter category include ones that declare program blocks (like the "begin-end" in Pascal) and that declare functions and procedures. The declaration of functions and procedures and other related concerns are the focus of this section.

Functions and procedures are units of code that perform a well-defined unit task that usually is not further subdivided. Consider this simple function:

```
function factorial(n:integer):integer;
var t:integer;
      if n >= 0 then
          if n = 0 then
              t:=1
          else
              t:=factorial(n-1) * n
      else
          t:=-99;
      factorial:=t
end;
```

The first line of the function is called the *function declaration*. It names the function and provides the function's *signature*, which gives its input and output (i.e., domain and range) information. In this case the name is "factorial."

The first line also indicates the *formal parameters* of the function. In this case the formal parameter is *n*. An argument for *n* must be supplied when the function is invoked.

Assume the following context for the function "factorial":

```
program main(input,output);

var x,y,z,f:integer;

function factorial(n:integer):integer;
var t:integer;
      if n >= 0 then
          if n = 0 then
              t:=1
          else
              t:=factorial(n-1) * n
      else
          t:=-99;
      factorial:=t
end;
```

begin
       readln(x,y,z);
       f:=factorial(x);
          :
end.

The function is invoked within an executable statement. In this example the function is invoked in an assignment statement. The value read in for x in the previous statement serves as the argument for the "factorial" function. Suppose the value 3 has been read in for variable x. When the function is invoked, execution in the main program is suspended, and an activation record for this execution of the function is established. The current activation record would be placed in the dynamic region of memory as shown in Figure 5.4 and would contain the information the function requires for its execution. The allocation and deallocation of activation records occurs with the invocation of and return from subprograms. Thus, the memory management is handled explicitly, requiring no garbage collection.

With the activation record is a structure called a *display*. For each declared unit of code (procedure or function) the display has an entry that serves as a pointer to the currently active activation record. Notice in Figure 5.9 the information stored in the activation record (AR). All input parameters, local variables, and the return address of a function or procedure are stored in its activation record. If the function or procedure is recursive, (i.e., if it calls itself), links to previous ARs are provided in the "pointer to previous AR" field.

Since $n > 0$, a recursive call is made, resulting in the configuration shown in Figure 5.10. (This is an abbreviated form from Figure 5.9.) Still, n is greater than 0; therefore, another recursive call results in the ARs shown in Figure 5.11, and the final recursive call results in the ARs shown in Figure 5.12. Notice that no further calls are made to the function "factorial," and a direct answer of 1 is

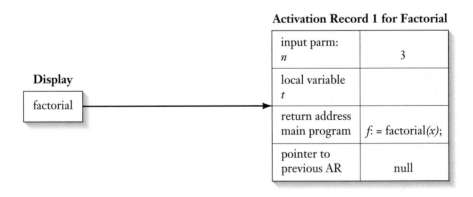

FIGURE 5.9   Activation record, initial call.

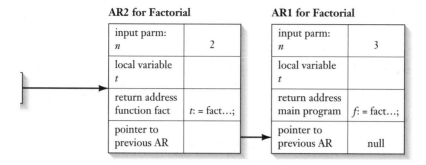

FIGURE 5.10 Activation record, first recursive call.

assigned to local variable *t*, as reflected in AR 4 in Figure 5.12. Up to this point, calls have been made to the function. As a call is executed, a new AR is allocated in the dynamic region of memory and is *pushed* onto a stack of ARs for which the function's display serves as the header.

For each return from the function, the AR stack is popped. In the lowest level of recursion, represented by AR4 in Figure 5.12, an assignment is finally made to "factorial" and the function returns its result to the return address indicated by AR4, as shown in Figure 5.13.

The assignment of 1 to "factorial results" in the return and the removal of AR3ₜ from the AR stack is shown in Figure 5.14. The assignment of 2 to "factorial" results in the return and the removal of AR2 from the AR stack, shown in Figure 5.15. And finally, "factorial" is assigned the value 6, and return is made to the main program, where the value 6 is assigned the main program variable *f*.

The display provides the static structure of the procedures and functions in a program. Thus, global variables and other *scoping* considerations are represented by the display. Consider the following program skeleton and its associated display:

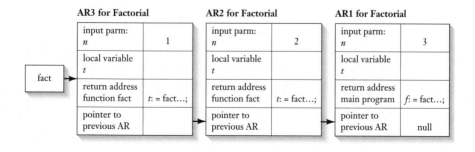

FIGURE 5.11 Activation record, second recursive call.

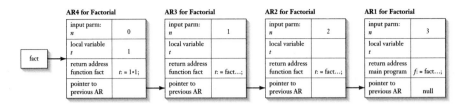

FIGURE 5.12 Activation record, third recursive call.

```
program main(input,output);
var x,y,z,f:integer;
procedure p1(n:integer);
var p1_t:integer;
    procedure p2(...)
    var p2_t:integer;
    begin
    :
           p2(...);
    :
    end;
begin
    :
end;

begin    {main}
    :
end      {main}.
```

Assume (1) that the main portion of the program in this display has called $p1$, (2) that $p1$ has executed one call to function $p2$, and (3) that $p2$ has executed one

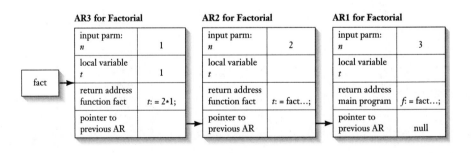

FIGURE 5.13 Activation record, first return.

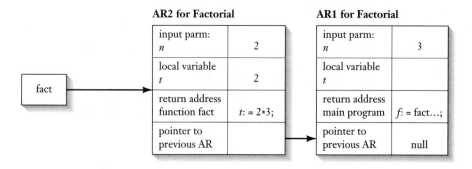

FIGURE 5.14   Activation record, second return.

recursive call to itself (Figure 5.16). At this point, if *p2* references variable *p2_t*, it will reference it from its own AR2. If *p2* references variable *p1_t* it will obtain its value from *p1*'s currently active AR. If *p2* references any variable, *x*, *y*, *z*, or *f*, it will obtain appropriate values from the main program's data area. It is worth noting that if procedure *p1* (or *p2*) declared a variable, *x*, as local, reference to *x* would be from the nearest AR rather than from the main program's data area.

PARAMETER PASSING

When arguments are passed in Pascal, they are passed as call-by-value or call-by-reference. In a *call-by-value argument*, the value of the argument is passed, or is copied, into an AR entry. In a *call-by-reference argument*, the function or procedure instead is provided direct access to the memory location associated with the argument passed.

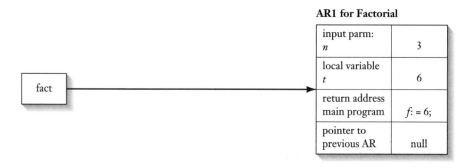

FIGURE 5.15   Activation record, third return.

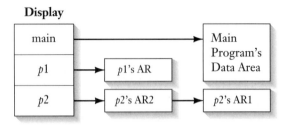

Display

FIGURE 5.16   Program display.

Consider the following procedure definition:

procedure p1(x,y:integer; var z:integer);

Variables prefixed with the keyword "var" are call-by-reference, and those not so prefixed are call-by-value. If *p1* is called with the arguments of *p1*(2,3,*r*), copies of integers 2 and 3 are stored in *p1*'s AR entries for variables *x* and *y*, respectively. Also, reference or assignment to variable *z* in *p1* will actually result in assignment to variable *r* in the calling program. With some compilers, trouble will arise with the call *p1*(2,3,4). A change to *z* in *p1* can potentially change the value of the constant 4. Consider the following example:

```
program main(output);
procedure px(var n:integer);
begin
        n:=9
end;


begin                {main}


        px(4);
        writeln(4)


end                  {main}.
```

Some FORTRAN compilers will allow this type of assignment. As a result, the "writeln" will write value 9, given a FORTRAN program similar to that presented here.

CONCLUDING REMARKS

In this chapter the evolution from an algorithm-oriented abstraction to one where data structure and algorithm serve as equals was presented. In accordance with the principle of reuse, the Pascal abstraction was extended to produce an object-oriented abstraction in which data structures are better isolated. The next chapter focuses on that object-oriented abstraction.

- -

REFERENCES

N. Wirth. "On the Design of Programming Languages." In *Information Processing 74*, edited by Jack Rosenfeld, North-Holland, Amsterdam, 1974, pp. 386–393.

P. Zave. "An Insider's Evaluation of PAISLey." *IEEE Transactions on Software Engineering* 17, no. 3 (March 1991):212–225.

QUESTIONS AND EXERCISES

1. Consider the following FORTRAN code segment. Write a Pascal program that will solve the problem with better control structures.

```
10      READ(,)(N,GPA)
        IF(N.EQ.-1)GO TO 50
        IF(GPA.GT.3.5)GO TO 40
        IF(GPA.GT.3.0)G0 T0 30
        IF(GPA.GT.2.5)GO TO 20
        WRITE(,15)N,GPA
15      FORMAT(' ','STUDENT CANNOT GRADUATE: ', I6,F4.2)
        GO TO 10
20      WRITE(,25)N,GPA
25      FORMAT(' ','STUDENT CAN GRADUATE: ', I6,F4.2)
        GO TO 10
30      WRITE(,35)N,GPA
35      FORMAT(' ','STUDENT GRADUATES WITH HONRS: ',
            I6,F4.2)
        GO TO 10
40      WRITE(,45)N,GPA
45      FORMAT(' ','STUDENT GRADUATES WITH HIGH HONRS:
            ', I6,F4.2)
        GO TO 10
50      CONTINUE
        :
```

2. Provide the full display/activation record history for the following program:

```
program main(input,output);

var n:integer;

function fib(x,y: integer):integer;
```

```
var x1,y1:integer;
        if y <= n then
                begin
                y1:=x+y;
                x1:=y;
                fib:=fib(x1,y1)
                end
        else
                fib:=x
end;

begin
        n:=20;
        writeln(fib(0,1))
end.
```

3. Explain the importance of stream I/O as compared with FORTRAN's I/O facility.

4. Assume an array implementation of a binary tree. Give a formula that will provide the worst-case size of the array needed to store *n* elements in the binary tree.

5. Given the following, write an equivalent unit of code in Pascal:

```
        READ(5,10) N
10      FORMAT(I2)
        DO 20 I=1,N
        READ(5,10) A(I)
20      CONTINUE
        S=0
        DO 30 I=1,N
        S=S+A(I)
30      CONTINUE
        AVE = S / N
```

6

OBJECT-ORIENTED
LANGUAGES

Recall the discussion of ordinary and extraordinary science from Chapter 1. A good example of the result of ordinary science in computer-language research is the object-oriented abstraction. Among other concerns, the object-oriented approach to programming grew out of a desire to encapsulate and reuse program and data structures. To accomplish these goals, the procedural programming paradigm was modified in a well-thought-out manner. In fact, to be a good object-oriented programmer in Java or C++, an individual must first be a good procedural programmer.

The object-oriented approach solved many technical problems of the procedural programming paradigm. Data structures in Pascal and other procedural languages exhibit two major problems. First, the variables holding the data structure must be held globally so that the structure will persist throughout the life of the program using the structure. These variables cannot exist as local variables in the functions and procedures defined to operate on the data structure because local variables are deallocated upon return from the subprogram. Object-oriented languages allow for a type of variable different from a local or global variable, called an *instance variable*, which allows for the necessary middle ground between local and global variables.

Second, the object-oriented languages allow for *polymorphism*, which facilitates software reuse by permitting the construction of "generic" data structures that will hold data of differing types. The *inheritance* constructs also facilitate the reuse of code. All of these additions to the procedural paradigm were needed in order to solve technical problems encountered by procedural programmers and to address Parnas's information-hiding concerns. In Kuhn's terms, the procedural theory was extended in a natural way to solve some technical problems. In fact, one could argue that there was little or no effort expended in developing a new computational model. Instead, object-oriented language designers have concentrated on the concern of how to communicate problem solutions in a language.

Many advantages from the object-oriented extensions have accrued to the computing profession. Foremost among these advantages is the ease with which one can now develop sophisticated graphical user interfaces. A by-product of the capabilities to reuse the objects that implement the interfaces is a growing standardization of the "look and feel" of computer applications. These are major advantages that make object-oriented languages a significant contribution to the state of the art and state of the practice in computing.

Now consider one of the motivating technical problems exhibited by Pascal and addressed by the object-oriented languages. The interpreter presented in Chapter 4 includes the Pascal code to implement a stack:

```
program zwhile(prog,dat,output);
type
    ptr2 = ^node2;
    node2 = record
        right:ptr2;
        val:integer
        end;
var result,p2:ptr2;

procedure push(i:integer);
begin
    new(p2);
    p2^.val:=i;
    p2^.right:=result;
    result:=p2
end;

function pop:integer;
begin
    if result <> nil then
        begin
        p2:=result;
        result:=result^.right;
        return p2^.val
        dispose(p2)
        end
    else
        return error
end;
    :
```

The important point to note in the preceding code is that the stack operators, namely *push* and *pop*, are implemented with reference to global types and variables, "node2" and "ptr2," respectively. Global variables referenced in procedures and functions lead to *side effects*, outputs that cannot be documented in the *signature*. (Signatures are discussed later in this chapter in more detail.) For example, the procedure signature for push is

```
procedure push(i:integer);
```

This signature indicates the procedure's input, but its output—a change in the state of the stack—is a side effect and therefore goes undocumented. To understand this procedure, therefore, a programmer must inspect its body. Given the general situation—that some problems cannot be solved without side effects—programmers must inspect the body of *any* procedure or function in *any* program they are trying to understand.

SOFTWARE REUSABILITY

A more specific problem with global structures is that in order to reuse the function or procedures for the stack, a programmer must implement the global type and variable declarations referenced by the stack operations:

```
type
    ptr2 = ^node2;
    node2 = record
        right:ptr2;
        val:integer
        end;
    var result,p2:ptr2;
```

In 1972 David Parnas summarized these concerns in two statements that have come to be known as the *Parnas information-hiding principles:*

- The user of a module should be provided with all the information needed to *use* the module and with nothing more.
- The implementer of the module should be provided with all the information needed to *complete* the module and with nothing more.

This means that the user should know only the *what* of the module and none of the *how*. The *what* tells the user what the module does, but not *how* it accomplishes its functionality, information that is unnecessary for the user and would only make using the module more complicated. Clearly, however, the person implementing the module must know both the *what* and the *how* of the problem solution. The information hidden from this person would be the intended purpose, or use, of the module. The goal of hiding this particular information is to force the person implementing the module to make its application as general, or generic, as possible.

Reusability increases for the user because there are few strings attached to the reuse of a more generic module. The user does not have to declare global variables and structures referenced by the module's procedures and functions. Hence, certain information is hidden from the implementer and other information is hidden from the user, both factors working together to increase reusability.

The notion of *encapsulating* data structures to further their reusability was another outcome of the Parnas information-hiding principles. Languages like Ada added new program structures designed to be orthogonal to other language features. For example, the Ada *package* implementation of the stack is able to distill and remove the problematic side effects that occur in the Pascal implementation. The package is a program structure that contains function, procedure, and data declarations.

```
package body STACK is
    type ptr2 is access node2;
    type node2 is record
        right:ptr2;
        val:integer
        end record;
    p2,top:ptr2;

procedure push(i:in ELEMENT)is
begin
    p2:=new ptr2;
    p2.val:=i;
    p2.right:=top;
    top:=p2
end push;

procedure pop(i:in out ELEMENT) is
begin
    if top <> null then
        i:=top.val;
        top:=top.right
    else
        writeln('stack underflow');
    end if
end pop;
end STACK
```

The package allows the person implementing the module to encapsulate the operations and the structures they reference. The types and variables declared in the package are local to the package and are not available globally to the program containing the package. However, the variables in the package remain active throughout the execution life of the program containing the package.

Recall that variables local to procedures and functions come and go as activation records are created and deleted corresponding to subprogram invocations and returns. The implemented package, as seen in the preceding example, can be hidden from the user of the package. Instead, the user sees only a specification:

```
generic
        type ELEMENT is private;
package stack is
        procedure push(i:in ELEMENT);
        procedure pop(i:in out ELEMENT);
end stack;
```

Notice that reusability is increased through the introduction of a generic type. The stack can be instantiated with any variable type and thus does not have to be reimplemented for other types.

Clearly, the encapsulation of data structures was an important step in advancing a paradigm wherein data structures interact on a more or less equal basis with algorithms in solving problems. Object-oriented programming was a natural step in advancing this view. The encapsulation and reuse of often used program structures has been accomplished in several languages, including Simula, Smalltalk, C++, and Java. In this chapter we focus on Java.

EVOLUTION OF LANGUAGES

Thus far languages providing definitive forms of executable constructs have been reviewed. FORTRAN defined the assignment statement and the arithmetic expression. No language since FORTRAN has altered the basic form of the arithmetic expression or the assignment statement. In other words, if you know the operational semantics and basic syntactic forms of FORTRAN's arithmetic expressions, you will not need to learn anything more about this type of statement or expression for any new language, even Java. The only differences will be syntactic nuances.

Likewise, languages like Algol and Pascal defined, for the most part, the remaining executable constructs. The input/output (I/O) and control structures were established in a definitive way by the forms they took in Algol and Pascal. Pascal's stream I/O—as opposed to a strictly formatted I/O—has not been subsequently improved upon in any revolutionary way. Similarly, the block-structured sequences and the selective (e.g., IF-THEN-ELSE and CASE or SWITCH statements) and iterative (e.g., the WHILE and the FOR statements) constructs have not been modified in a major way by subsequent languages. The only major changes in control constructs is that (1) parallel control structures have been added in many languages, including Concurrent Pascal, Modula, Ada, and Java; and (2) the way in which encapsulated program structures are declared, instantiated, and invoked is different.

It can be argued that encapsulation of program structures is less a change in control structures than in the commands a programmer gives to a language interpreter or compiler to establish data and program structures. The view taken in this text is that in terms of the procedural paradigm (including the paradigm's object-oriented extensions), the declaration of program and data structures—the set of nonexecutable constructs—is the one area of a language that continues to undergo substantive change in conventional languages. Therefore, in exploring Java, this text focuses on explanations of the nonexecutable constructs and assumes the reader, from earlier discussions of the executable constructs, will have no difficulty understanding the procedural aspects of Java.

THE SUBSTANTIAL CHANGES INTRODUCED IN OBJECT-ORIENTED LANGUAGES

Attempts to satisfy the Parnas information-hiding principles led to a view of programming in which real-world *objects* are represented by program *objects*, a term that will be explained in this section.

The fundamental ideas that led to the object-oriented abstraction came from early work on a language called Simula. [Nygaard] The Simula programming language was designed and built by Ole-Johan Dahl and Kristen Nygaard at the Norwegian Computing Centre (NCC) in Oslo between 1962 and 1967. It was originally designed and implemented as a language for discrete event simulation but was later expanded and reimplemented as a full-scale, general-purpose programming language. As a simulation language, Simula introduced the concept of an *object* to serve as an abstract construct capable of representing the entities to be simulated. These entities could be any item or concept. Objects are categorized in *classes* and are described in terms of their variables and *methods* (methods are explained later in this section).

Suppose you declare a class of objects representing bank tellers. Multiple bank tellers can be operating at any given point in the simulation. Each bank teller is represented by its own occurrence of an object. Each of these objects is called an *instance* of the class of bank teller. Whereas much of the specification of an object thus far described is accomplished through the use of nonexecutable statements, executable statements allow for the *instantiation* of a given object.

There might also be customers, each represented by an object belonging to the class of "customer." Bank tellers would interact with customers and other tellers on an abstract level by sending and responding to *messages* (messages are explained later). Beyond representing the behavior of physical items, objects can also represent conceptual notions, such as how we organize customers to interact with tellers. In other words, *queues* can also be established as objects, behaving according to statistical distributions for arrival rates of customers. Notice also that the object-oriented abstraction extends easily to classical data structures. An object of type "stack" can provide access through messages to push and pop items to and from the stack.

The object-oriented abstraction focuses on the *external* (or *observable) behavior* of the abstract objects and attempts to hide the implementation details. In other words, the abstraction focus is on what is done to solve a problem, not how it is done. Of course, in implementing the objects, you must focus on the "how" of the problem solution as well. Therefore, whereas part of a problem solution might be solved at the object, or specification, level, other parts are usually solved through the implementation of new objects.

The implementation of objects is through the use of standard procedural constructs. These constructs appear in program units called *methods*, which, when taken together with data structures needed for the implementation, constitute the implementation of an object. The *messages*, which are often parameterized procedure or function calls, occur between methods to provide the way in which objects are to interact with each other. The set of messages are the focus of a computation, which, as mentioned earlier, provides visibility to the external behavior of a problem solution. Obviously, the reuse of objects is central to the use of existing objects in a problem solution.

Object-oriented languages typically provide capabilities for organizing objects already implemented. Some classes of objects share many similarities yet also have differences. *Class hierarchies* allow for the sharing of similar characteristics or behaviors. For example, two or more list-based data structures could share the notion of linearity as well as the behaviors of insertion to, deletion from, and access to elements of the list, yet have some differences in the *manner* of insertion, deletion, and access. Thus, different objects might constitute one class of lists.

Figure 6.1 shows a hierarchy for a list class composed of two different lists, one a queue type and one a stack type. In this hierarchy, the list class is a *superclass* for the subclasses of "queue" and "stack." These subclasses presumably share attributes and behaviors that are described in the superclass. Distinguishing behaviors and attributes are described in the individual subclasses.

In order to place a new node (e.g., an array class) under the list superclass, a declarative facility to *extend* the superclass must be available in the language. Likewise, to specify distinguishing attributes and behaviors, the facility to override general characteristics of the superclass must be available. Also, a given class might belong to multiple superclasses, a situation of *multiple inheritance*. For example, the subclass of bats could inherit characteristics from the two superclasses of mammals and flying creatures, since the bat is a mammal that can fly.

The notions of Simula led to the idea that all programming can be generalized as a simulation of the behavior of real-world objects. Real-world models are

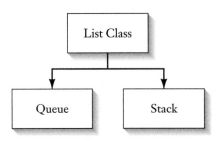

FIGURE 6.1   List class.

constructed as class hierarchies in which behaviors are modeled as message-passing among the objects. Classes of objects are categorized based on shared attributes. Consider the partial tree of objects in Figure 6.2. At each node of the tree are attributes shared by all descendants. For example, the node containing "steam-powered" would describe the pertinent attributes of most, if not all, steam-powered vehicles. These attributes need not be repeated in the definitions of objects under the "steam-powered node"—they can be *inherited*.

Inheritance is a key concept in object-oriented approaches to programming. It is a natural way for viewing reusability. The basic idea is that there are classes of objects that share features. Once the features are defined, they can be reused through inheritance.

Features of an object are available through *methods*. Methods are implemented in Java as functions. Functions have *signatures*, as mentioned earlier, indicating inputs and outputs. The push operator's signature is in boldface in the following. Notice that the push's output is empty, or "void."

public void push(Object n)
    {Stackn t;
    t = new Stackn( );
    t.x = n;
    t.next = top;
    top = t;}

A *void* function can be viewed as a procedure. Functions also have *bodies*, which specify how a method carries out its function. The push's body is in boldface in the following:

public void push(Object n)
    {Stackn t;
    t = new Stackn();
    t.x = n;

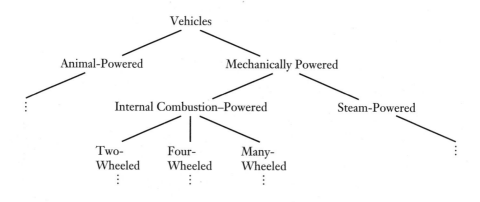

FIGURE 6.2   A hierarchy of vehicles.

```
    t.next = top;
    top = t;}
```

Methods communicate with one another using messages, which in Java are passed through a function's I/O parameters.

A descendant of some class of objects could have some exceptional properties that cause it to deviate from the norm, the norm being defined by the class of which it is a member. Object-oriented languages allow descendants of a class to *override* any such definitions that do not apply.

OBJECT-ORIENTED PROGRAMMING IN JAVA

Consider the implementation of the following stack in Java:

```
class Stackn implements Stackz{
private Object x;
private Stackn next, top;

Stackn( ) //A CONSTRUCTOR METHOD
    {top = null;}

public void push(Object n)
    {Stackn t;
    t = new Stackn( );
    t.x = n;
    t.next = top;
    top = t;}

public boolean mt( )
    {if (top == null) return true;
        else
                return false;}

public Object pop( ) {Object n;
    if (mt( )) {n = null;}
    else
        {n = top.x;
        top = top.next;}
    return n;
    }}
```

The class definition encapsulates the operations and the hidden structure upon which the operations do their work. In this implementation, the hidden structure of the stack is a linked list of objects. The data type of the stack is type Object, which means we can stack any object on the stack, including any nonprimitive data type, user-defined objects, or any object below the Object class in the Java-environment hierarchy. This stack's object is, by default, beneath the Object node, since it does not place itself in the hierarchy with an *extends* clause in the class definition (more on the extends clause later).

Variables that provide attributes associated with the class being defined are declared inside the class and are called *instance variables*. The variables *x*, *next*, and *top* are instance variables for the class Stackn. To create a new instance of Stackn, one would declare a *reference variable* in the set of instructions in which the stack is to be used. For example,

```
Stackn s = new Stackn( );
```

declares a new instance of Stackn, and the variable *s* references the new instance. The instance variables of *next*, *x*, and *top* are declared as *private variables*, meaning they are unavailable outside the scope of the object in which they are declared. If they were *public* (rather than private) *variables*, one could refer to *s*'s instances of the attributes through *dot notation*. For example, "s.top" refers to *s*'s instance of top.

The variables of *next* and *top*, which are instance variables for the current Stackn object, also serve as variables referencing new instances of Stackn. Thus, linked structures (i.e., structures akin to linked lists) are built not through the use of pointer variables but through the use of variables (recursively) *referencing* new instances of the Stackn class.

The operations on the stack are, by default, public. The only information the user of this object will have to work with is the stack specification. Through the stack specification, the user can access the stack only through the generic operations of push, mt, and pop. Notice that Stackn "implements" the Stackz interface. Through the use of the keyword "implements," the implementation and its specification are tied together.

```
public interface Stackz{

public void push(Object n);
public boolean mt( );
public Object pop( ); }
```

The full view of a simple user-defined program that makes use of the Stackz class follows:

```
import Stackz;

class Stacku{
public static void main (String args[ ]) {
        int i,m=10;

        Stackn s = new Stackn( );

        for (i=0;i<=m−1;i++)
```

```
                 {   s.push(new Integer((i+1)*10));                    }

   for (i=0;i<=m−1;i++) .
                 {   System.out.println(s.pop( )); }

   s.push(new Double(1.1));
   s.push(new Double(2.2));
     System.out.println(s.pop( ));
}}
```

The stack interface is referenced in "import Stackz," which provides the stack user with access to the stack implementation in Stackn. In terms of the Java environment hierarchy, both Stackz and Stackn are at the same level under the Object class. They are under the Object class because neither class declares its position in the hierarchy. By default, then, both exist under the Object class (Figure 6.3).

The user is thus able to reuse the stack structure and can instantiate any number of stack objects. In this program the user instantiates one stack object—accessible with the class reference variable *s:*

```
Stackn s = new Stackn( );
```

SEMANTIC NOTE

The Java FOR statement in the preceding example is easily incorporated into the language defined in Chapter 3.

SYNTAX CHANGE

$S ::= V:=E \mid read(V) \mid write(V) \mid$ while C do S od $\mid S;S \mid$
$\quad$ for$(V=E;C;V++)\{S\}$

SEMANTIC CHANGE

Σ « for$(V=E;C;V++)\{S\}$ » γ $\quad = \Sigma$ « while C do $S; V: = V + 1$ od » °
$\quad \Sigma$ « $V:=E$ » γ

Notice also that all of the loop structures can be defined in terms of the WHILE loop construct.

Looking back at the stack implementation in Stackn, you can see that a constructor method,

```
Stackn( )      {top = null;}
```

is executed, setting the class variable of top to null. Even the existence of the top variable is hidden from the user. When a constructor method is defined for an

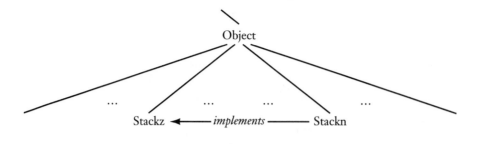

FIGURE 6.3   Object class, containing stack example 1.

object, it is executed so as to initialize the object whenever a new instance is declared by the object's user. Once the stack is initialized, the user is free to push items onto, and pop items off, the stack referenced by *s*. These operations are performed by "s.push(new Integer((i+1)*10))" and "s.pop( )," respectively.

Pushes and pops are also performed later in the program using *double-precision items*—demonstrating the fact that the stack implemented is capable of holding heterogeneous values. This capability allows the stack, as implemented here in Java, to be a better realization of the abstract notion of the stack.

The example also indicates some aspects of data typing in Java. To stack an object, the item input must be a subclass of Object. Both Integer and Double are subclasses of the Object class—as opposed to the primitive types of integer and double. Constants are, by default, primitive types. Therefore, to stack the constants, one must first convert the constants to their equivalent objects with the Integer and Double conversion functions.

There is another way in which the Stack object can be reused. By extending the stack implementation, Stackn, a user is able to inherit the stack functionality.

```
class Stacku2 extends Stackn{
public static void main (String args[ ]) {
        int i,m=10;

        Stackn s = new Stackn( );

        for (i=0;i<=m−1;i++)
            {    s.push(new Integer((i+1)*10));                    }

        for (i=0;i<=m−1;i++)
            {    System.out.println(s.pop( )); }

        s.push(new Double(1.1));
        s.push(new Double(2.2));
        System.out.println(s.pop( ));
}}
```

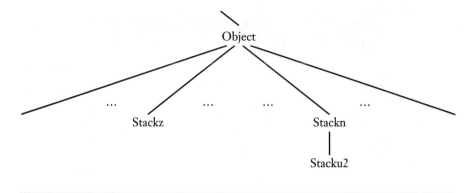

FIGURE 6.4 Object class, extending the stack hierarchy.

Figure 6.4 shows the defined relationship in the hierarchy; the Stacku2 function is placed beneath the Stackn object in the Java class hierarchy. Given this configuration, the user is able to make use of all the Stackn functionality as specified in the Stackz interface.

Thus, a Java object can be reused in two ways: it can be *imported* or *extended*. In the latter case, the user can actually place the class beneath the extended object in the class hierarchy. This way the functionality is inherited. Multiple inheritance is not allowed in Java, but, in addition to its role in information hiding, "implements" allows the user to realize the benefits of multiple inheritance while avoiding the problems that accompany it.

USING *EXTENDS* AND *IMPLEMENTS* FOR MORE COMPLICATED APPLICATIONS

A *Java applet* is a self-contained application that can run on the World Wide Web through the use of a web browser or on the host through the use of a Java utility called *appletviewer*. To create an applet, you must extend the applet class so that the appropriate environment for an applet can be established. Notice that the applet in Figure 6.5 also imports a lot of functionality from the Java graphics package.

The applet window shown in the figure allows the user to draw rectangles on it by pointing (with a mouse-click), dragging the mouse (while its button remains depressed), and pointing again (by releasing the mouse button). The mouse click and release establish opposite corners of the box. The code to implement the applet follows. It is based on an example from Lemay.

```
public void paint(Graphics g) {

    // Draw existing lines
    for (int i = 0; i < currline; i++) {
```

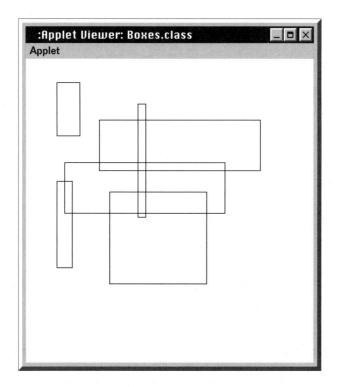

FIGURE 6.5 Applet viewer.

```
        g.drawLine(starts[i].x,starts[i].y,ends[i].x,starts[i].y);
        g.drawLine(starts[i].x,starts[i].y,starts[i].x,ends[i].y);
        g.drawLine(ends[i].x,starts[i].y,ends[i].x,ends[i].y);
        g.drawLine(starts[i].x,ends[i].y,ends[i].x,ends[i].y);
    }

    // draw current line
    g.setColor(Color.blue);
    if (currentpoint != null)   {
        g.drawLine(anchor.x,anchor.y,currentpoint.x,anchor.y);
        g.drawLine(anchor.x,anchor.y,anchor.x,currentpoint.y);
        g.drawLine(currentpoint.x,anchor.y,currentpoint.x,currentpoint.y);
        g.drawLine(anchor.x,currentpoint.y,currentpoint.x,currentpoint.y);}
}
```

The applet code makes good use of the Java environment. A couple of features warrant explanation. The imported Paint class provides a data structure for storing the x, y coordinates of a point on a graph. The *paint* method is a standard method in the applet superclass. However, the standard method is overridden here by virtue of the fact that the programmer has provided his own paint class.

Therefore, when the applet begins execution, the local paint method is invoked. The paint method uses point data defined in the *event handlers*, mousePressed, mouseReleased, and mouseDragged. When the mouse events have occurred, the paint method draws existing rectangles (ones that were previously drawn based on prior mouse events) as well as the new rectangle, which is based on the current mouse events. Four *drawlines* must occur for all rectangles. When the user depresses the mouse button in the applet, an anchor for the rectangle is defined. While holding the mouse button down, the applet user defines a diagonal line as shown in Figure 6.6. Thus, two sets of x, y point coordinates are defined. The four drawlines connect the points in a fashion that is appropriate for the rectangle drawn with the mouse as shown in Figure 6.7. The first set of drawlines redraw the previously drawn rectangles (up to nine) that are stored in an array.

The mouse events define the rectangle coordinates through the use of a user-defined method called *addline*. The addline method stores the coordinates' input in arrays of point data called *starts* and *ends*. As the applet is refreshed, the paint method redraws the lines forming the rectangles based on this data. The drawing of the rectangles makes use of the *drawLine* method defined in the "Graphics" superclass.

The basic design of the applet is now clear. Mouse inputs from the user interrupt the applet's execution. Mouse movements relevant to the drawing of the rectangles are intercepted by the user-defined event handlers, mousePressed,

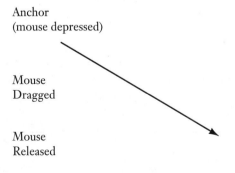

FIGURE 6.6 Anchor: diagonal line.

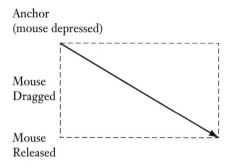

Anchor
(mouse depressed)

Mouse
Dragged

Mouse
Released

FIGURE 6.7   Anchor: four drawlines.

mouseReleased, and mouseDragged. In other words, input actions are handled by appropriate event handlers.

Event handling can be viewed as an extension of the control construct of the language. It is similar to the interrupt processing that takes place in an operating system. When an event, or interrupt, is triggered, the computer temporarily *suspends* execution of the program that was running at the time the event occurred. Triggering events are often caused by input-output devices such as a mouse. When the event occurs, control is transferred, in real time, to the *handler* that is registered as the code that responds to the event. When the event handler has completed execution, control returns to the suspended task. Thus, an event handler is similar to a procedure in that the invoking routine is suspended while the handler executes, and control is returned to the suspended routine after the handler completes execution. The significant difference is that the suspended routine does not do the invoking. Rather, a run-time environment does the invoking based on some condition that may occur external to the suspended routine—and the invoking/return point can exist *anywhere* in the suspended routine.

Output action for the applet is implemented through the user-defined paint method already described, which is invoked by the applet class to refresh the applet's contents. Thus, the drawing of rectangles is accomplished through an interaction between event handlers and the applet refresh activity.

The basic design of the control flow associated with the applet is shown in Figure 6.8. To accomplish the applet's functions, a user would need to extend the MouseListener and MouseMotionListener, but neither of these can be extended, because it is necessary that we extend the applet class when building an applet (e.g., in order to have our paint method invoked for the applet). Recall that multiple inheritance is disallowed in Java. Therefore, we must implement these other classes. (Recall that "implements" is also the command used to implement a specification as stated in a Java interface.)

When implementing a class, one must provide the signature for each function in the implemented class. A method in an implemented class can be overridden by providing a new function body. We default to the class's definition of all its methods except the following:

```
public void mousePressed(MouseEvent e)
public void mouseReleased(MouseEvent e)
public void mouseDragged(MouseEvent e)
```

For those exceptions we provide our own function bodies:

```
/* draw boxes at each click and drag */
import java.awt.Graphics;
import java.awt.Color;
import java.awt.Point;
import java.awt.event.*;

public class Boxes extends java.applet.Applet
    implements MouseListener,MouseMotionListener {
```

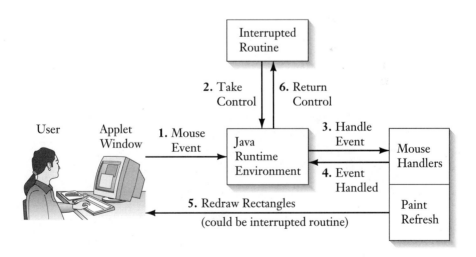

FIGURE 6.8   Control flow of applet.

```
final int MAXLINES = 10;
Point starts[ ] = new Point[MAXLINES]; // starting points
Point ends[ ] = new Point[MAXLINES]; // endingpoints
Point anchor; // start of current line
Point currentpoint; // current end of line
int currline = 0; // number of lines

public void init( ) {
   setBackground(Color.white);
      // register event listeners
      addMouseListener(this);
      addMouseMotionListener(this);
}

   // needed to satisfy listener interfaces
public void mouseMoved(MouseEvent e) {}
public void mouseClicked(MouseEvent e) {}
public void mouseEntered(MouseEvent e) {}
public void mouseExited(MouseEvent e) {}

   // same as mouseDown
public void mousePressed(MouseEvent e) {
   if (currline < MAXLINES)
      anchor = new Point(e.getX( ),e.getY( ));
   else
      System.out.println("Too many lines.");
}

   // same as mouseUp
public void mouseReleased(MouseEvent e) {
   if (currline < MAXLINES)
      addline(e.getX( ),e.getY( ));
}

   // same as mouseDrag
public void mouseDragged(MouseEvent e) {
   if (currline < MAXLINES) {
   currentpoint = new Point(e.getX( ),e.getY( ));
   repaint( );
   }
}
}

   void addline(int x,int y) {
   starts[currline] = anchor;
```

```
ends[currline] = new Point(x,y);
currline++;
currentpoint = null;
anchor:=null;
repaint( )
}

public void paint(Graphics g) {

// Draw existing lines
for (int i = 0; i < currline; i++) {
    g.drawLine(starts[i].x,starts[i].y, ends[i].x,starts[i].y);
    g.drawLine(starts[i].x,starts[i].y,starts[i].x,ends[i].y);
    g.drawLine(ends[i].x,starts[i].y,ends[i].x,ends[i].y);
    g.drawLine(starts[i].x,ends[i].y,ends[i].x,ends[i].y);
}

// draw current line
g.setColor(Color.blue);
if (currentpoint != null)     {
    g.drawLine(anchor.x,anchor.y,currentpoint.x,anchor.y);
    g.drawLine(anchor.x,anchor.y,anchor.x,currentpoint.y);
    g.drawLine(currentpoint.x,anchor.y,currentpoint.x,currentpoint.y);
    g.drawLine(anchor.x,currentpoint.y,currentpoint.x,currentpoint.y);}
}

}
```

The prohibition against multiple inheritance in Java is due to inconsistencies that can arise from its use. In particular, inconsistencies resulting from naming conflicts can lead to serious problems. For example, suppose we establish a new class, "Locomotive," relative to the Hierarchy of Vehicles presented in Figure 6.2. Since some locomotives can be steam-powered and others diesel-powered, we might want the locomotive class to extend both the Steam-powered and Internal combustion–powered classes in the figure. It is quite possible for each of these two superclasses to possess a definition for a method named "engine." If someone now instantiates Locomotive,

```
Locomotivel = new Locomotive( );
```

and then attempts to invoke the "engine" method as follows,

```
l.engine( );
```

there is a conflict. Which definition of "engine" should respond: the Steam-powered or the Internal combustion–powered?

Some of these so-called conflicts can be handled based on the notion of *polymorphism*, which means, literally, "many forms." Consider the fact that you could define two classes, "Integer" and "Boolean," as defining the plus (+) operator. The integer definition is for integer addition, whereas the Boolean definition is for the logical OR. The apparent name conflict can be resolved based on the specific operands to which the plus operator is applied. When integer operands are supplied, the plus operator responds with integer arithmetic. When Boolean operands are supplied, it responds with the Boolean OR operation.

Similarly, if "steam" and "diesel" were declared as types and a variable *(e)* declared to be one of the types, you could allow for the appropriate selection of the engine with "l.engine(*e*)."

Returning to the applet example, the user must provide an HTML file for each applet defined. Minimally, the file must provide the size of the window and the name of the associated class, which is the file produced when the source is interpreted by the Java intpreter.

```
<HTML>
<BODY>
<P>
<APPLET CODE5"Boxes.class" WIDTH=300 HEIGHT=300>
</APPLET>
</BODY>
</HTML>
```

RECURSION

Methods can contain recursive calls, just as functions and procedures in most procedural languages permit recursion. The following factorial method is an example:

```
int fact(int n) {
        if (n==0) return 1;
        else
        return fact(n−1)*n;
        }
```

As in other languages, the return addresses, input arguments, and local variables constitute the stacked activation records.

A NONRECURSIVE SYNTAX ANALYSIS EXAMPLE

Because of the overhead involved in recursion (recall the activation records from Chapter 5) one often strives to discover simple iterative approaches to solving recursive problems. Recall the Chapter 4 grammar for which a recursive-descent interpreter was built.

$$
\begin{array}{ll}
E & ::= T\ E1\ \$ \\
E1 & ::= +\ T\ E1 \\
 & ::= -T\ E1 \\
 & ::= \\
T & ::= F\ T1 \\
T1 & ::= *\ F\ T1 \\
 & ::= /\ F\ T1 \\
 & ::= \\
F & ::= \mathrm{id}
\end{array}
$$

In this section a different approach to syntax analysis is presented on the simplified grammar,

$$
\begin{array}{ll}
E & ::= T\ X\$ \\
X & ::= +\ T\ X \\
 & ::= \\
T & ::= F\ Y \\
Y & ::= *\ F\ Y \\
 & ::= \\
F & ::= \mathrm{id}
\end{array}
$$

Furthermore, for the sake of simplicity, selection sets are ignored. In this approach, recursive calls are not made in the parsing of a sentence. Instead, a stack is maintained containing the grammar information that must be satisfied in order to validate an input sentence. The resulting program with the hard-coded input $a + a * a\$$ follows:

```
1    import Stack6;
2
3    class Lang{
4    public static void main (String args[ ]) {
5        String s1 = "a+a*a$";
6        Stack6 s = new Stack6(100);
7        char ch,next;
8        s.push('e');
9        ch = s.pop( );
10       int n = s1.length( );
11       next = s1.charAt(0);
12
13       while(ch != '$')
14       {    next = s1.charAt(0);
15            if(ch=='e')
16                {s.push('$'); s.push('x'); s.push('t');}
17            else
18            if(ch=='t')
19                {s.push('y'); s.push('f');}
```

```
20              else
21              if(ch=='x')
22                {if(next == '+')
23                      {s1 = s1.substring(1,n);
24                       next = s1.charAt(0);
25                       s.push('x'); s.push('t');}
26                 else
27                 if(next == '$')
28                       {s1=s1;};     }
29              else
30              if(ch=='y')
31                {if(next == '*')
32                      {s1 = s1.substring(1,n);
33                       next = s1.charAt(0);
34                       s.push('y'); s.push('f');}
35                 else
36                 if(next == '+')
37                       {s1=s1;};         }
38              else
39              if(ch=='f')
40                {if(next == 'a')
41                      {s1 = s1.substring(1,n);
42                       next = s1.charAt(0);     }     };
43              n = s1.length( );
44              ch=s.pop( );     };
45  }
```

In the preceding code, lines 5–11 show the initialization for the parsing. First, a string, *s1*, is declared and defined to contain the hard-coded input of *a* + *a* * *a*$. Next, two-character variables are declared. The variable *ch* will contain the left-hand side of the next rule to be applied at any given point in the parse. The left-hand side is obtained by popping the stack, *s*, which is declared in line 6 and initialized with the grammar start symbol, *e*, in line 8. Next *n* is initialized to the value of the length of the input string, obtained through the built-in string method, length( ). The next token is obtained by selecting the *s1*'s first character: *s1*.charAt(0).

To simplify the example, all tokens and nontokens are one character in length. The subscripting on a string begins at position 0. The length of the string is the true length in terms of the number of characters in the string. Therefore, for the string input, the subscripts and length information shown in Figure 6.9 are true.

The basic algorithm here is an iterative structure that processes the *s* stack. The top of the stack is popped into the variable *ch*. For each left-hand side there is an IF-THEN structure. The basic process is to stack nonterminals in the right-hand side. Stacking is performed from right to left in order to preserve the order of the right-hand side in the stack. For example, in lines 15–16, the rule,

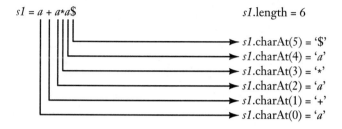

$s1 = a + a*a\$$ $s1$.length = 6

$s1$.charAt(5) = '$'
$s1$.charAt(4) = 'a'
$s1$.charAt(3) = '*'
$s1$.charAt(2) = 'a'
$s1$.charAt(1) = '+'
$s1$.charAt(0) = 'a'

FIGURE 6.9   String input.

$$E \quad ::= T\, E1\ \$$$

is handled. The sequence of pushes begins with the symbol $ and ends with t. In order to preserve the one-character limit on tokens, $e1$ and $t1$ are changed to x and y, respectively, in the code.

When a terminal is matched in the input, it is consumed through the following actions:

```
s1 = s1.substring(1,n);
next = s1.charAt(0);
```

The terminal is consumed by taking the substring of $s1$. Recalling the axiomatic approach to semantics, for the initial string the state change is reflected in the following:

```
s1 = a+a*a$ {s1 = s1.substring(1,n); } s1 = +a*a$
```

The substring extracts the string beginning at the second character in the string (remember, subscripts begin at position 0) up to but not including n. Recall that the length of the string obtained in the $s1$.length( ) operation will contain a value 1 beyond the valid range of the subscripts.

The next token is then updated to reflect the change in the input:

```
next = 'a' & s1 = +a*a${ next = s1.charAt(0);} next = '+' & s1 = +a*a$
```

The processing of the input string continues until the top of the stack is $, at which time the next token should also be $.

DEVELOPING USEFUL REUSABLE PROGRAM STRUCTURES

Java allows the encapsulation of often-used program structures as well as data structures. Our applet example demonstrated the ease with which a developer can produce Windows-based user interfaces. The mouse, graphics, and applet classes provide reusable functions that facilitate the construction of good GUI (graphical user interface)-type applications.

In a similar vein, one can develop environments in Java that make it easy to write codes of interest to a particular organization. For example, in some business environments, primitives for inventory or accounting transactions are implemented for subsequent reuse by application developers. The same potential exists in engineering and scientific environments.

CONCURRENT PROGRAM STRUCTURES

Concurrent, or parallel, features of a language are an extension to the control constructs. In addition to sequence, selective, and iterative structures, you can develop parallel control structures in Java. These structures typically require the ability to establish the codes that can run concurrently—in Java you do this in a special method called *run*—together with an ability to *fork* the concurrent paths and an ability to *join* them together when they have completed executing.

In order to develop concurrent routines in Java, you first extend the Java thread class. All concurrent paths are placed in the special method called "run." Then you can fork concurrent paths with the start command and join them with a join command. Examples follow.

TASK PARALLELISMS

Task parallelisms exist when different components of the same computation are executed in parallel. [Kennedy] A simple example of task parallelism is the computation of a vector of slopes. Suppose the following Java-code segment is found in a program:

```
for (i=0;i<=m-1;i++)
    {slope[i] = (y2[i]-y1[i])/(x2[i]-x1[i]);}.
```

Through an analysis of the code, which involves analyzing the arithmetic statement computing the slope and the fact that the statement's context is a loop statement, one can see that components of the computation can be executed in parallel. Detecting the parallelism is not a simple matter, even in this simple example. Detecting parallelisms in procedural-like code often requires a data flow and context-oriented analysis.

Once the analysis is completed, one can see that the tasks to compute the difference in the *x*-pair and the *y*-pair are noninterfering and can be accomplished concurrently. Figure 6.10 presents a concurrent solution to the problem using threads in Java. In statements 37–38 two reference variables, *n1* and *n2*, are defined. These variables are used to reference the two instances of the *numden* class that are to execute concurrently. The *numden* class is placed in the Thread hierarchy with the EXTENDS. When the *numden* class is instantiated, the vectors to be subtracted (for the numerator and denominator of the slope formula) are initialized. The initialization is accomplished via the *constructor* method, called numden (lines 7–12). Next, the two instances are initiated in lines 40–41.

```
1   class numden extends Thread{
2
3   float[ ] x2;
4   float[ ] x1;
5   public float[ ] diff;
6
7   numden(float[ ] a, float[ ] b)        {
8
9          x2=new float[a.length];
10         x1=new float[b.length];
11         x2=a;
12         x1=b;
13  }
14
15
16  public void run( )       {
17
18  diff = new float[x2.length];
19  int i;
20
21         for(i=0;i<=x2.length-1;i++)
22                {diff[i] = x2[i]-x1[i];}
23
24  }
25
26  public static void main (String args[ ]) {
27         int i;
28         int m = 100;
29
30         float[ ] x2 = new float[m];
31         float[ ] x1 = new float[m];
32         float[ ] y2 = new float[m];
33         float[ ] y1 = new float[m];
34
35  /*          Code to obtain the values of vectors: x1, x2, y1,
                        and y2      */
36
37         numden n1 = new numden(x2,x1);
38         numden n2 = new numden(y2,y1);
39
40         n1.start( );
41         n2.start( );
42
43         try {n1.join( );
44             try {n2.join( );
45                 for (i=0;i<=m-1;i++)
46                 {System.out.println((n2.diff[i]/n1.
                        diff[i])); }
47             }
48             catch (InterruptedException ignored) { }
49          }
50         catch (InterruptedException ignored) { }
51  }}
```

FIGURE 6.10 Task parallelism in a slope calculation problem.

These statements initiate the run( ) methods for the instances referenced by *n1* and *n2*. The methods initiated (i.e., *n1*.run( ) and *n2*.run( )) will run concurrently with the main program. The run( ) methods cannot have parameters and cannot return results. These constraints are inherited from the Thread object. Because of these constraints, the data upon which the concurrently run methods will operate must be set up using the constructor method. Likewise, their results will exist as public reference variables in the form of the diff array.

Here is a problem with the design of this language. The fact that one must establish the inputs and outputs for the run method with variables that are for all intents and purposes global goes against the information-hiding principles that govern the rest of the language. Hence, there is a lack of uniformity between classes that extend the Thread superclass and any other class extensions.

The nested *try* statements (43 and 44) await the completion of the concurrent tasks. When the try statements succeed, the remainder of the *slope* calculation (i.e., the division) is performed.

The gain achieved in concurrency is at the expense of readability and writability of the solution. In particular, the components of the computation are divided and separated, resulting in an overall loss in the intuitiveness of the solution. Therefore, even in a modern language like Java, one can see that finding, designing, and understanding concurrent problem solutions is not an easy undertaking.

DATA PARALLELISMS

The key to achieving high performance on distributed-memory machines is to allocate data to various processor memories in such a way as to maximize locality and minimize communication. *Data parallelism* is parallelism that derives from subdividing the data domain in some manner and assigning the subdomains to different processors. [Kennedy] Data parallelisms are those characteristic of SIMD (single instruction multiple data) architectures. They usually result in the same computation being performed simultaneously on subdivided data sets as opposed to dividing up the computation itself.

Consider the following word-search problem as written for sequential execution in Java:

```
String s = "here is a test string";
String s1 = "test";

char[ ] sample = s.toCharArray( );
char[ ] find = s1.toCharArray( );

System.out.println(sample);

n = sample.length;
n1 = find.length;

for(i=0;i<=n−n1;i++)
```

```
{System.out.println(s.substring(i,i+n1));
if(s.substring(i,i+n1).equals(s1))
{System.out.println(" TRUE == FOUND ");}
}
```

The sample text is a 21-character string. In this problem, the goal is to determine if the four-character string "test" is in the sample. The linear search involves checking each unique four-character substring of the sample to see if it is equal to the string test. Given the parameters of the problem, the IF statement is executed 18 times.

A data-parallel solution to this problem involves the separation of the 18 unique four-character substrings as accomplished in Figure 6.11. An array of reference variables is declared in line 33. The size of the array is based on the difference in length of the string being searched and the length of the string for which the search is being conducted (i.e., in this example, the array will consist of 18 elements). The general rule for determining the number of unique substrings of size n_t that exist in some larger string of size n_L is obtained by: $(n_L - n_t) + 1$.

In lines 35–38, the string being searched is subdivided using the substring operator and is used to initialize the reference variables as the 18 references to the class are instantiated via the class constructor method, wrdsrch2 (lines 7–12). Once the 18 instances are set up, the concurrent processes to compare the strings are initiated (in lines 42–43). The 18 comparisons are executed concurrently, and execution proceeds no further until the 18 processes are joined (in lines 45–48). The 18 instances of the Boolean variable *found* are then written.

ADDED DIFFICULTIES IN VERIFYING CONCURRENT PROGRAMS

The problem of software quality assurance is made more complicated with the addition of concurrent, or parallel, program structures. There are special problems like *race*, *deadlock*, and *starvation* that are unique to the concurrent program. Deadlock occurs when two or more concurrent processes are awaiting resources held exclusively by the other process(es). Starvation occurs when a process becomes permanently blocked from a needed resource. These problems may not appear when the software is tested, their incidence being statistically low.

Traditionally, software verification is accomplished with respect to a specification of the software. If sufficiently precise and complete, the specification serves as a mathematical model of the intended consequences of the software, given its field of inputs. At the end of Chapter 3 the reader was introduced to the notion of formal verification where a mathematical specification of a problem, together with axiomatic semantics of the programming language used, were employed to prove the program correct. Such formal verification of a program is usually unfeasible, though, so statistical approaches to software testing are performed instead. The mathematical models used to determine if a program is correct, whether by testing or by proof, are also necessary for the verification of

```
1  class wrdsrch2 extends Thread{
2  String text;
3  String target;
4  boolean found;
5  int i;
6
7  wrdsrch2(String in, String targ, int k)   {
8          target=targ;
9          text=in;
10         found=false;
11         i=k;
12 }
13
14 public void run( )   {
15         if(text.equals(target))
16                 {found = true;}
17 }
18
19 public static void main (String args[ ]) {
20         int i, j, k, n, n1;
21
22         String s = "here is a test string";
23         String s1 = "test";
24         char[ ] sample = s.toCharArray( );
25         char[ ] find = s1.toCharArray( );
26
27         System.out.println(sample);
28
29         n = sample.length;
30         n1 = find.length;
31         String send;
32
33         wrdsrch2 w[ ] = new wrdsrch2[(n−n1)+1];
34
35         for(i=0;i<=n−n1;i++)
36                 {send = s.substring(i,i+n1);
37                 w[i] = new wrdsrch2(send,s1,i);
38                 }
39
40         System.out.println("To Run ");
41
42         for(i=0;i<=n−n1;i++)
43                 {w[i].start( );}
44
45         for(i=0;i<=n−n1;i++)
46                 {try {w[i].join( );
47                 catch (InterruptedException ignored) { }
48                 }
49
50         System.out.println("The answer is: ");
51
52         for(i=0;i<=n−n1;i++)
53                 {System.out.println(w[i].found);}
54
55 }}
```

FIGURE 6.11 Data parallelism in word search-problem.

concurrent programs. However, the standard verification approaches taken alone are not sufficient for verification of concurrent programs.

The problem of concurrent design was ably pointed out in Leveson's study of the famous Therac-25 accidents. Although the Therac software was tested, a race condition was apparently not detected and eventually manifested when the machine was put into practice. Consequently, the Therac-25 administered overdoses of radiation therapy to patients, several of whom died as a result.

Consider the concurrent configuration in Figure 6.12. Here are the possible ways (or orders) in which the instructions in those paths might execute:

$t_1 \, t_2 \, t_3 \, t_4$
$t_1 \, t_3 \, t_2 \, t_4$
$t_1 \, t_3 \, t_4 \, t_2$
$t_3 \, t_4 \, t_1 \, t_2$
$t_3 \, t_1 \, t_4 \, t_2$
$t_3 \, t_1 \, t_2 \, t_4$

Suppose it is the t_4 writing of "dose" that provides the correct dosage for a treatment. In the configuration given there is a fifty-fifty chance that an erroneous condition—where t_2 writes the dosage—will occur. Thus, testing alone might not reveal the error.

Even worse is the configuration in Figure 6.13. Possible orderings for that configuration are

$t_5 \, t_1 \, t_2 \, t_3 \, t_4$
$t_1 \, t_5 \, t_2 \, t_3 \, t_4$
$t_1 \, t_2 \, t_5 \, t_3 \, t_4$
$t_1 \, t_2 \, t_3 \, t_5 \, t_4$
$t_1 \, t_2 \, t_3 \, t_4 \, t_5$

Here there is only a 20 percent chance that the error will occur during testing—the error being when t_4 does not write the dosage. Notice that we could easily reduce the probability of detecting the error through testing even further by adding instructions to the beginning of TASK 1.

The basic problem is that there is an additional control-flow construct in a concurrent program—a construct not possible in a sequential system. Sequential

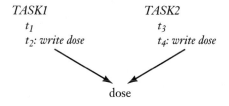

FIGURE 6.12 Concurrent configuration, example 1.

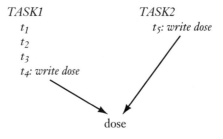

FIGURE 6.13 Concurrent configuration, example 2.

systems are usually *deterministic*, meaning that every execution of the program on the same data establishes the same computation. *Nondeterminism* occurs in concurrent systems because different executions of the system may indeed result in different computations. [Sehti] Nondeterminism can be viewed as an extension of control flow. When concurrent pathways of execution exist, a number of orderings are possible for execution. For example, suppose two tasks, each consisting of three instructions (t_i), are to be executed concurrently:

TASK1   *TASK2*

t_1 t_4
t_2 t_5
t_3 t_6

In this program there are "instructions" t_1, t_2, t_3 in one path and "instructions" t_4, t_5, t_6 in a separate path. This small example results in the following possible orderings of execution:

$t_1, t_2, t_3, t_4, t_5, t_6$
$t_1, t_2, t_4, t_3, t_5, t_6$
$t_1, t_2, t_4, t_5, t_3, t_6$
$t_1, t_2, t_4, t_5, t_6, t_3$
$t_1, t_4, t_2, t_3, t_5, t_6$
$t_1, t_4, t_2, t_5, t_3, t_6$
$t_1, t_4, t_2, t_5, t_6, t_3$
$t_1, t_4, t_5, t_2, t_3, t_6$
$t_1, t_4, t_5, t_2, t_6, t_3$
$t_1, t_4, t_5, t_6, t_2, t_3$
$t_4, t_1, t_2, t_3, t_5, t_6$
$t_4, t_1, t_2, t_5, t_3, t_6$
$t_4, t_1, t_2, t_5, t_6, t_3$
$t_4, t_1, t_5, t_2, t_3, t_6$
$t_4, t_1, t_5, t_2, t_6, t_3$
$t_4, t_1, t_5, t_6, t_2, t_3$
$t_4, t_5, t_1, t_6, t_2, t_3$

$t_4, t_5, t_1, t_2, t_6, t_3$
$t_4, t_5, t_1, t_2, t_3, t_6$
$t_4, t_5, t_6, t_1, t_2, t_3$

The number of orderings is a function of the number, n, of paths of execution and the length, L, of the paths. Assuming, for the sake of simplicity, that concurrent paths are of equal lengths, the number of possible orderings for execution O is obtained by

$$O = \frac{(nL)!}{(L!)^n}$$

In this example $n = 2$ and $L = 3$. Notice the growth in orderings as n or L increase. For example, when $n = 3$ and $L = 2$, $O = 90$.

Because of the nondeterminism in concurrent systems, problems like race, deadlock, and starvation might not be uncovered by testing alone. The orderings in which the problems occur might not arise during the testing phase. In order to fully scrutinize a concurrent program, one should not only test, but also *model* the system. Often a separate engineering model is required to analyze a concurrent program. An *engineering model* of a program provides an abstraction that focuses on some phenomenon of the system. In the case of a concurrent program, the phenomenon to be understood is the control and data-flow view of the program. Through this view, one can understand the concurrent behavior. *Petri net modeling* of concurrent programs provides a suitable and versatile approach to the discovery of problems unique to concurrent programs.

PROBLEMS WITH THE OBJECT-ORIENTED APPROACH

Certain disadvantages to object-oriented programming are becoming clear. An example of a simple problem that can fester in any reuse environment is the freedom to ruin the language design. As pointed out in Chapter 1, a requirement of a language is that it exhibit regularity and consistency in its features. Although the original design of an object-oriented language might be regular, when objects are added to extend the language, the language can become inconsistent.

In Java, for example, there is a String class that provides a wide array of powerful String-processing methods. These methods become (and really should be viewed as) a part of the language itself. The substring method provided is of the form

string_name.substring(begin,end)

where "string_name" is the name of the string from which the substring is to be taken, "begin" is an integer argument indicating the beginning of the desired substring, and "end" is an integer indicating one character position beyond the end of the desired substring. In plain English, the programmer is requesting a substring of "string_name" beginning at "begin" and encompassing characters up to *but not including* the "end" argument. It turns out that all of the built-in String processing methods specifying a substring are consistent in the way the range is specified.

However, users can extend the String class at any time, adding their own methods to process strings. In doing so, they are arguably extending the language itself. (An advantage of an object-oriented language is that it is extensible.) Clearly, the freedom to extend brings with it the freedom to corrupt the language design. A user extension might require a subrange of a string (or, for that matter, some other object), and the ranges might specify object elements from "begin" up to and *including* the "end." Now the programmer using the built-in methods and the methods of the extension must remember which type of subrange to use with which method. A technical distraction of this sort is a burden to programmers.

Another problem that arises out of software reuse has to do with the profession's desire to reuse software beyond the point of effectiveness. Although identifying and reusing objects that possess an understood functionality is not difficult (e.g., a prior understanding of the pull-down menu function in a Windows-based human interface facilitates effective reuse of these objects), programmers are sometimes tempted to reuse objects possessing functionality that they do not understand well, in which case they must often review the code that implements the objects. The difficulty encountered when reusing objects from an unfamiliar domain is reflected in "specifications" or "interfaces" written in a way that fails to convey exactly *what* the identified objects do. For example, Java interfaces specify only the names and the inputs and outputs of reused methods. This information alone is insufficient to understand the functionality of objects in an unfamiliar domain. Truly effective attempts to reuse software require a high-level language capable of precisely identifying objects to be reused in a program under development.

As pointed out earlier, software reuse can be likened to automatic programming. In automatic/declarative programming, the programmer specifies what problem is to be solved, and then the programs that solve the problem are automatically generated. Software reuse has the same goal: the programmer specifies, at a high level, what needs to be done, and rather than being generated, the appropriate reusable object is identified in a table-lookup. Until objects can be precisely identified and understood at a high level, the goal of software reuse will not be completely realized.

Of course, when a high-level language exists that solves the software reuse problem, software reuse may become unnecessary. The same high-level language could be used for automatic programming instead—and the same productivity gains would be realized.

Another problem with object-oriented languages like Java is the multithreading capability that results in a method structure that departs from the information-hiding principles governing the development of other classes and their methods. Reusability is therefore reduced.

REFERENCES

Ken Kennedy. "Compilers, languages, and libraries." In *The Grid, Blueprint for a New Computing Infrastructure* (Ian Foster and Carl Kesselman, editors). San Francisco: Morgan Kaufmann Publishers, 1999.

Laura Lemay and Charles L. Perkins. *Teach Yourself Java 1.1 in 21 Days.* Indianapolis: Sams.net Publishing, 1997.

Nancy G. Leveson and Clark S. Turner. "An investigation of the Therac-25 accidents." *Computer* 26, no. 7 (July 1993):18–41.

K. Nygaard and O.-J. Dahl. "The development of the Simula languages." In R. Wexelblat (Ed.), *History of Programming Languages.* New York: Academic Press, 1981, pp. 439–491.

D. L. Parnas, "On the criteria to be used in decomposing systems into modules." *CACM* 15, no. 12 (1972):1053–1058.

Ravi Sehti. *Programing Languages: Concepts and Constructs.* Reading, MA: Addison-Wesley Publishing Company, 1996.

Download: A version of Java can be obtained at: http://java.sun.com/j2se/1.3/docs.html

QUESTIONS AND EXERCISES

1. Create an inputFloat method similar to the following inputInteger method. Create a reusable class called "myInputs," and then write a Java program that imports your new class and uses it by reading/writing an array of integers and an array of floats.

```java
import java.io.*;

class Prt{

int inputInteger( ) throws IOException
    {

    String s = "";
    char x =' ';
    System.out.print("Input an integer: End with CRNL ");
    while((int) x != 10 & (int) x != 13)
        {
        if (x != ' ' & (int) x != 10 & (int) x != 13)
                {s = s + x;}
        x = (char) System.in.read( );

        }
```

```
        System.in.skip(1);
        return Integer.valueOf(s).intValue( );
        }

    public static void main (String args[ ]) throws IOException {
        Prt p = new Prt( );
        int x = p.inputInteger( );
        System.out.println("x is " + x);
        System.out.println("x+1 is " + (x+1));

}}
```

2. Create a class called "Mat". In this class allow for the definition (i.e., initialization) of up to two matrices (of type float) through the use of constructor methods. Then write methods to input and output the matrix via the desktop computer screen and keyboard. Enter and display the matrices in row-major order. Next, provide methods to perform the functions of "square" and "transpose" on single matrices. Also provide a method to perform matrix multiply on two matrices.

3. Write an equivalent unit of code in Java for the following:

```
        READ(5,10) N
10      FORMAT(I2)
        DO 20 I=1,N
        READ(5,10) A(I)
20      CONTINUE
        S=0
        DO 30 I=1,N
        S=S+A(I)
30      CONTINUE
        AVE = S / N
```

7

FUNCTIONAL LANGUAGES—
PROGRAMMING IN LISP

Thus far we have concentrated on a single language paradigm (the procedural, or imperative) and its extensions to allow for reusability and concurrency. The remainder of this book focuses on totally different approaches to programming. In this chapter we consider the functional programming paradigm, in particular, the *LISt Processing language (LISP)*. Developed mainly by John McCarthy, LISP is a truly landmark achievement in computer science.

THE IMPORTANCE OF LISP

LISP was developed in the late 1950s at a time when most of the computer science community was focused on the revolution brought about by the introduction of FORTRAN and COBOL. LISP stands out as a supremely elegant approach to programming, and it is truly a marvelous achievement considering that it was introduced so early in the history of high-level languages.

LISP is also important for having introduced an abstraction that is a far simpler and, for many people, more natural approach to programming than what had gone before. LISP has a single data structure, the list. The list is the most primitive of nonscalar structures. All data structures can be reduced to a list structure. Consider the following examples as evidence of the versatility of the list.

Assume that items s_1 and q_1 represent components existing in the data structure exemplified. First is the *stack:*

$$(s_1, s_2, s_3, \cdots, s_n)$$

The stack structure is easily represented as a list where the top item is s_1 and, after a *pop*, the stack becomes $(s_2, s_3, \cdots, s_n)$. Also, given the stack $(s_1, s_2, s_3, \cdots, s_n)$, and a new item, s_0, a *push* results in $(s_0, s_1, s_2, s_3, \cdots, s_n)$.

Now look at the *queue:*

$$(q_1, q_2, q_3, \cdots, q_n)$$

The queue structure is easily represented as a list where the end item is q_n, the beginning item is q_1, and, after a *delete*, the queue becomes $(q_2, q_3, \cdots, q_n)$. Also, given the queue, $(q_1, q_2, q_3, \cdots, q_n)$, and a new item, q_{n+1}, an *insert* results in $(q_1, q_2, q_3, \cdots, q_n, q_{n+1})$.

Finally, consider the structure of the *binary tree* (Figure 7.1) and its equivalent list representation of $(b_1, (b_2, (b_4), (b_5)), (b_3, (b_6), ()))$, where () represents a null item.

Even these few simple examples show the potential for powerful list-processing primitives. In fact, two categories of list-processing primitives were identified in the preceding examples: a primitive for extracting elements of a list and a primitive for constructing a new list. In order to develop these primitives, a distinction between a list and an element of a list is necessary. To break a list down to its most primitive elements, one needs the notion of an *atomic element*. Atomic elements in LISP are the fundamental scalar data types, e.g., integers and characters.

Reconsider the stack example with a concrete example. Suppose we have a stack such as (1,2,3,(4,5,6)). Notice that there are atomic and nonatomic elements in this list:

$1 \in (1,2,3,(4,5,6))$ & 1 is atomic
$2 \in (1,2,3,(4,5,6))$ & 2 is atomic
$3 \in (1,2,3,(4,5,6))$ & 3 is atomic
$(4,5,6) \in (1,2,3,(4,5,6))$ & (4,5,6) is nonatomic

In order to extract a component of the stack, we would like to be able to obtain the first component and maintain the remaining elements of the list:

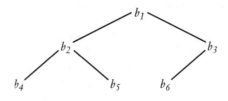

FIGURE 7.1   Binary tree.

First = 1 and remainder = (2,3,(4,5,6))

Fundamentally, given the operators to obtain these items and a tight interaction with a recursive construct, one is in possession of the basic building blocks to process any conceivable data structure. The list-processing primitives in LISP are the *car* and the *cdr*. The car operation extracts the first element from the list operand:

LISP prompt> (*car* '(1 (2 3) 4))
1

The answer is provided in boldface type:

LISP prompt > (*cdr* '(1 (2 3) 4))
((2 3) 4)

The single quote in front of the list operand is necessary so that LISP does not try to evaluate the argument. Notice that LISP operations are themselves list structures. The cdr obtains the remainder.

The car and cdr operators owe their names to mnemonic information associated with the machine on which LISP was originally implemented.

The ability to construct lists is obtained with the *cons* operator. It allows you to place an element at the beginning of a list:

LISP prompt > (*cons* '1 '(2 3 *a* 4))
(1 2 3 *a* 4)
LISP prompt > (*cons* '(1 2) '(*a* 3 4))
((1 2) *a* 3 4)

Notice that it is possible to mix data types in the same list structure. There is no requirement that lists be homogeneous in terms of the data types they contain. Thus, a heterogeneous stack is implemented with a push, top, and pop in the following way:

(*defun* push *(X Y)*   (*cons X Y*))
(*defun* top *(X)*   (car *X*))
(*defun* pop *(X)*   (*cdr X*))

The *defun* operator permits you to define your own functions. The function parameters follow the function name, and the function body follows the function parameters—in total, a function is a nested list structure. If you attempted to pop from an empty list, the interpreter would return nil. Examples of the uses of these functions are

LISP prompt > (push 1 '(2 3))
(1 2 3)
LISP prompt > (top '(1 2 3))
1
LISP prompt > (pop '(1 2 3))
(2 3)
LISP prompt > (pop '( ))
nil

When first introduced, LISP was shown to be Turing-complete. [McCarthy] This result is significant, because LISP reduced data structure and program structure to an elegant and concise form—to a form with very few orthogonal primitives. Yet in this primitive language and with a single data structure you have the power needed to solve any solvable problem.

SEMANTIC NOTE

Assuming all atoms to be integers and a mapping from a syntactic list, L, to a corresponding semantic list, ϕ, consider these examples of denotational definitions of the car, cdr, and cons:

SYNTAX
E ::= *car*(list) | *cons*(atom,list) | *cdr*(list)

SYNTACTIC DOMAIN
E: *Exp*

SEMANTIC DOMAIN
ϕ: $Fi = N^*$
v: $N = \{\cdots,-2,-1,0,1,2,\cdots\}°$

SEMANTIC FUNCTION DECLARATION
ε: $(Exp \to Fi \to N + Fi) + (Exp \to N \times Fi \to Fi)$
$\beta2$: list $\to Fi$
$\beta1$: atom $\to N$

$\beta1$ « atom »   =   element of N corresponding to atom
$\beta2$ « list »   =   element of Fi corresponding to list

ε « *car*(list) »   = $hd(\beta2$ « list »$)$
ε « *cdr*(list) »   = $tl(\beta2$ « list »$)$
ε « *cons*(atom, list) » = ϕ
         where $\beta1$ « atom » = $hd(\phi)$ & $\beta2$ « list » = $tl(\phi)$

S-EXPRESSIONS

In LISP, the fundamental construct is the *symbolic expression*, better known as the *S-expression*. Data and functions in LISP are S-expressions. These expressions have structure not unlike the binary tree structure shown in Figure 7.1. Thus, you could nest the car and cdr operators in the following ways:

LISP prompt > (car (cdr (car '((1 2 3 4) 5 6 7))))
2

The structure of the operation of the S-expression is shown in Figure 7.2. The evaluation of the operation proceeds as shown in Figure 7.3.

Any nested car/cdr combination can be abbreviated. For example, the nested sequence in Figure 7.3 can also be stated as (cadar '((1 2 3 4) 5 6 7)). The single quote's purpose should now be easier to understand: it designates a leaf in the S-expression's tree organization.

Now consider the basic mathematical operations in LISP:

LISP prompt > (+ 4 4)
8
LISP prompt > (* 4 4)
16
LISP prompt > (− 4 4)
0
LISP prompt > (/ 4 4)
1

Notice that constants need not be preceded by the quote because a constant evaluates to itself. More complicated expressions can easily be built in a prefix notation:

LISP prompt > (/ (−25 3) (− 12 5))
3.14286

The S-expression tree organization is shown in Figure 7.4. When evaluated, it becomes that shown in Figure 7.5.

Boolean-valued S-expressions are permitted. Built into versions of LISP are the standard relational operators. Booleans return "t" for true and "nil" for false:

LISP prompt > (> 5 4)
t
LISP prompt > (< 5 4)
nil

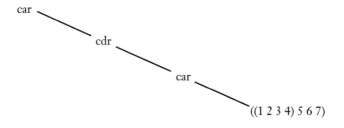

FIGURE 7.2   Operation structure of S-expression.

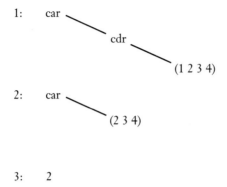

FIGURE 7.3   Operation evaluation of S-expression.

LISP prompt > (< 2 3)
t
LISP prompt > (equal 4 4)
t

In addition to the typical relational operators, there are a host of special predicates meant to perform type checking and other operations:

LISP prompt > (INTEGERP 3)
t
LISP prompt > (FLOATP 4)
nil
LISP prompt > (SYMBOLP 4)
nil
LISP prompt > (SYMBOLP +)
nil
LISP prompt > (SYMBOLP 'cat)
t
LISP prompt > (NULL 'cat)
nil

One can compose more sophisticated Boolean expressions using the conjunctions AND, OR, and NOT:

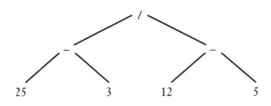

FIGURE 7.4   S-expression tree.

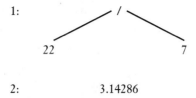

FIGURE 7.5 Evaluation of S-expression tree.

LISP prompt > (AND t t)
t
LISP prompt > (AND t nil)
nil
LISP prompt > (NOT t)
nil
LISP prompt > (NOT nil)
t
LISP prompt > (AND (< 3 4) (> 5 6))
nil
LISP prompt > (AND (< 3 4) (> 6 5))
t

See Figure 7.6 for the final expression in tree form and Figure 7.7 for its evaluation.

COMPOSING MORE SOPHISTICATED FUNCTIONS

By pairing Boolean expressions with other expressions, you can compose conditional expressions. Here we use the keyword COND to develop these more powerful expressions:

(COND ((> X 90) '(a)) (t '(b)))

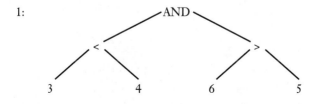

FIGURE 7.6 Tree form of Boolean expression.

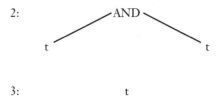

2: AND

t   t

3:       t

FIGURE 7.7   Evaluation of Boolean expression.

This expression is composed of two conditional expressions. They are evaluated from left to right, and the first Boolean expression that evaluates to "t" returns the result of its paired expression. For example, suppose the variable X has a value of 95 (Figure 7.8). In this case, the result shown in "(a)" is returned. For any $X <= 90$, the value shown in "(b)" is returned. The conditional expressions together with the unconditional expressions arm the programmer with a complete array of capabilities for writing LISP functions.

COMPOSING FULL LISP FUNCTIONS

We are now equipped with the necessary constructs to elaborate full LISP functions. Introduced earlier was the keyword employed for declaring a function and establishing its signature, *defun*. A function *signature* provides the function's name and the parameters it requires. Consider the function *factorial* in LISP:

```
(defun fact ( X )
        (cond ((EQUAL X 0) 1)
              (t ( * X (fact (− X 1))) ) ))
```

The function itself can be viewed as a list. For example, consider the following uses of the car and cdr.

LISP prompt > (car '(defun fact (X) (cond ((EQUAL X 0) 1) (t (* X (fact (− X 1)))))))
defun

$$
\text{Result}(X) = \begin{cases} \text{(a)} & \text{if } X > 90 \\ \text{(b)} & \text{otherwise} \end{cases}
$$

FIGURE 7.8   Representation of two conditional expressions.

The function name is obtained with a car of a cdr of the function:

> LISP prompt > (cadr '(defun fact (X) (cond ((EQUAL X 0) 1) (t (* X (fact
> (− X 1)))))))
> **fact**

The function signature is obtained with a car of two cdr operators of the function:

> LISP prompt > (caddr '(defun fact (X) (cond ((EQUAL X 0) 1) (t (* X (fact
> (− X 1)))))))
> **(x)**

The function body is obtained with three cdr operators of the function:

> LISP prompt > (cdddr '(defun fact (X) (cond ((EQUAL X 0) 1) (t (* X (fact
> (− X 1)))))))
> **(cond ((EQUAL *X* 0) 1) (t (* X (fact (− X 1)))))**

Looking back at the function definition, one can see that the function and its signature are declared in the first line:

> defun fact (X)

The remainder is a conditional expression that provides the function's body:

> (cond ((EQUAL X 0) 1)
>   (t (* X (fact (− X 1))))))

The first condition gives the function's nonrecursive definition, or base case. When input argument equals 0, the constant expression 1 is returned. Otherwise, which is denoted by true, or t, for the condition, *X* is to be multiplied by the result of "fact"'s application to the argument, obtained by subtracting 1 from *X*.

Consider the following evaluation of the preceding function. After the function is edited, it can be loaded into the interpreter's workspace:

> LISP prompt > (load "fact.lsp")
> ; reading fact.lsp
> t

The function is executed by referring to it and an argument:

> LISP prompt > (fact 6)
> 720

Now consider a full trace of the function:

> LISP prompt > (trace fact)
> fact
> LISP prompt > (fact 6)
> fact (6)

```
fact (5)
fact (4)
fact (3)
fact (2)
fact (1)
fact (0)
fact = 1
fact = 1
fact = 2
fact = 6
fact = 24
fact = 120
fact = 720
```

The recursive steps occur up through the line containing "fact (0)." Thereafter the base case applies, and the values for "fact" are returned until the original invocation is reached and evaluated. Consider the following smaller example of the trace:

```
LISP prompt > (fact 4)
fact (4)
fact (3)
fact (2)
fact (1)
fact (0)
fact = 1
fact = 1
fact = 2
fact = 6
fact = 24
LISP prompt >
```

The tree formed by the S-expressions denoting the series of recursive calls is shown in Figure 7.9. Evaluation proceeds according to the seven steps shown in Figure 7.10 through 7.16.

One can see from this introduction of the LISP primitives that this language is well suited for solving complicated problems. The remainder of the chapter focuses on some more sophisticated features of LISP.

ADVANCED FEATURES OF LISP

Even the earliest writings concerning LISP refer to at least two advanced data structures: association lists and property lists. [Berkeley] These advanced lists provide guidance to the programmer when attempting to solve problems involving table look-ups or record processing.

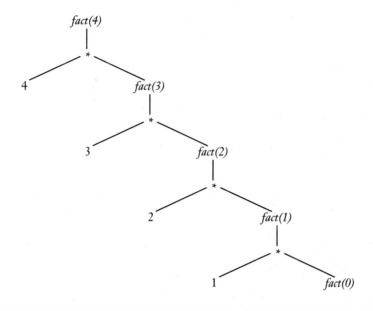

FIGURE 7.9 S-expression tree.

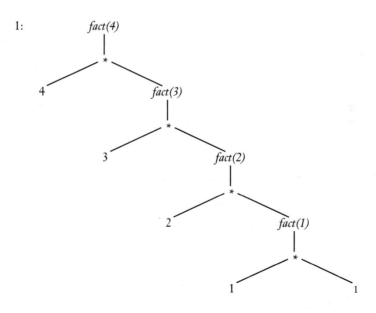

FIGURE 7.10 Step 1 of evaluation.

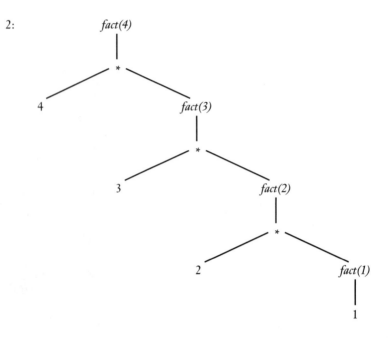

FIGURE 7.11 Step 2 of evaluation.

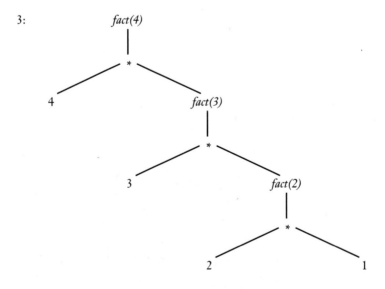

FIGURE 7.12 Step 3 of evaluation.

4:

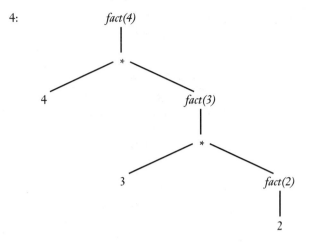

FIGURE 7.13   Step 4 of evaluation.

5:

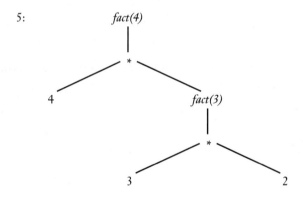

FIGURE 7.14   Step 5 of evaluation.

6:

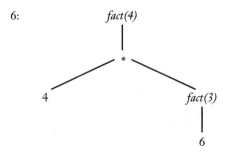

FIGURE 7.15   Step 6 of evaluation.

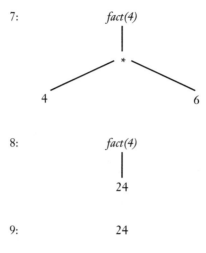

7:      *fact(4)*

8:      *fact(4)*
          |
          24

9:          24

FIGURE 7.16   Step 7 of evaluation.

ASSOCIATION LISTS

Association lists allow for the definition of mappings. For example, you can define simple table-lookup mappings such as

m = ((1 one) (2 two) (3 three) · · ·)

Now m can be used to associate the domain of a mapping to its range:

(assoc m 2)   =   two

You can define, globally, an association list, or any other kind of list, using the *setq* command in LISP:

(setq m '((1 one)(2 two) (3 three)))

After the association list is defined, you can perform the associations using the built-in *assoc* function. This function is an elegant, short piece of LISP code composed with the more primitive elements of the language already presented:

```
(defun assoc ( X Y )
     (cond ((null X) X)
           ((equal (caar X) Y) (cdar X))
           (t (assoc (cdr X) Y) )))
```

Suppose that rather than mapping from a domain to a range in terms of **values,** you choose to map from a domain to a specific function that is to be applied to a second domain:

(setq m '((add +) (minus −)))

A small change to the assoc function is all that is needed in order to map to the appropriate function to accomplish addition or subtraction. The modification makes use of the *eval* function that causes the evaluation of its term:

```
(defun assoc ( X Y A B )
    (cond ((null X) X)
            ((equal (caar X) Y) (eval '((cadar X ) A B)) )
            (t (assoc (cdr X) Y) )))
```

The boldface portion of the preceding contains the required modification. If *Y* matches the car of the car of *X* (e.g., add), the car of the cdr of the car of X will be the operator to apply to the second domain *A* and *B*. Here is an execution of the function:

```
LISP prompt > (assoc m 'add 4 5)
9
```

PROPERTY LISTS

Property lists establish relations between atoms and lists. The relational structures can be established in a way that allows you to define what are effectively *record structures*. Suppose, for example, you wish to define a record of information associated with a woman named Mary. This can be accomplished by relating "mary" with some *attribute* of information. Such relationships can be established through the use of the *put* function in LISP:

```
LISP prompt > (put 'mary 'age 21)
21
LISP prompt > (put 'mary 'child 'sam)
sam
LISP prompt > (put 'mary 'salary 65000)
65000
```

There are several ways of viewing the resulting structure. One way is to view it as a set of relations:

```
age(mary, 21)
child(mary,sam)
salary(mary,65000)
```

The structure can also be viewed as a record in a database, in which the relation names serve as the names of record fields or attributes (see Figure 7.17).

The put function *injects* the values to be related. In other words, the put establishes the relationships. The *get* function allows you to obtain, or *project*, the values in a relation. (Both injection and projection are explained further later on.)

```
LISP prompt > (get 'mary 'age)
21
LISP prompt > (get 'mary 'child)
sam
```

name	age	child	salary
⋮	⋮	⋮	⋮
mary	21	sam	65000
⋮	⋮	⋮	⋮

FIGURE 7.17

Additional relations can be established through the use of rules that can be cast into LISP functions. Suppose the following relations have been previously defined:

LISP prompt > (put 'mary 'child 'sam)
sam
LISP prompt > (put 'sam 'child 'bob)
bob

The put functions can be viewed as a declaration that "Mary's child is Sam" and "Sam's child is Bob." To obtain grandparent information associated with Mary, do the following:

LISP prompt > (get (get 'mary 'child) 'child)
bob

You can establish the grandparent rule in a LISP function as follows:

```
(defun gp (X)
        (cond
                ((null (get X 'child)) (get X 'child))
                ((null (get (get X 'child) 'child))
                        (get (get X 'child) 'child))
                ( t (get (get X 'child) 'child) )))
```

The grandparent relation exhibits a limited closure function. The first two cases handle the situations in which the individual, X has no child, or in which X has a child but that child has no children. Under these conditions, "null" is returned, signifying there are no grandchildren of X. The default case will get X's child, and having done so, will get X's child's child.

Consider the following trace, which establishes parent relationships between Mary and Sam, and between Sam and Bob. As you can see, child relationships succeed when Mary is the parent and fail when Bob is the parent.

LISP prompt > (put 'mary 'child 'sam)
sam
LISP prompt > (put 'sam 'child 'bob)
bob

LISP prompt > (get 'mary 'child)
sam
LISP prompt > (get 'bob 'child)
nil
LISP prompt > (gp 'mary)
bob

■ ■

EXPRESSION INTERPRETER

Recall the interpreter developed in Pascal in Chapter 4. In LISP you will find
that is easier to express the functionality of an interpreter in a more intuitive and
concise manner. Following is a function to evaluate postfix arithmetic expressions. First stack operations are provided. As numbers are parsed by the interpreter, they will be pushed onto a stack using the cons operator as before. The
push has two parameters: the item X to be stacked, followed by the stack itself, S.

```
(defun push (X S)
    (cons X S))
```

When an operator is parsed, the top two items on the stack must be obtained,
to which the operator is to be applied. The second operand is obtained by a top
operation, and the first operand is obtained by a top following a pop, that is,
top(pop(S)). Here are the top and pop operations:

```
(defun pop (S)
        (cond      ((equal S nil) '( ))
                   (t (cdr S))))
```

```
(defun top (S)
        (cond      ((equal S nil) '( ))
                   (t (car S))))
```

The interpreter is a simple function we will call *ev*. This function's state is
manifested by the state of the input, X, and the state of the stack, S, which is initially empty.

```
(defun ev (X S)
    (cond    ((equal X nil) S)
             ((integerp (car X)) (ev (cdr X) (push (car X) S)) )
             (t (ev (cdr X) (push (eval (cons (car X)
                (cons (top (pop S)) (cons (top S) '( ) ) ) )) (pop (pop S)) )))))
```

The first case handled,

```
((equal X nil) S)
```

is the situation when the input is empty. In this case the current state of the stack is the answer. If a valid expression has been input, the stack should contain exactly one value, the value of the result obtained by evaluating the input expression. If the input is initially empty, an empty stack is obtained. If the input contains an invalid postfix expression, the stack may contain multiple items.

The next case handled is when the first item in the input is an integer. When this case, (integerp (car X)), arises, the correct response is to push the integer onto the stack, (push (car X) S)), remove the integer from the input, (cdr X), and reinvoke *ev*, with the resulting two structures as input:

((integerp (car X)) (ev (cdr X) (push (car X) S)))

The final (and default) case is when an operator is the next item in input. When this occurs, the top two items must be obtained from the stack (as was mentioned earlier):

cons (top (pop S)) (cons (top S) '( ))

Two cons operators are employed in order to begin the construction of a list to be arithmetically evaluated. The second operand is obtained by performing a top on the stack and performing a cons with an empty list. A cons is then performed on the resulting list, with the result of a pop to eliminate the second operand from the stack and a top, which can now return the first operand. This list, containing the operands, can now be subjected to a cons with the operator obtained by a (car X), with which they will be evaluated:

(eval (cons (car X) (cons (top (pop S)) (cons (top S) '( )))))

The result of the evaluation is pushed onto the stack after the two operands are popped from it. This resulting stack,

(push (eval (cons (car X) (cons (top (pop S)) (cons (top S) '( ))))) (pop
 (pop S)))

serves as the second argument for the next recursive call to *ev:*

(ev (cdr X) (push (eval (cons (car X)
 (cons (top (pop S)) (cons (top S) '( ))))) (pop (pop S))))

The first argument is simply the input list X with the operator removed:

(cdr X)

The following trace of the evaluation of the postfix expression (5 6 + 4 −) ends this section. Notice how the input expression (the first argument) and the stack (the second argument) change over the course of the evaluation and reflect the total computation space in terms of state, for the evaluation of the example expression:

LISP prompt > (ev '(5 6 + 4 −) '( ))

ev ((5 6 + 4 −) nil)
ev ((6 + 4 −) (5))
ev ((+ 4 −) (6 5))
ev ((4 −) (11))
ev ((−) (4 11))
ev (nil (7))
ev = (7)
ev = (7)
ev = (7)
ev = (7)
ev = (7)
ev = (7)

METAINTERPRETER

We end this chapter with a short introduction to *metaprogramming*, a form of programming based on the features of LISP and allowing problem solving at a higher level, or order, of abstraction. Hill described it this way: "A meta-program, regardless of the nature of the programming language, is a program whose data denotes another (object) program." Metaprogramming can be explained best in context of the types of argument that a function can take.

We have already observed that the LISP abstraction allows program units to be treated just like data. The fact that we can pass program or function structures to functions that, in turn, can process these structures, indicates that the LISP environment accommodates *higher-order functions*, or functions that can accept other functions as arguments.

Metaprogramming can be demonstrated by the fact that one can easily build a LISP interpreter in LISP. To do so, you must be able to evaluate LISP functions, and to evaluate them, you must process their interactions with their state. The functions to process a function's interaction with its state are described in this section. The state will be termed the function's *environment* and will be represented by an association list.

The two primitive functions to process the state are the *inject* and *project* functions. *Injection* takes place when a variable and its associated value are inserted into the environment:

```
(defun inject ( X Y Z )
        ( cons (cons Y (cons Z '( ))) X))
```

Injection of a variable, *Y*, and its value, *Z*, into an environment, *X*, requires a series of cons. The inner cons associates the variable and its value. The outer cons places the pair in the environment.

```
(inject '((a 4)(b 5)) 'c '6)            =
(cons (cons 'c (cons '6 ( )))'((a 4)(b 5)))    =
```

```
(cons (cons 'c (6))'((a 4)(b 5)))          =
(cons (c 6)'((a 4)(b 5)))                  =
((c 6)(a 4)(b 5))
```

In *projection*, an environment, X, and a variable, Y, are taken as arguments, and the value associated with Y is returned if Y is paired with a value in environment X.

```
(defun project ( X Y )
        (cond   ((null X) (cons Y X) )
                ((equal (car (car X)) Y) (cdr (car X)))
                (t (project (cdr X) Y) )))
```

Project is a recursive search function. The two nonrecursive cases are when the variable is either found or not found. The variable is not found whenever the environment is empty, or null:

LISP prompt> (project *m* 5)

```
project (((1 one) (2 two) (3 three)) 5)
project (((2 two) (3 three)) 5)
project (((3 three)) 5)
project ( nil 5)
project = (5)
project = (5)
project = (5)
project = (5)
```

The variable is found when the car of the car of the environment equals the variable in Y:

LISP prompt> (project *m* 1)

```
project (((1 one) (2 two) (3 three)) 1)
project = (one)
```

Otherwise the remainder (i.e., the cdr) of the environment is searched for the variable:

LISP prompt> (project *m* 2)

```
project (((1 one) (2 two) (3 three)) 2)
project (((2 two) (3 three)) 2)
project = (two)
project = (two)
```

A function to instantiate variables with their respective values is used to create the environment of a function:

```
(defun instance (expr env)
    (cond ((null expr) expr )
```

((equal (car expr) 'cond) (cons 'cond (instance (cdr expr) env)))
((consp (car expr)) (cons (instance (car expr) env) (instance (cdr expr)
     env)))
((op (car expr))   (cons (car expr) (instance (cdr expr) env)))
((atom (car expr)) (cons (car (project env (car expr))) (instance (cdr
     expr) env)))))

The instance function takes a LISP function body and instantiates all variables in the body with associated values from the environment. This function
handles conditional expressions. It makes use of a built-in *consp* function,
which returns "true" when its argument is a list and "nil" otherwise. It also
uses a built-in function, *atom*, which returns "nil" when the argument is a list
and "true" otherwise. The function *op* checks to see if its argument is an
operator:

```
(defun op (x)
        (cond    ((equal x '+) t)
                 ((equal x '−) t)
                 ((equal x '*) t)
                 ((equal x '/) t)
                 ((equal x '<) t)
                 ((equal x '>) t)
                 ((equal x 'equal) t)
                 (t nil) ))
```

A trace of the execution of instance follows. The function replaces variables
(using the project function) in a function body with their associated values from
the environment. Notice that much of the work involves breaking down the
original body containing the variables and then faithfully reconstructing the
body with the values of the variables, as found through projection:

```
instance ((+ (+ (+ a b) a) 3) ((a 2) (b 3)))
instance (((+ (+ (+ a b) a) 3) ((a 2) (b 3)))
instance ((+ (+ a b) a) ((a 2) (b 3)))
instance (((+ (+ a b) a) ((a 2) (b 3)))
instance ((+ a b) ((a 2) (b 3)))
instance ((a b) ((a 2) (b 3)))
project (((a 2) (b 3)) a)
project = (2)
instance ((b) ((a 2) (b 3)))
project (((a 2) (b 3)) b)
project (((b 3)) b)
project = (3)
project = (3)
instance ( nil ((a 2) (b 3)))
instance = nil
instance = (3)
```

```
instance = (2 3)
instance = (+ 2 3)
instance ((a) ((a 2) (b 3)))
project (((a 2) (b 3)) a)
project = (2)
instance ( nil ((a 2) (b 3)))
instance = nil
instance = (2)
instance = ((+ 2 3) 2)
instance = (+ (+ 2 3) 2)
instance ((3) ((a 2) (b 3)))
project (((a 2) (b 3)) 3)
project (((b 3)) 3)
project ( nil 3)
project = (3)
project = (3)
project = (3)
instance ( nil ((a 2) (b 3)))
instance = nil
instance = (3)
instance = ((+ (+ 2 3) 2) 3)
instance = (+ (+ (+ 2 3) 2) 3)
```

After the basic functions handling the environment are defined, a capability to define functions is needed. Following is a function that defines a global variable—the function's name as obtained with (car (cdr expr))—with the function's body, which is obtained by (car (cdr (cdr (cdr expr)))). The function also extracts the parameters of the function—(car (cdr (cdr expr))))—and associates them with a variable called *parms*.

```
(defun deffunc (expr)
    (set (car (cdr expr)) (car (cdr (cdr (cdr expr)))))
    (set 'parms (car (cdr (cdr expr))) ) )
```

Thus, given the goal of (deffunc '(def F (a b) (cond ((> a b) a) (t b)))), we set two global variables to the following values:

LISP prompt> *f*
(cond ((> a b) a) (t b))
LISP prompt> parms
(a b)
LISP prompt>

After a function is defined, it can be executed. To execute the function, we must invoke it with an argument list. The function to perform the evaluation of a function follows:

```
(defun evfunc (func args)
        (set 'env (crtenv parms args '( )) )
        (set 'opf (instance (symbol-value func) env) )
        (evbody opf ))
```

The "crtenv" uses the instance function to set the variable *env*. This is used to pass a function's arguments by matching parameters with the values passed when the function is invoked.

```
(defun crtenv (parms args env)
       (cond ((null parms) env)
             (t (crtenv (cdr parms) (cdr args) (inject env (car parms) (car args)) ))))
```

The following trace indicates the construction of the environment given the previous definitions and the argument list (4 3):

```
crtenv ((a b) (4 3) nil )
crtenv ((b) (3) ((a 4)))
crtenv ( nil nil ((b 3) (a 4)))
crtenv = ((b 3) (a 4))
crtenv = ((b 3) (a 4))
crtenv = ((b 3) (a 4))
```

Symbol-value, referenced in evfunc, returns the current value of the referenced variable based on a prior *set* operation. An error occurs if the symbol has no value. With the previous definition of function, f, one can evaluate the f with, for example, (evfunc 'f '(4 3)). Prior to invoking the *evbody* function, two more global variables are set:

```
LISP prompt> opf
(cond ((> 4 3) 4) (t 3))
LISP prompt> env
((b 3) (a 4))
```

Notice that opf receives the value of the function body after variables are instantiated with the instance function.

The "evbody" determines whether there is a conditional or unconditional function body and invokes the appropriate function accordingly. All three of these functions follow. Notice that "evconds" evaluates a conditional and invokes the appropriate unconditional. Also notice the special "inv" in "evunconds," which permits one to invoke a function.

```
(defun evbody (body)
        (cond ((equal (car body) 'cond) (evconds (cdr body)))
              (t (evunconds body)) ))

(defun evunconds (body)
        (cond ((atom body) (eval body))
```

```
        ((equal (car body) 'inv) (evfunc (car (cdr body)) (cons
                    (eval (car (cdr (cdr body)))) '( )) ))
            (t eval body)))

    (defun evconds (body)
            (cond ( (eval (car (car body))) (evunconds (car (cdr (car body)))))
                ( t (evconds (cdr body))) ))
```

Follow now the definition and invocation of a recursive function. The function is a *succ* function with the following body and parameter list:

```
LISP prompt > succ
(cond ((> a 5) a) (t (inv succ (+ a 2))))
LISP prompt > parm
(a)
```

The *succ* function is invoked with argument 3 and results in the following trace:

```
evfunc (succ (3))
crtenv ((a) (3) nil )
crtenv ( nil nil ((a 3)))
crtenv = ((a 3))
crtenv = ((a 3))
evbody ((cond ((> 3 5) 3) (t (inv succ (+ 3 2)))))
evconds ((((> 3 5) 3) (t (inv succ (+ 3 2)))))
evconds (((t (inv succ (+ 3 2)))))
evunconds ((inv succ (+ 3 2)))
evfunc (succ (5))
crtenv ((a) (5) nil )
crtenv ( nil nil ((a 5)))
crtenv = ((a 5))
crtenv = ((a 5))
evbody ((cond ((> 5 5) 5) (t (inv succ (+ 5 2)))))
evconds ((((> 5 5) 5) (t (inv succ (+ 5 2)))))
evconds (((t (inv succ (+ 5 2)))))
evunconds ((inv succ (+ 5 2)))
evfunc (succ (7))
crtenv ((a) (7) nil )
crtenv ( nil nil ((a 7)))
crtenv = ((a 7))
crtenv = ((a 7))
evbody ((cond ((> 7 5) 7) (t (inv succ (+ 7 2)))))
evconds ((((> 7 5) 7) (t (inv succ (+ 7 2)))))
evunconds (7)
evunconds = 7
evconds = 7
evbody = 7
evfunc = 7
```

```
evunconds = 7
evconds = 7
evconds = 7
evbody = 7
evfunc = 7
evunconds = 7
evconds = 7
evconds = 7
evbody = 7
evfunc = 7
7
LISP prompt >
```

CONCLUSION

The simplicity and elegance of LISP have served as an inspiration to computer scientists for decades. The abstraction has stood the test of time. It represents the genesis of the very important functional-language segment of programming languages. LISP also serves as the language of choice for many who do research in artificial intelligence. So significant is LISP that so-called LISP machines have been manufactured by major companies like Texas Instruments.

REFERENCES

E. C. Berkeley, (LISP—A Simple Introduction). In E. C. Berkeley and D. G. Bobrow, editors. *The Programming Language LISP: Its Operation and Applications.* Cambridge, MA: MIT Press, 1964.

P. M. Hill and J. Gallagher. In *Handbook of Logic in Artificial Intelligence and Logic Programming* (D. M. Gabbay, C. J. Hogger, and J. A. Robinson, editors). London: Oxford University Press, 1998, pp. 421–498.

J. McCarthy. "Recursive functions of symbolic expressions and their computation by machine." *Communications of the ACM* 3, no. 4 (April 1960):184–195.

The version of LISP used to interpret the LISP functions presented in this chapter can be obtained at http://www.ozemail.com.au/~birchb/reflisp.html

QUESTIONS AND EXERCISES

1. Write a LISP function that will perform the preorder traversal of a binary tree in which the tree is (a (b (c d)) (e (f g))).

2. With which feature of LISP does one accomplish the sequence structure, the selective or the iterative? Show how each of the following Pascal code segments would be implemented in LISP:

   a. $s:= a+b; t:=c+d; r:=s/t;$

   b. if $x > m$ then $m:=x;$

   c. $s:=0;$ for $i:=1$ to 10 do $s:=s+i;$

3. Given the command (set 'DS '(a (b (d (h i) e) c (f g)))), write a LISP function that will take "DS" as input and return the list (a (b (d (h i) e (x y)) c (f g))).

4. Write a set of LISP functions to sort a list in ascending order.

5. What is the significance of the fact that LISP was shown to be equivalent to a Universal Turing Machine? Relate your answer to the idea of problem-solving involving abstractions.

6. Given the invocation (s '0 '(10 20 30 40 50 60)), trace the execution of the following LISP program. Your answer should include a history of the values associated with the variables of the function:

   (defun s (X Y)
       (cond ((null Y) X)
               (t (s (+ X (car Y)) (cdr Y)))))

7. What does the following LISP routine do?

   (defun what (X)
   (cond ((null X) nil)
   ((atom (car X)) (princ (car X)) (what (cdr X)))
   (t (what(car X)) (what (what X))))))

8. Write an equivalent LISP function where A and N in the following code are arguments of a function rather than input values using an I/O construct.

```
           READ(5,10) N
10         FORMAT(I2)
           DO 20 I=1,N
           READ(5,10) A(I)
20         CONTINUE
           S=0
           DO 30 I=1,N
           S=S+A(I)
30         CONTINUE
           AVE = S / N
```

8

LOGIC PROGRAMMING USING PROLOG

....

BRIEF OVERVIEW OF LOGIC

Although the study of logic dates back to the time of Aristotle, we will begin our discourse on logic with the advancements that were made in the nineteenth century by mathematicians such as Boole and Frege. For a thorough and very accessible history of the logical foundations of computer science, the reader is encourage to read *The Universal Computer: The Road from Leibniz to Turing*, by Alan Davis.

The *propositional calculus* provides a language and semantic that allows for reasoning about objects in a *domain of discourse*, that is, a formalized subject area. The pure approaches developed in logic were an effort to develop a symbolic form of reasoning that could be mathematically manipulated without it being necessary to interpret the symbols used. In other words, the reasoning could be performed independently of knowledge of the domain of discourse to which the symbols mapped. The resulting form of logic gave rise to some of the most important results ever obtained in mathematics, including Gödel's *incompleteness theorem* and Turing's results concerning solvability and computability, which ultimately led to the development of the computer.

The most atomic term in propositional logic is the *proposition*, a statement of facts that can be viewed as axiomatic. For example, the following statements of fact could be assigned proposition variables as shown:

S = the sun shines 75% of the daylight hours in the spring and summer.
R = the rain falls 20% of spring and summer.
C = the corn grows.

Having assigned these variables intuitive meanings, we now have the beginnings of a domain of discourse that provides a framework for discussion and proof. We can construct logical sentences using the connectives of AND (&), OR (OR), NOT (~), and implication (→). The meaning of these terms can be determined from the truth or falsity of the propositions to which they are applied.

Assume $\pi1$ and $\pi2$ are metasymbols that can represent any conceivable proposition variable. The table in Figure 8.1 provides an exhaustive enumeration of the possible truth values the propositions could have and, based upon these assignments, the truth of the statement connective.

Given the truth-table semantics in Figure 8.1 and a set of axioms represented by proposition variables, one can extend the domain of discourse by providing rules:

$$S \ \& \ R \rightarrow C$$

The truth of the implication is determined according to the appropriately constructed tables. So, for example, if S and R are true, then the implication as shown in Figure 8.2 is true. The italicized rows in each truth table provide the truth assignments needed to make the implication true. From the information provided in these rows, one can "reason" about implications. Recalling the sentences to which the proposition variables are assigned, one can see that for the corn to grow, the sun must shine *and* the rain must fall in the percentages stated. From the second table one can see that there may be other conditions under which the corn may grow. For example, maybe the percentages of sunshine and rainfall need not be exactly those stated.

One other significant fact arises out of the observation that if we know that the implication holds, then C *must* be true whenever S and R are true. This fact is embodied in a fundamental rule of inference called *modus ponens*, which states that if the left-hand side (i.e., the antecedent) of an implication is true, then the

$\pi1$	$\pi2$	$\sim\pi1$	$\pi1 \ \& \ \pi2$	$\pi1$ OR $\pi2$	$\pi1 \rightarrow \pi2$
T	T	F	T	T	T
T	F	F	F	T	F
F	T	T	F	T	T
F	F	T	F	F	T

FIGURE 8.1 The semantics of the logical connectives.

S	R	S & R
T	T	T
T	F	F
F	T	F
F	F	F

S & R	C	S & R → C
T	T	T
T	F	F
F	T	T
F	F	T

FIGURE 8.2   Truth tables for domain of disclosure.

right-hand side (i.e., the consequent) of the implication must be true. The modus ponens is symbolized by the following:

If A and $A{\rightarrow}B$ are axioms, then B can be concluded; OR, stated symbolically:

A
$A{\rightarrow}B$
_____

B by modus ponens

To advance the usability of logic, propositional expressions were expanded, and proposition variables were allowed to have arguments:

Sunshine_amount(X)
Rainfall_amount(X)

A proposition variable together with its arguments is termed a *literal*. A literal has an *arity*, which refers to the number of arguments it takes. The literals in our example each have an arity of 1. A *constant literal* (i.e., a proposition) has an arity of zero. The resulting *first-order predicate calculus* clearly subsumes and expands on the propositional calculus. The range of legal values for the arity of literals can be expressed as

If an arity $= n$, then $n \in$ Integers & $n \geq 0$

In fact, we can state the definition logically when we introduce two additional connectives. The definition of arity is

$(\forall n)$arity$(n) \rightarrow n \in$ Integers & $n \geq 0$

Additional connectives are required in order to provide a precise expression of propositional statements containing variables. The additional connectives are called *quantifiers*. They express information concerning the truthfulness of the quantified expression in terms of number. There are two quantifiers, the universal and the existential. The one shown in the preceding expression, $\forall$, is the *universal quantifier*. That expression can be read, "For every n, if n serves as an arity, then n must be an integer greater than or equal to zero." For an arbitrary statement, Σ, containing a variable, Δ, that ranges over the full set of values, $\{\delta1,$ $\delta2, \cdots, \delta n\}$, the universal quantifier can be defined by

$$(\forall\Delta)\Sigma(\Delta) \equiv \Sigma(\delta1) \ \& \ \Sigma(\delta2) \ \& \ \cdots \ \& \ \Sigma(\delta n)$$

The domain of discourse need not be finite. That is, Δ ranges over $\{\delta1, \delta2, \cdots,$ $\delta i, \cdots\}$:

$$(\forall\Delta)\Sigma(\Delta) \equiv \Sigma(\delta1) \ \& \ \Sigma(\delta2) \ \& \ \cdots \ \& \ \Sigma(\delta i) \ \cdots$$

The *existential quantifier* (i.e., $\exists$) is read as "there exists." For an arbitrary statement, Σ, and a variable, Δ, that ranges over a domain of discourse, $\{\delta1, \delta2,$ $\cdots, \delta n\}$, the existential quantifier can be defined by

$$(\exists\Delta)\Sigma(\Delta) \equiv \Sigma(\delta1) \ OR \ \Sigma(\delta2) \ OR \ \cdots \ OR \ \Sigma(\delta n)$$

Once again, the domain of discourse need not be finite. That is, Δ ranges over $\{\delta1, \delta2, \cdots, \delta i, \cdots\}$:

$$(\exists\Delta)\Sigma(\Delta) \equiv \Sigma(\delta1) \ OR \ \Sigma(\delta2) \ OR \ \cdots \ OR \ \Sigma(\delta i) \ OR \ \cdots$$

Comparing the definitions of $\exists$ and $\forall$ with the simple truth-table semantics of the connectives for propositional expressions that do not contain variables, one readily sees how these additional features complicate the semantics of the resulting language, which is called the *first-order predicate calculus*. Clearly, the truth-table semantic is not capable of handling the translations needed for this much more sophisticated language. In fact, many advances were required to find a semi-decidable approach to these translations. [Robinson] These advances led to development of the Prolog language.

Prolog represents a truly revolutionary approach to programming. In this chapter, we will focus on the elements of Prolog one must master in order to program effectively with it. First, though, a brief example of a proof based on formal definitions in predicate calculus is appropriate. Suppose there is a statement such as

$$(\forall\Delta)\Sigma(\Delta)$$

You can prove the statement false if you can find a single δi where $\sim\Sigma(\delta i)$. The proof is one consisting of a counterexample that makes the conjunction defining the universal quantifier false. This sort of proof is also clear based on the equivalence,

$$\sim(\exists\Delta)\sim\Sigma(\Delta) \equiv (\forall\Delta)\Sigma(\Delta)$$

which also makes it clear that if an element Δ is found that satisfies $\sim\Sigma(\Delta)$, then one has proved that $\forall\Delta\Sigma(\Delta)$ is not a true statement.

PROGRAMMING IN PROLOG

Prolog possesses two primitives for the definition of data structures: the term and the assertional data structures. The *assertional* data structure allows one to assert literals to a database, as follows:

a(1,10).
a(2,30).
a(3,40).

Numbers and lowercase alphabetic letters denote constant information. The *functor* of this literal is "*a*," and "*a*" has an arity of 2, or is binary. Assert is a built-in predicate that takes another predicate as an argument, *assert (Σ(Δ))*, and adds its argument to the Prolog database.

After the facts have been asserted to a database, Prolog provides the capability to *query* the database. Think of the database in our example as consisting of a three-element array. Consider the following formatted Prolog session in SWI Prolog, which occurs after double-clicking on a file containing the facts previously presented. SWI Prolog is a free version of Prolog that can be downloaded from the internet.

Welcome to SWI-Prolog (Version 3.2.0)
Copyright(c)1993-1998 University of Amsterdam. All rights reserved.

For help, use ?- help(Topic). or ?- apropos(Word).

c:/PROGRA~1/PL/ARRAY.PL compiled, 0.00 sec, 768 bytes.

?- a(2,X).

X = 30

Yes
?- a(I,10).

I = 1

Yes
?- a(2,20).

No
?- a(3,40).

Yes
?- a(X,Y).

X = 1
Y = 10 ;

X = 2
Y = 30 ;

X = 3

Y = 40 ;

No

Queries are typed to the right of the "?-" prompt and are highlighted in bold-face. They are the original *goals* of a Prolog program. As Prolog attempts to sat-isfy a goal, new goals may be introduced in the bodies of conditional assertions (as will be seen later).

We will begin by considering the two *closed queries*. A query is closed if it con-tains only constant information, that is, no variables as arguments. The goal of a closed query is to determine if the constant arguments of the literal are true, that is, whether the literal with said constants is asserted in the database. Therefore, closed queries receive answers of either yes or no:

?- a(2,20).

No
?- a(3,40).

Yes

Open queries include variables as arguments. The goal here is to find values (for the variables) as asserted in the database that make the literal true. If none are found, the literal is false. Therefore, one either gets the value of the variable that leads to a yes answer or receives the answer no:

?- a(2,X).

X = 30

Yes
?- a(8,X).

No

The preceding queries are made to determine what value is held in the second or eighth element of the array.

Prolog is based on a *closed-world assumption*, which, informally stated, is the assumption that a goal (or literal) is true if and only if its database (or program) can satisfy the goal. If it cannot prove the goal, Prolog states that the goal is false. This assumption is not equivalent to the way we intuitively feel about negation. If we are asked if X is true, we answer "yes" if we know it to be true, "no" if we know it to be false. If we have no information about X, we answer that we do not know whether it is true. Notice how Prolog differs from the intuitive response: in the absence of any information, Prolog answers "no."

Most versions of Prolog have a *not(P)* predicate, in which *P* is itself a predi-cate. The *not* implements the so-called closed-world assumption, succeeding when P cannot be satisfied in the current database, and failing if P can be satisfied. Much work has been done to extend Prolog to handle true forms of negation and thus deal with uncertain information, a very important capability in the more sophisticated forms of model-based reasoning.

The open query that follows is different from the previous open query in that all arguments contain variables. It is also different in that after each answer Prolog provides, the user enters a semicolon, which denotes a logical OR, to see if there are additional answers. The semicolon forces Prolog to perform *backtracking* to see if there are new values for the arguments of a literal that will result in differing answers. In this example, we exhaustively search the database containing binary literals with the *functor "a"*:

?- a(X,Y).

X = 1
Y = 10 ;

X = 2
Y = 30 ;

X = 3
Y = 40 ;

No

The "no" answer following the input of the final semicolon indicates that we have exhausted the binary "a" database.

An enumeration of literals, like the binary "a" database, results in a set of unconditional assertions. Prolog programs are formed through the use of unconditional literals and what might be viewed as conditional assertions. *Conditional assertions* take the form of

literal:- body.

The literal can be viewed to be asserted *if* (denoted by :-) the associated body is satisfiable. The body consists of other literals, some defined by the programmer and others that are built into the language. In Prolog the conditional assertion is typically called a *rule* or a *procedure*. The literal is called the *head*, and the body is called the *body*. The body of a procedure consists of predicates that, serving as goals, must be satisfied before the head is satisfied. Suppose the following procedures exist in a Prolog database:

p_1:-q_1, q_2, $\cdots$, q_n
p_1:-r_1, r_2, $\cdots$, r_m
remainder of q and r assertions

Now suppose the goal, p_1, serves as a query. What follows is a trace that shows the top-down/left-to-right evaluation of a Prolog procedure set. To satisfy the query one of the p_1 procedures must succeed. Consequently, the original goal results in new goals that arise from the body of the p_1 procedure.

```
:- p₁
:- q₁, q₂, · · · , qₙ
```

The goals q_1 through q_n will be evaluated from left to right. If one of these goals fails, backtracking will possibly force Prolog to try to satisfy the next p_1 procedure in the database (an example of the top-down part of the execution strategy):

```
:- p₁
:- q₁, q₂, · · · , qₙ,
:- fail,
:- next p₁
:- r₁, r₂, · · · , rₘ,
:- r₂, · · · , rₘ,
        : :
:- rₘ,
:- yes
```

The execution strategy provides for a top-down/left-to-right evaluation of literals. Consider now a nongeneralized example of the execution strategy. The following code consists of a set of numbers asserted in a literal with functor "*n*". The conditional assertion, "larger," identifies a number, if any, that is larger than the input number, which is provided by the user in variable *C*:

```
n(20).
n(2).
n(234).
n(4).
n(97).
n(8).
```

```
larger(C,M):-n(M),C < M.
```

A trace of a session in which this program was run follows. The number input for variable *C* is 200. The session demonstrates the top-down/left-to-right execution strategy as well as backtracking. The backtracking leads to the *redo* step following each step (in boldface) labeled "fail."

Welcome to SWI-Prolog (Version 3.2.0)
Copyright (c) 1993-1998 University of Amsterdam. All rights reserved.

For help, use ?- help(Topic). Or ?- apropos(Word).

C:/PROGRA~1/PL/GREATER.PL compiled, 0.00 sec, 1,180 bytes.

?- trace,larger(200,X).
```
    Call: ( 7) larger(200, _G214) ? creep
    Call: ( 8) n(_G214) ? creep
```

```
Exit: ( 8) n(20) ? creep
Call: ( 8) 200<20 ? creep
Fail: ( 8) 200<20 ? creep
Redo: ( 8) n(_G214) ? creep
Exit: ( 8) n(2) ? creep
Call: ( 8) 200<2 ? creep
Fail: ( 8) 200<2 ? creep
Redo: ( 8) n(_G214) ? creep
Exit: ( 8) n(234) ? creep
Call: ( 8) 200<234 ? creep
Exit: ( 8) 200<234 ? creep
Exit: ( 7) larger(200, 234) ? creep
```

X = 234

In order to gain a better understanding of the execution strategy, including backtracking, consider the modified and annotated trace in Figure 8.3.

Moving on to a more complicated example, see Figure 8.4, which shows a simple directed graph that will form the basis for considering the closure of paths among the nodes. Following is Prolog code that defines the graph in terms of connectivity and will perform closure under the direction of the programmer, using semicolons to find all paths:

```
g(a,b).
g(a,d).
g(b,c).
g(d,e).
g(e,b).
g(c,f).

close(X,Y):-g(X,Y).
close(X,Y):-g(X,Z),close(Z,Y).
```

The binary database with functor "g" gives the complete definition of the directed graph in Figure 8.3 in terms of directed connectivity. For example, "g(a,d)" indicates there is an edge beginning at node "a" and ending at node "d." The *close* clauses will—if guided by semicolons after each answer—give the paths of any lengths connecting one node to another. Following is a trace of this program:

Copyright (c) 1993-1998 University of Amsterdam. All rights reserved.
For help, use ?- help(Topic). or ?- apropos(Word).
c:/pl/close.pl compiled, 0.00 sec, 1,256 bytes.

?- close(X,Y).

X = a
Y = b ;

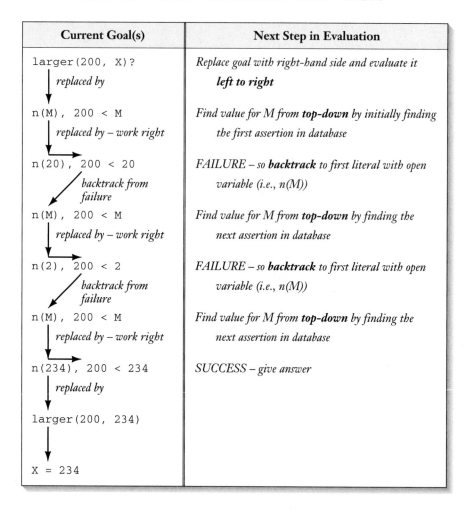

Current Goal(s)	Next Step in Evaluation
larger(200, X)?	*Replace goal with right-hand side and evaluate it*
↓ *replaced by*	**left to right**
n(M), 200 < M	*Find value for M from **top-down** by initially finding*
↓ *replaced by – work right*	*the first assertion in database*
n(20), 200 < 20	*FAILURE – so **backtrack** to first literal with open*
↙ *backtrack from failure*	*variable (i.e., n(M))*
n(M), 200 < M	*Find value for M from **top-down** by finding the*
↓ *replaced by – work right*	*next assertion in database*
n(2), 200 < 2	*FAILURE – so **backtrack** to first literal with open*
↙ *backtrack from failure*	*variable (i.e., n(M))*
n(M), 200 < M	*Find value for M from **top-down** by finding the*
↓ *replaced by – work right*	*next assertion in database*
n(234), 200 < 234	*SUCCESS – give answer*
↓ *replaced by*	
larger(200, 234)	
↓	
X = 234	

FIGURE 8.3 Modified and annotated trace.

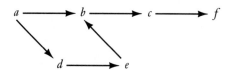

FIGURE 8.4 Simple directed graph.

X = a
Y = d ;

X = b
Y = c ;

X = d
Y = e ;

X = e
Y = b ;

X = c
Y = f ;

X = a
Y = c ;

X = a
Y = f ;

X = a
Y = e ;

X = a
Y = b ;

X = a
Y = c ;

X = a
Y = f ;

X = b
Y = f ;

X = d
Y = b ;

X = d
Y = c ;

X = d
Y = f ;

X = e

Y = c ;

X = e
Y = f ;

No
?-

Now here is an annotated and modified trace:

close(X,Y) replaced by g(X,Y) replaced by answer
close(a,b) user enters semicolon
close(X,Y) replaced by g(X,Y) replaced by answer
close(a,d) user enters semicolon
close(X,Y) replaced by g(X,Y) replaced by answer
close(b,c) user enters semicolon
close(X,Y) replaced by g(X,Y) replaced by answer
close(d,e) user enters semicolon
close(X,Y) replaced by g(X,Y) replaced by answer
close(e,b) user enters semicolon
close(X,Y) replaced by g(X,Y) replaced by answer
close (c,f) user enters semicolon

At this point the first close rule has been completely satisfied, and further evaluation results in failure, so that the process continues by evaluating the second close rule. From here on, we will present the trace in terms of a tree (Figure 8.5). As we proceed downward through the tree, literals are rewritten by their associated right-hand sides. For example, close(X,Y) is rewritten by either g(X,Y) or g(X,Z),close(Z,Y). The edges that ascend the tree indicate how a literal is resolved in terms of finding answers to its arguments. The final answer is given to the right of the graph in Figure 8.5.

Now when the user enters the semicolon, we first backtrack only on the close(Z,Y) portion of the initial right-hand side to the close(X,Y) query. The italicized portions of the tree in Figure 8.6 indicate items that are not different from the tree in Figure 8.5—that is, the point to which backtracking will go.

Notice that the execution strategy for trying to satisfy a literal begins at the top of a database and works downward, and from the left to the right within the right-hand side of a conditional assertion. Backtracking reverses the process until the first point where a literal's argument can take on new values, at which time the top-down/left-to-right execution strategy continues. Backtracking halts when all values for all variables for affected clauses have been found. The remaining execution graphs (that follow as the programmer enters semicolons) are left as an exercise for the reader.

DATA STRUCTURES

As mentioned earlier, Prolog has two primitive data structures: the assertional and the term. Examples of the assertional data structure have been shown. Any

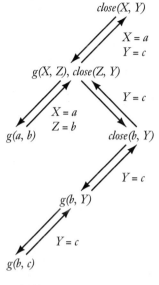

ANSWER: $X = a$, $Y = c$

FIGURE 8.5   Closure of node 'a' to 'c.'

fact added to a database is viewed as an assertional data structure—for example, the facts in the array structure seen earlier. We will now look at more advanced structures implemented using the assertional data structure, and in doing so will introduce two built-in Prolog procedures, the asserta/assertz and the retract.

The *asserta/assertz* allows a user to assert to the beginning or the end of "database." Databases are organized in Prolog by putting facts with the same functor and arity together in the Prolog workspace. The *retract* predicate allows the programmer to remove items from a database. To gain an understanding of these predicates, consider the Prolog assertional implementation of the stack and the queue.

First the stack:

```
push(X):-asserta(s(X)).
pop(X):-retract(s(X)).
```

We begin execution of these procedures by pushing three items, of differing types, onto the stack:

Welcome to SWI-Prolog (Version 3.2.0)
Copyright (c) 1993-1998 University of Amsterdam. All rights reserved.

For help, use ?- help(Topic). or ?- apropos(Word).

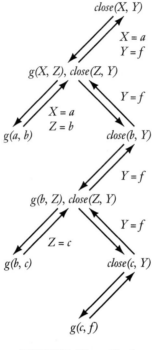

close(X, Y)

$X = a$
$Y = f$

g(X, Z), close(Z, Y)

$X = a$
$Z = b$

$Y = f$

g(a, b)

close(b, Y)

$Y = f$

g(b, Z), close(Z, Y)

$Z = c$

$Y = f$

g(b, c)

close(c, Y)

$Y = f$

g(c, f)

ANSWER: $X = a, Y = f$

FIGURE 8.6 Closure of node 'a' to 'f.'

c:/pl/stack.pl compiled, 0.00 sec, 988 bytes.

?- **push(a).**

Yes
?- **push(10).**

Yes
?- **push(4.3).**

Yes

At this point in the execution, we will ask the Prolog interpreter to "list" the items in any database with the functor name "*s*." This request allows us to see the state of the stack at the time the request is made:

?- **listing(s).**

s(4.3).

s(10).
s(a).

Notice the stack can consist of items of any type. Accordingly, we are able to build heterogeneous stacks that can logically grow to any size. Now we perform a pop, and list the state of the stack after the pop:

Yes
?- pop(X).

X = 4.3

Yes
?- listing(s).

s(10).
s(a).

Yes
?-

The code to perform the assertional implementation of a queue differs from the stack in only one way. Rather than performing an *asserta*, which places items at the beginning of a database, as the push does in the stack implementation, the *enq* performs an *assertz*, which places items at the end of a database:

enq(X):-assertz(q(X)).
deq(X):-retract(q(X)).

Now consider a trace of the execution of the queue code:

Welcome to SWI-Prolog (Version 3.2.0)
Copyright (c) 1993-1998 University of Amsterdam. All rights reserved.

For help, use ?- help(Topic). or ?- apropos(Word).

c:/pl/queue.pl compiled, 0.00 sec, 984 bytes.

?- enq(9).

Yes
?- enq(r).

Yes
?- enq(4.5).

Yes
?- enq(a(9)).

After performing these operations, we inquire about the state of the stack using, once again, the built-in *listing* predicate:

Yes
?- listing(q).

q(9).
q(r).
q(4.5).
q(a(9)).

Yes

Notice the end of the queue is at the bottom of the database (due to the assertz), and the beginning of the queue is at the top of the database. Thus, the following *deq* operation retracts the element of "q" containing the first item enqueued:

?- deq(X).

X = 9

Yes
?- listing(q).

q(r).
q(4.5).
q(a(9)).

Yes
?-

Returning to the stack, we will introduce Prolog's *term* data structure. The list in Prolog is a heterogeneous nonscalar structure contained in square brackets, for example, [1,2,*a*,3.67]. Prolog possesses a powerful operator that allows one to perform the car, cdr, and cons of LISP based on the instantiation of arguments. The general form of the operator is [Head | Tail]. Because of the power of the operator, one can implement the stack push and pop with the single rule,

push_pop(H,T,[H|T]).

Consider the following uses of the operator. In the first use, the first and second arguments are instantiated and the third operator acts as a LISP cons, which puts together a new list based on the first two arguments:

?- push_pop(4,[1,2,a,3.67],S).

S = [4, 1, 2, a, 3.67]

Yes

In the next use, the first and second arguments are uninstantiated and the third operator acts as a LISP car and cdr, which takes a list apart providing the list head (car) and the tail of the list (cdr):

?- push_pop(Top,Stack,[4,1,2,a,3.67]).

Top = 4
Stack = [1, 2, a, 3.67]

Yes
?-

SET OPERATIONS

In introducing the *set operations*, we will see further examples of the term data structure. The basic primitive of set operations is *set membership*. This fact will be clear when we define the more advanced set operations like union and intersection.

Membership tests in Prolog can be accomplished through an interaction of recursion and the list operator *[H | T]*.

member(X,[X | _]).
member(X,[_ | Y]) :- member(X,Y).

The basic intuition here is that if the head of the list matches the first argument, then the *member* rule succeeds, and the tail of the list is irrelevant (the underscore is an anonymous variable that matches anything). If the head does not match, the second rule responds and, through recursion, an attempt is made to see if the first argument matches an element of the tail of the list. If the first argument is not an element of the second argument, the empty list becomes the final version of the second argument, to which neither of the rules above can respond:

```
?- trace,member(3,[p,7,d,2,set,7.8]).
    Call: (  7) member(3, [p, 7, d, 2, set, 7.8]) ? creep
    Call: (  8) member(3, [7, d, 2, set, 7.8]) ? creep
    Call: (  9) member(3, [d, 2, set, 7.8]) ? creep
    Call: ( 10) member(3, [2, set, 7.8]) ? creep
    Call: ( 11) member(3, [set, 7.8]) ? creep
    Call: ( 12) member(3, [7.8]) ? creep
    Call: ( 13) member(3, []) ? creep
    Fail: ( 13) member(3, []) ? creep
    Redo: ( 12) member(3, [7.8]) ? creep
    Call: ( 13) member(3, []) ? creep
    Fail: ( 13) member(3, []) ? creep
    Fail: ( 12) member(3, [7.8]) ? creep
    Redo: ( 11) member(3, [set, 7.8]) ? creep
```

```
Call: ( 12) member(3, [7.8]) ? creep
Call: ( 13) member(3, []) ? creep
Fail: ( 13) member(3, []) ? creep
        :
```

No
[debug] ?-

Of course, subset and the other set operations are defined based on the set-membership primitive:

```
subset([A|X],Y) :- member(A,Y),subset(X,Y).
subset([ ],Y).
```

```
diff([ ],Y,[ ]).
diff(X,[ ],X).
diff([X|R],Y,[X|Z]) :- not(member(X,Y)),diff(R,Y,Z).
diff([X|R],Y,Z) :- diff(R,Y,Z).
```

```
intersection([ ],X,[ ]).
intersection([X|R],Y,[X|Z]) :- member(X,Y),intersection(R,Y,Z).
intersection([X|R],Y,Z) :- intersection(R,Y,Z).
```

```
union([ ],X,X).
union([X|R],Y,Z) :- member(X,Y),union(R,Y,Z).
union([X|R],Y,[X|Z]) :- union(R,Y,Z).
```

The definitions required to find the *cardinality* of a set needs explanation, as follows:

```
card(X,[ ],X).
card(X,[H|R],Y):- Z is X+1,card(Z,R,Y).
```

The rule is invoked with a goal like "card(0,[some_list],N)." If the list is empty, the first rule responds and returns 0 for N. If nonempty, the list is recursively decomposed, one item at a time, and the running count contained in X is incremented until the empty list is obtained and the current count is returned:

?- trace,card(0,[1,2,d,a,3],N).
```
    Call: (  8) card(0, [1, 2, d, a, 3], _G278) ? creep
    Call: (  9) _L134 is 0+1 ? creep
    Exit: (  9) 1 is 0+1 ? creep
    Call: (  9) card(1, [2, d, a, 3], _G278) ? creep
    Call: ( 10) _L148 is 1+1 ? creep
    Exit: ( 10) 2 is 1+1 ? creep
    Call: ( 10) card(2, [d, a, 3], _G278) ? creep
    Call: ( 11) _L162 is 2+1 ? creep
    Exit: ( 11) 3 is 2+1 ? creep
    Call: ( 11) card(3, [a, 3], _G278) ? creep
```

Call: (12) _L176 is 3+1 ? creep
Exit: (12) 4 is 3+1 ? creep
Call: (12) card(4, [3], _G278) ? creep
Call: (13) _L190 is 4+1 ? creep
Exit: (13) 5 is 4+1 ? creep
Call: (13) card(5, [ ], _G278) ? creep
Exit: (13) card(5, [ ], 5) ? creep
Exit: (12) card(4, [3], 5) ? creep
Exit: (11) card(3, [a, 3], 5) ? creep
Exit: (10) card(2, [d, a, 3], 5) ? creep
Exit: (9) card(1, [2, d, a, 3], 5) ? creep
Exit: (8) card(0, [1, 2, d, a, 3], 5) ? creep

N = 5

Yes
[debug] ?-

LANGUAGE CONSTRUCTS

Examples of Prolog's versions of all of the standard language constructs have been introduced with the exception of the *input/output* constructs. First, let us review the constructs already seen. The assignment and arithmetic constructs can be seen in the preceding cardinality example. In general, the assignment statement in Prolog is

identifier is **arithmetic_expression**

The sequence and selection constructs are implemented by the top-down/left-to-right execution strategy that is built into Prolog. A sequence of actions is provided in the body of a rule, which will be evaluated from left to right:

predicate :- *s1, s2, · · · , sn*.

The predicates "*s1, s2, · · · , sn*" will serve as goals and will be evaluated in the order in which they occur.

Selective structures can be composed in a number of ways, based on Prolog's effort to try to satisfy a goal from the top of the database to the bottom. The simplest decision construct one can implement in Prolog is a form of the CASE statement. Consider an interpreter to evaluate prefix expressions in Prolog. This code is given in contrast to the Chapter 4 interpreter for evaluating infix expressions.

```
e(N,N):-number(N).
e(+(X,Y),N):-e(X,X1),e(Y,Y1),N is X1+Y1.
e(*(X,Y),N):-e(X,X1),e(Y,Y1),N is X1*Y1.
e(-(X,Y),N):-e(X,X1),e(Y,Y1),N is X1-Y1.
e(/(X,Y),N):-e(X,X1),e(Y,Y1),N is X1/Y1.
```

The procedures, *e*, provide for the evaluation of an expression. Prolog's pattern-matching capability is the basis for the selections. If the argument is a number, the first *e* procedure responds by returning that number. The remaining procedures simply indicate that given a prefix arithmetic expression, select the matching operator (i.e., +, −, *, and /) find the value of the first term of the expression (*X*), the value of the second term (*Y*)—both obtained through recursive calls to *e*—and then apply the matched operator to the resulting values. Consider the trace associated with the evaluation of the expression: *(+(4,5),+(5,7)):

?- trace,e(*(+(4,5),+(5,7)),X).
```
    Call: (   7) e( (4+5)* (5+7), _G397) ? creep
    Call: (   8) number( (4+5)* (5+7)) ? creep
    Fail: (   8) number( (4+5)* (5+7)) ? creep
    Redo: (   7) e( (4+5)* (5+7), _G397) ? creep
    Call: (   8) e(4+5, _L147) ? creep
    Call: (   9) number(4+5) ? creep
    Fail: (   9) number(4+5) ? creep
    Redo: (   8) e(4+5, _L147) ? creep
    Call: (   9) e(4, _L162) ? creep
    Call: ( 10) number(4) ? creep
    Exit: ( 10) number(4) ? creep
    Exit: (   9) e(4, 4) ? creep
    Call: (   9) e(5, _L163) ? creep
    Call: ( 10) number(5) ? creep
    Exit: ( 10) number(5) ? creep
    Exit: (   9) e(5, 5) ? creep
    Call: (   9) _L147 is 4+5 ? creep
    Exit: (   9) 9 is 4+5 ? creep
    Exit: (   8) e(4+5, 9) ? creep
    Call: (   8) e(5+7, _L148) ? creep
    Call: (   9) number(5+7) ? creep
    Fail: (   9) number(5+7) ? creep
    Redo: (   8) e(5+7, _L148) ? creep
    Call: (   9) e(5, _L162) ? creep
    Call: ( 10) number(5) ? creep
    Exit: ( 10) number(5) ? creep
    Exit: (   9) e(5, 5) ? creep
    Call: (   9) e(7, _L163) ? creep
    Call: ( 10) number(7) ? creep
    Exit: ( 10) number(7) ? creep
    Exit: (   9) e(7, 7) ? creep
    Call: (   9) _L148 is 5+7 ? creep
    Exit: (   9) 12 is 5+7 ? creep
    Exit: (   8) e(5+7, 12) ? creep
    Call: (   8) _G397 is 9*12 ? creep
    Exit: (   8) 108 is 9*12 ? creep
```

Exit: (7) e((4+5)* (5+7), 108) ? creep

X = 108

Yes
[debug] ?-

This interpreter is only one example of the expressiveness and simplicity of Prolog. Prolog is easy to use to develop ideas and concepts, and the author has used Prolog in a wide variety of applications, including the development of language interpreters and software modeling tools.

The IF-THEN-ELSE structure is better suited for situations where a selection is based on a range of values. For example, if you wished to know a proper word to describe the ambient temperature, you might use the following IF-THEN-ELSE type of structure:

temp(T,freezing)	:- T =< 32.
temp(T,cold)	:- T > 32, T =< 45.
temp(T,cool)	:- T > 45, T =< 60.
temp(T,mild)	:- T > 60, T =< 80.
temp(T,warm)	:- T > 80, T =< 89.
temp(T,hot)	:- T > 89, T =< 99.
temp(T,scorching)	:- T > 99.

In the procedural paradigm there are two types of loop structures: the counting and the conditional loop. The *counting loop* is easily established in Prolog as a non–tail recursive procedure set. Consider the following counting loop to compute *factorial* in Pascal:

```
f:=1;
for i:=n down to 1 do
        f:=f * i;
```

The same purpose is accomplished in Prolog with the following procedure set:

```
fact(0,1).
fact(A—B,F):-N is A—B,fact(N,F).
fact(N,F):-fact(N-1,N1),F is N * N1.
```

This example demonstrates selection based on the value of the first argument (i.e., zero or nonzero in the first and third procedures) or the form of the argument. The middle procedure handles the subtraction based on matching two arguments with the minus sign between them. The first and third procedures handle the nonrecursive and recursive definitions. The *fact* procedure set is a non–tail recursive, recursive definition. That is, the final answer is not obtained at the lowest recursive point, but is obtained in steps as returns from the recursive calls occur. This can be seen in the following trace:

?- trace,fact(4,F).
    Call: (7) fact(4, _G190) ? creep

```
Call: (   8) fact(4-1, _L132) ? creep
Call: (   9) _L146 is 4-1 ? creep
Exit: (   9) 3 is 4-1 ? creep
Call: (   9) fact(3, _L132) ? creep
Call: ( 10) fact(3-1, _L158) ? creep
Call: ( 11) _L172 is 3-1 ? creep
Exit: ( 11) 2 is 3-1 ? creep
Call: ( 11) fact(2, _L158) ? creep
Call: ( 12) fact(2-1, _L184) ? creep
Call: ( 13) _L198 is 2-1 ? creep
Exit: ( 13) 1 is 2-1 ? creep
Call: ( 13) fact(1, _L184) ? creep
Call: ( 14) fact(1-1, _L210) ? creep
Call: ( 15) _L224 is 1-1 ? creep
Exit: ( 15) 0 is 1-1 ? creep
Call: ( 15) fact(0, _L210) ? creep
Exit: ( 15) fact(0, 1) ? creep
Exit: ( 14) fact(1-1, 1) ? creep
Call: ( 14) _L184 is 1*1 ? creep
Exit: ( 14) 1 is 1*1 ? creep
Exit: ( 13) fact(1, 1) ? creep
Exit: ( 12) fact(2-1, 1) ? creep
Call: ( 12) _L158 is 2*1 ? creep
Exit: ( 12) 2 is 2*1 ? creep
Exit: ( 11) fact(2, 2) ? creep
Exit: ( 10) fact(3-1, 2) ? creep
Call: ( 10) _L132 is 3*2 ? creep
Exit: ( 10) 6 is 3*2 ? creep
Exit: (   9) fact(3, 6) ? creep
Exit: (   8) fact(4-1, 6) ? creep
Call: (   8) _G190 is 4*6 ? creep
Exit: (   8) 24 is 4*6 ? creep
Exit: (   7) fact(4, 24) ? creep
```

F = 24

The following *conditional loop* is set up as a tail recursive procedure set in Prolog. Consider the following Pascal conditional loop implementing Euclid's *greatest common divisor* algorithm. Given two values greater than zero, this algorithm takes the two values and iteratively subtracts the lesser of the two values from the greater until they are equal. They are equal when the final subtraction results in a zero:

```
while u <> 0 do
        begin
        if u < v then
                begin
```

```
                         t:=u;
                         u:=v;
                         v:=t
                         end
            u:=u-v
           end;
gcd:=v;
```

Assuming that *U* and *V* have initial values greater than zero, the Prolog version of the procedure is

```
gcd(0,V,V).
gcd(U,V,D):−U < V,U1 is V−U,gcd(U1,U,D).
gcd(U,V,D):−U1 is U−V,gcd(U1,V,D).
```

As in all recursive procedures, the test for the nonrecursive point occurs first. If it succeeds (when the first argument has become zero), the answer is contained in the variable *V*. If, on the other hand, the test fails, the nonrecursive points containing the logic for the IF-THEN are implemented.

Now consider the *Fibonacci sequence program* in Prolog. The first rule, "fib," with no arguments, contains examples of the input commands in Prolog. The "print" allows one to print text and the values associated with variables in the workspace of the Prolog session. The "nl" command causes the line to advance to a new line. The "read" allows the user to input a value that instantiates the argument.

Most versions of Prolog require the user to place a period after the entered value. Once the input/output is performed, the "fib" procedures requiring arguments are invoked, with a 0 and 1 as initial values in the sequence and *U* instantiated with an upper bound—the number up to which the sequence is computed:

```
fib:-print('enter upper bound followed by a period: '),
      nl,read(U),nl,print('the sequence follows: '),nl,fib(0,1,U).

fib(X,Y,U):− Y > U,print(X),nl.
fib(X,Y,U):− Y1 is X + Y,print(X),nl,fib(Y,Y1,U).
```

Once initiated with the goal "fib," the session begins by entering an upper bound of 40,000,000 in the following example. From there the values are computed and printed:

```
?- fib.
'enter upper bound followed by a period:'
l: 40000000.

'the sequence follows:'
0
1
1
```

```
2
3
5
8
13
21
34
55
89
144
233
377
610
987
1597
2584
4181
6765
10946
17711
28657
46368
75025
121393
196418
317811
514229
832040
1346269
2178309
3524578
5702887
9227465
14930352
24157817
39088169

Yes
?-
```

CONCLUSION

Prolog is a very expressive language, quite good for prototyping formally defined concepts, including new languages and software, hardware, and database models. The experiments in this chapter are meant to demonstrate its expressiveness and versatility.

■ ■

REFERENCES

Alan Davis. *The Universal Computer: The Road from Leibniz to Turing.* New York: W.W. Norton and Company, 2000.

J. A. Robinson. "A machine-oriented logic based on the resolution principle." *Journal of the ACM* 12, no. 1 (1965):23–41.

Download: A version of Prolog can be obtained at: http://www.swi.psy.uva.nl/projects/SWI-Prolog/

QUESTIONS AND EXERCISES

1. Explain the duplicate answers in the session involving the *close(X,Y)* query.

2. With which feature of Prolog does one accomplish the sequence structure, the selective or the iterative? As an example, show how each of the following Pascal code segments would be implemented in Prolog:

   a. $s:= a+b;\ t:= c+d;\ r:= s/t;$
   b. if $x > m$ then $m:=x;$
   c. $s:=0;$ for $i:=1$ to 10 do $s:=s+i;$

3. Implement a binary tree as an assertional structure and then provide the Prolog code to perform an inorder traversal of the tree.

4. Do the same for a term data structure.

5. Extend the prefix interpreter to allow for WHILE expressions such as $(:=(x,10),while(<(x,5),(:=(x,-(x,1)))))$.

6. Define, in Prolog, set union and intersection in terms of set difference.

7. Write the Prolog code to sort an assertional list in ascending order.

8. Write the Prolog code to sort a term list in ascending order.

9. Write an equivalent piece of Prolog code for the following:

```
         READ(5,10) N
   10    FORMAT(I2)
         DO 20 I=1,N
         READ(5,10) A(I)
   20    CONTINUE
         S=0
         DO 30 I=1,N
         S=S+A(I)
   30    CONTINUE
         AVE = S / N
```

10. Following is the code for a Universal Turing Machine that is implemented as two stacks. Included in the code is input/output code to allow the user to trace the execution of a given machine:

```
/* The Universal Turing Machine                                          */

push(X,S,[X|S]).
pop(X,S,[X|S]).


/* Code to convert a tape—view as a list—to two stacks and a value for the
current position of the tape head                                        */

go:-retract(tape(L)),retract(head(I)),linit(1,I,L,[ ], Tape,Left),pop(X,Tape2,Tape),
    asserta(head(X)),reverse(Tape2,Tape3),rinit([ ],Right,Tape3),
    asserta(right(Right)),asserta(left(Left)).

linit(N,N,Tape,Left,Tape,Left).
linit(I,N,[H|Tape],Left,Tape2,Left2):-I1 is I + 1,
    linit(I1,N,Tape,[H|Left],Tape2,Left2).

rinit(R,R,[]).
rinit(R1,R2,[H|Tape]):-rinit([H|R1],R2,Tape).


/* Code to convert the two stacks and the tape head back to a single list for
output                                                                    */

recon:-retract(left(L)),retract(right(R)),retract(head(H)),doleft(1,N,L,T1),
    asserta(head(N)),reverse(T1,T2),append(T2,[H],T3),doright(R,T3,T4),
    asserta(tape(T4)).

doleft(N,N,[ ],[ ]).
doleft(I,N,[H|L],[H|T]):-I1 is I + 1,doleft(I1,N,L,T).

doright([ ],T,T).
doright([H|Right],T,Tape):-append(T,[H],T2),doright(Right,T2,Tape).

/* Code move left or right on the tape                                    */


movel(H):-retract(head(_)),retract(right(R)),push(H,R,R1),asserta(right(R1)),
    retract(left(L)),pop(H1,L1,L),asserta(head(H1)),asserta(left(L1)).

mover(H):-retract(head(_)),retract(left(L)),push(H,L,L1),asserta(left(L1)),
    retract(right(R)),pop(H1,R1,R),asserta(head(H1)),asserta(right(R1)).
```

```
/*        Code to run the machine                              */

turing:−listing(tape),head(X),spacing(X),nl,doit(i).

spacing(X):−write(' '),N is 3 * X,place(0,N).

place(N,N):−write('^'),nl.
place(I,N):−write(' '),I1 is I + 1,place(I1,N).

doit(f).
doit(S):−go,head(H),m(S,H,R,Direction,S1),nl,print('state= '),print(S),
    print(' head= '),print(H),print(' replace= '),print(R),print(' direction= '),
    print(Direction),print(' new state= '),print(S1),nl,nl,recon,listing(tape),
    head(X),spacing(X),get(_),nl,doit(S1).


/*        A Turing Machine to reverse the elements of a string    */

tape([n,n,n,n,n,n,n,d,1,0,1,1,0,f]).
head(8).

m(i,d,d,right,i):−mover(d).
m(i,0,d,left,z):−movel(d).
m(i,1,d,left,o):−movel(d).

m(z,d,d,left,z):−movel(d).
m(z,0,0,left,z):−movel(0).
m(z,1,1,left,z):−movel(1).
m(z,n,0,right,a):−mover(0).

m(o,d,d,left,o):−movel(d).
m(o,0,0,left,o):−movel(0).
m(o,1,1,left,o):−movel(1).
m(o,n,1,right,a):−mover(1).

m(a,0,0,right,a):−mover(0).
m(a,1,1,right,a):−mover(1).
m(a,d,d,right,b):−mover(d).

m(b,0,d,left,z):−movel(d).
m(b,1,d,left,o):−movel(d).
m(b,d,d,left,b):−mover(d).
m(b,f,f,left,c):−movel(f).

m(c,0,0,left,c):−movel(0).
m(c,1,1,left,c):−movel(1).
```

m(c,d,d,left,c):−movel(d).
m(c,n,d,none,f).

m(f,d,d,none,f).

Run the machine given in order to become acquainted with what is involved in providing a Turing Machine. Then replace the machine with one that will add two binary numbers.

9

EXPERIMENTING WITH LANGUAGES

Computer science researchers and practitioners have an obligation to experiment with the languages they study and use. This text aims to encourage such experimentation by demonstrating how to empirically study a language in terms of the features it shares with other languages and the features unique to it. All languages have nuances and subtleties that should be fully explored as a part of studying and applying them. Just as an athlete practices their sport to the point that the mechanics of any play become second nature, allowing them to focus on winning the game, so software developers should practice with their languages until they can be used with minimal conscious effort, allowing them to focus on solving a problem.

Language designers spend a great deal of time developing the theoretical foundations for their languages. They need to spend equal time empirically studying the language so as to make the necessary modifications. Experimentation will usually reveal ways that any language can be improved.

Even in the simple experiments one conducts to learn a language, the *theory-experiment* interactions seen in other sciences are evident. For example, recall the experiment suggested in Chapter 5 to discover when the test for a FOR loop is done, at the beginning of the loop body or at the end.

```
flag:=false;
for i:=2 to 1 do
    flag:=true;
```

```
if flag then
        writeln('for-loop test done at the end of the loop')
else
        writeln('for-loop test done at the beginning of the loop');
```

Prior to executing the experiment, one might develop an hypothesis about where the test should occur. Then the experiment is designed and instrumented to test the hypothesis.

Another good example can be seen in the Prolog term-based stack. Suppose the scientist develops the standard definition of the stack:

```
push(X,S,[X|S]).
pop([X|S],S).
top([X|S],X).
```

The stack operations would be employed in a manner similar to that seen in the following trace:

```
?− push(3,[s,t,a,c,k],S).
```

S = [3, s, t, a, c, k]

Yes
```
?− pop([3,s,t,a,c,k],S).
```

S = [s, t, a, c, k]

Yes
```
?− top([s,t,a,c,k],T).
```

T = s

Yes

Studying the preceding top, pop, and push definitions, you can see that the entire set of operations can be reduced to exactly one, seemingly elegant rule:

```
ptp(X,S,[X|S]).
```

Just as is done with the standard definitions, the instantiation of arguments when using the *ptp* operation determines its functionality:

```
?− ptp(X,S,[s,t,a,c,k]).
```

X = s
S = [t, a, c, k]

Yes
```
?− ptp(3,[s,t,a,c,k],S).
```

S = [3, s, t, a, c, k]

Yes
?−

Through the theory-experiment exchange, one is able to discover the expressiveness of languages as well as more elegant ways in which to express problem solutions. Other types of experiments might lead to more efficient problem solutions in terms of the amount of execution time or memory required. In other words, improved algorithms represent the result of the *theoretical* efforts, whereas tests to determine functionality or efficiency represent *experimental* work.

In the next chapter, you will find an overview of the design of the author's language, *SequenceL*. This language is the result of a decade of effort. What the reader does not see are the formal definitions underlying the language or the series of versions of the language: several sets of formal definitions providing the "language theory" and the several prototype interpreters that have been employed in order to experiment with and study the language.

10

DESIGN OF SEQUENCEL:
A CASE STUDY

The effort to develop the SequenceL language was influenced at different points by the language paradigms presented in this book. SequenceL provides an approach to computing in which the parallelisms in a problem solution can be automatically generated. Other approaches to declarative parallel programming, including pH [Nikhil], NESL, Scampi, and Eden [Hammond], have resulted in languages that do not require the programmer to provide the full extent of specification and guidance in developing a parallel problem solution. In these languages, the programmer often specifies *what* is to be performed in parallel, but need not specify *how* the parallelisms are to be implemented.

SequenceL possesses a semantic that permits the problem solver to specify a simple problem solution. Parallelisms in SequenceL are implicit, so much (if not all) of the detail in specifying parallel problem solutions—even the specification of what is to be performed in parallel—is stripped away. The focus of the SequenceL research has been to remove detail, so that the problem solver ends up specifying only a definition of what is to be solved, leaving the *how* of the problem solution to the language interpreter. And in SequenceL the specification of iterative and parallel control structures is considered to be part of the *how* of problem solution.

A STARTING POINT:
PROCEDURAL PROGRAMMING

Rather than trying to enter an established area of language research, the effort to develop SequenceL began with a simple, basic question that lies at the heart of computer science: to what extent can we strip away nonessential detail in problem-solving? Can we discover an abstraction that is more fundamental and primitive than current language abstractions? Clearly, the Turing Machine is the most primitive problem-solving abstraction. Thus, the Turing Machine is a lower bound. The motivation in designing SequenceL was to have a more expressive language than that provided for the Turing Machine—a language that people would see as intuitive language, one that would provide straightforward approaches to problem solving.

We hoped for a language that would specify the *what* of a problem solution and not force the problem solver to determine *how* the problem would be solved. Obviously, the upper bound on our language goal was represented by high-level specification languages. The problem with these languages is the fact that they are often inherently ambiguous. That is, a problem definition in a very high-level language is often open to multiple, nonequivalent interpretations. [Cooke, 1996]

Thus, the stage was set: our goal was to develop a fundamental language that was more intuitive than a Turing Machine, and that allowed one to identify precisely the *what* of a problem solution. Two questions motivating the research were (1) what constitutes the *what* of a problem solution, and (2) can we begin at the procedural programming level and from that point strip away nonessential detail? If so, would we arrive at an unambiguous language for describing the *what* of the problem?

The first question can be rephrased this way: *What is the product of the programmer?* Clearly, the product is not the program, but rather the data product that is produced by the program. A data product is a generalized data structure. A generalized data structure is a report, a screen display, instrument readings on an aircraft, an internal data structure, and so on. Information contained in a data structure has a complexity that is associated with the algorithm required to produce the data structure.

Loops and recursive control structures are a focal point of the complexity one finds in producing a data product. The resulting data structures themselves possess recursive features that mirror the control structures employed in producing them. For example, we can envision a simple student record as follows:

Student Name:	Alan Turing
Student Address:	London
:	
Student Major:	Mathematics
Grades:	

Math 101	A
Math 102	A
:	:
Physics	A

The section of grades in the student record is repeated and produced by an iterative or recursive control structure algorithmically. Just as these control structures are the basis for determining the complexity of an algorithm—an indicator of the performance of the algorithm—they are also the areas of a program where the programmer spends the majority of effort in coding and testing. In other words, the iterative and recursive parts of a problem solution also dominate the productivity measures of the programmer.

Software engineers have long realized that the construction of loops is complex and costly. [Mills] Bishop noted that "Since Pratt's paper on the design of loop control structures was published more than a decade ago, there has been continued interest in the need to provide better language features for iteration." The fact that the data product is implied by the control structures is the heart of the complexity facing the programmer. *The hard part of programming is making the implied data product appear in the programmer's mind when reading or writing the explicit control structures that produce or process the data product.* [Cooke, 2000]

Given this view, the second question deals with what can be stripped away from a procedural language so that only the ability to state precise definitions of a data product remains. Furthermore, can we develop this language in a way that it remains Turing-computable?

First, recall the discussion in Chapter 2 concerned with the famous proof by Böhm and Jacopini. That proof showed that in terms of control structures, the ability to establish sequences of statements and the WHILE loop construct are all that is necessary to solve any solvable problem. Now recall that John McCarthy proved that LISP is Turing-computable. Thus, in terms of data structures, all one needs in order to solve a problem is the ability to establish lists and recursively nested lists. In SequenceL these lists are sequences.

A further simplification was to disallow atoms in SequenceL. Singleton sequences (i.e., sequences containing single values) supplant the need for atoms. With these questions resolved, the starting point for the definition of SequenceL is established. We begin with a language possessing the ability to form blocks of statements that can be controlled only with the WHILE construct and that interacts with one data structure—the list, or the sequence.

Study of this language led us to the following observations. First, loops always take an input and always produce an output, and typically one or the other is a nonscalar structure (i.e., a list). Clearly, the arguments and results of loops can be viewed as external files (which are also lists or sequences), so that input/output can be viewed as implicit to the operation of the loops. The second observation is that in order to specify a data product, one must be able to describe the following loop behaviors precisely [Cooke, 1991]:

- $S \rightarrow S$: Loops that take scalars (i.e., atoms) and produce as a result a scalar.
- $S \rightarrow N$: Loops that take scalars and produce as a result a nonscalar.

- $N \to S$: Loops that take a nonscalar and produce as a result a scalar.
- $N \to N$: Loops that take a nonscalar and produce as a result a nonscalar.

Examples of each type of loop follow:

- $S \to S$: *N*-Factorial.
- $S \to N$: Fibonacci numbers.
- $N \to S$: The sum of a list of numbers.
- $N \to N$: Sorting a list.

To specify a data product, new language constructs capable of expressing each of these loop behaviors are needed. SequenceL possesses such constructs. They are regular, irregular, and generative. Additionally SequenceL possesses a modified data-flow execution strategy. In the following sections each of the constructs is discussed, along with the manner in which they interact with the execution strategy.

REGULAR CONSTRUCT: *N → S*

The *regular construct* applies an operator to corresponding elements of normalized operand sequences and implements the loop behavior: $N \to S$. This construct provides for all forms of arithmetic processing as demonstrated in the following examples, which exhibit binary arithmetic, summation, and advanced forms of arithmetic processing.

USER SPECIFIES		SEQUENCEL SIMPLIFICATIONS		ANSWERS
Two singletons:				
+([4,4])	=	[4+4]	=	[8]
Nonscalar:				
+([4,4,3,2])	=	[4+4+3+2]	=	[13]
Nested nonscalars:				
+([[10,30,40],[4,6,7]])	=	[10+4,30+6,40+7]	=	[14,36,47]

In all cases these operations execute in a uniform way: the operator is applied to corresponding elements of the *normalized* operand sequences. Normalization affects nested operands that are of varying levels of nesting or cardinalities. Thus, in the examples, normalization has no effect.

EXAMPLES OF NORMALIZATION

The following example consists of two sequences that differ only in cardinality:

$$[[2,3,4,5,6],[10]] =_{normalize} [[2,3,4,5,6], [10, 10, 10, 10, 10]]$$

Now consider an example that demonstrates the effect of normalization when the operands differ in levels of nesting as well as cardinality. The levels of nesting are the basis of a sequence's *dimension*. The first component of the sequence is a two-dimensional structure ([[2,3],[4,5]]), the second contains a three-dimensional structure ([[[1,2],[3,4]], · · ·]), and the final structure is one-dimensional ([10,11]). The component sequences must also be normalized in terms of cardinality, since there is a three-element sequence among several two-element sequences:

$$
\begin{aligned}
&[\\
&\quad [[2,3],[4,5]], \\
&\quad [[[1,2],[3,4]],[5,6,7]], \\
&\quad [10,11] \\
&\qquad\qquad] \\
=_{\text{normalize}} &[\\
&\quad [[[2,3,2],[4,5,4]],[[2,3,2],[4,5,4]]], \\
&\quad [[[1,2,1],[3,4,3]],[[5,6,7],[5,6,7]]], \\
&\quad [[[10,11,10],[10,11,10]],[[10,11,10],[10,11,10]]] \\
&\qquad\qquad]
\end{aligned}
$$

Operands are normalized in terms of size and levels of nesting prior to carrying out the assigned operation. In terms of cardinality or nesting differences, the elements of the smaller operands are repeated in the order they occur until the smaller operand is equal in size to the largest operand.

$$
\begin{aligned}
*([[10,20,30,40,50],[2]]) \quad &=_{\text{normalize}} \\
*([[10,20,30,40,50],[2,2,2,2,2]]) & \\
&=_{\text{math}} \quad [20,40,60,80,100]
\end{aligned}
$$

- -

GENERATIVE CONSTRUCT: $S \rightarrow N$

The *generative construct* allows for the expansion of sequences implementing the $S \rightarrow N$ loop behavior. The simple form expands integers within some bounds. The complex version expands values within bounds when the values satisfy a constraining formula:

SIMPLE
gen([1, · · ·,5]) = [1,2,3,4,5]

COMPLEX
[0,1, · · ·,+([p(p(next)),p(next)]), · · ·,5] =
[0,1,1,2,3,5]
where p stands for **predecessor**

Generative terms can be nested. For example, let $m = 4$ and $n = 21$. The following term is evaluated as shown:

gen([[1, · · · , m], · · · , [n−m+[1], · · · , n]]) =
gen([[1, · · · , 4], · · · , [18, · · · , 21]]) =
gen([[1,2,3,4], · · · , [18,19,20,21]]) =

[[1,2,3,4],[2,3,4,5],[3,4,5,6],
         [4,5,6,7],[5,6,7,8],[6,7,8,9],
         [7,8,9,10],[8,9,10,11],[9,10,11,12],
         [10,11,12,13],[11,12,13,14],[12,13,14,15],
         [13,14,15,16],[14,15,16,17],[15,16,17,18],
         [16,17,18,19],[17,18,19,20],[18,19,20,21]   ]

IRREGULAR CONSTRUCT: $S \to S$ AND $N \to N$

The *irregular construct* applies an operator selectively, based on a WHEN clause. The irregular construct can actually specify any of the loop behaviors. When the condition of the WHEN clause is true, the corresponding operator is applied:

[s_1 **when** <>(mod([s_1,2]),0) **else** []   ]

In this case a null operation is specified: s_1 is produced when it contains an odd number; otherwise, an empty sequence is produced. This example demonstrates the $S \to S$ loop behavior. The next example returns a sequence if and only if it is in ascending sorted order. When it does, the code exemplifies the $N \to N$ loop behavior:

[list **when and**(<(list)) **else** []   ]

Consider the following trace of the code, when list = [2,3,4,5,6]:

[2,3,4,5,6] **when and**(<([2,3,4,5,6])) **else** []

First the condition is tested. A relational operator, like the less-than operator here, distributes among the corresponding elements of the operand sequences much the way arithmetic operators distribute under the regular construct:

[2,3,4,5,6] **when and**([2<3<4<5<6]) **else** []

The result is a sequence of Boolean (i.e., true or false) values:

[2,3,4,5,6] **when and**([true,true,true,true]) **else** []

Now an AND operator applies to corresponding elements of its operand sequence to reduce to a single Boolean value:

[2,3,4,5,6] **when** [true **and** true **and** true **and** true] **else** [] =
[2,3,4,5,6] **when** true **else** [] =
[2,3,4,5,6]

One should have noticed by now that SequenceL operators operate only on sequences and produce as results only sequences. Sometimes the sequences are singletons, for example, +([[2],[2]]) = [4]. User-defined functions satisfy the same constraint—they operate only on sequences and produce only sequences. As will be seen, this is an important simplifying feature of SequenceL.

The ability to selectively apply operators to the elements of nonsingleton sequences requires the specification of a complete function. SequenceL functions are built up using the regular, irregular, and generative constructs. These constructs can be combined in any manner, and the sequences they produce can be used as operands or subscripts to operands. Sequences and functions can both serve as results of a function's execution.

The next question to be answered is how do the SequenceL functions execute? The functions follow a modified version of a data-flow execution strategy.

CONSUME-SIMPLIFY-PRODUCE EXECUTION STRATEGY

Data flow is the underlying feature of SequenceL's execution strategy. In the data-flow approach to execution, operations can execute as soon as the data they require to complete execution are available. For example, this sequence of statements,

$n := y2 - y1;$
$d := x2 - x1$
$slope := n \,/\, d;$

will execute in the order they appear in a procedural language as indicated in the control-flow Petri net in Figure 10.1. A *Petri net* is an abstraction of flow characteristics through a graph. It is made up of places, tokens, transitions, in-degree, and out-degree information. The in- and out-degree information exists between transitions and places. *Places* are the circles in the graph. *Transitions* are the bars that are perpendicular to the edges of the graph. In the net in Figure 10.1, transitions are labeled by the assignment statements from the sequence of code under analysis. The token is the darkened circle in the initial place. Execution of a network moves the token through the places based upon the in- and out-degree of the transitions and places and a determination of the transitions that are ready to *fire*. A transition is ready to fire if and only if all incoming places are occupied by at least one token. Thus, in a control-flow representation of a program, the token represents the state information after one statement has executed and prior to the execution of the next.

Follow the execution of the control-flow graph in Figure 10.2. A predictably sequential flow is observed in this example. Based on a definition/reference analysis on the variables involved in the assignment statements, one can establish a data-flow graph as shown in Figure 10.3. However, the control-flow elements of the network (namely the control-flow places from the original net) force a sequential flow through the transitions. Subtracting out the control-flow places, one obtains the data-flow Petri net wherein data parallelisms are evident (Figure 10.4). The computations for the numerator and denominator can be computed in parallel if their respective arguments are available. There is a data-flow dependency between the numerator and denominator computation and the slope definition.

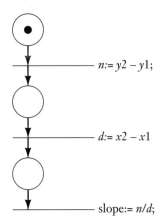

$n := y2 - y1;$

$d := x2 - x1$

slope $:= n/d;$

FIGURE 10.1   Control-flow Petri net.

In SequenceL, the data flow is between functions and operators and their arguments. Formally, there is a tableau that serves as an abstraction of a shared memory and is the workspace of a SequenceL program. In the tableau one finds references to SequenceL functions intermixed with sequences containing data. For example, consider the following function definitions:

function $p(X)$ = {plus(X)}
function $m(L)$ = {mul(L) }

Assume the following tableau with sequences of numbers behind the references to the function "m," and a not-yet-computed sequence, [m, [2, 2], m, [4, 3], m, [6, 1]], behind the function "p:"

initial tableau = [p, [m, [2, 2], m, [4, 3], m, [6, 1]]]

Due to the nesting of sequences, one can view the data-flow structure as follows:

initial tableau = [p, ← [m, ← [2, 2], m, ← [4, 3], m, ← [6, 1]]]

Figure 10.5 shows an equivalent data-flow Petri net.

What follows is a trace of the specified computation employing the functions in Figure 10.5. The trace is produced by a new SequenceL interpreter that was completed during the summer of 2001. In the discussion of the trace, we will focus on the execution strategy.

TRACE OF EXECUTION

In this section boxes show trace information produced by the SequenceL interpreter—that is, information not specified by the programmer. All SequenceL

State 1:

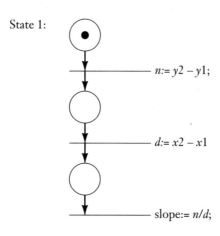

State 2:

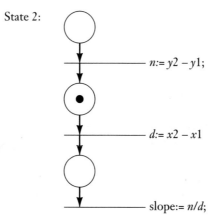

State 3:

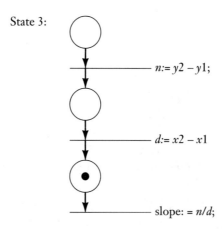

FIGURE 10.2 Control-flow Petri net graph: states 1 through 3.

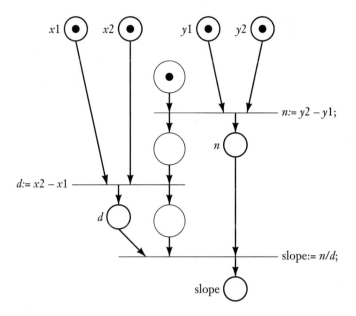

FIGURE 10.3 Data-flow Petri net graph.

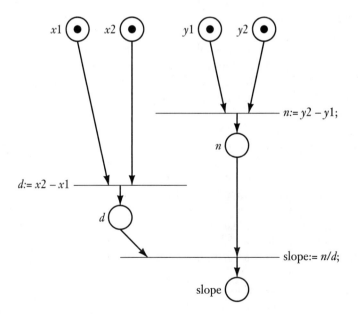

FIGURE 10.4 Data-flow Petri net, example 1.

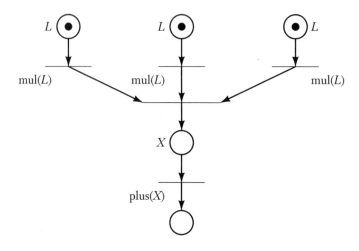

FIGURE 10.5   Data-flow Petri net, example 2.

computations are relative to a *tableau*, which maintains the state of a function's execution behind it. The tableau is an abstraction of a shared memory. In the abstraction the memory is shared among a theoretically infinite number of processing units. A function, or operator, is scheduled for execution whenever its required operands are fully computed and available behind the function or operator in the tableau. A process called *operand availability determination* determines whether an operator or function can be scheduled for execution.

Since sequences can contain references to functions and operators, the operand availability determination is based on whether the sequence following an operator is a *fully computed sequence*, meaning a sequence that contains only constants or nested, fully computed sequences. SequenceL operators take as operands only sequences and compute as results only sequences. The operators distribute themselves among the corresponding elements of operand sequences.

For example, in binary arithmetic the operator will distribute among the corresponding elements of two singleton sequences, for example, $*([2,2]) = [2] * [2] = [4]$. This semantic operates on sequences of any size or any level of nesting (i.e., of any dimension). The fact that operators take a single sequence as their only form of operand signifies how powerful the language is in terms of operand availability determinations for data flow and in terms of ease of specification of complicated computations.

For a user-defined function, the operand availability determination is based on the function's signature, which includes a specification of the function's domain. For example, the functions referenced in the initial tableau provided earlier (i.e., "p" and "m") each require exactly one argument. In the initial tableau, each of the three functions of "m" are followed by fully computed operands. Therefore, the "m" functions can execute in parallel.

SequenceL's execution strategy was influenced by the manner in which Petri net transitions consume tokens from incoming places and produce tokens in outgoing places. Furthermore, the analog between the consume/produce of the Petri net and the retract/assert from/to the Prolog database very much affected the SequenceL definition. When the SequenceL functions execute, the references to the functions and the function's operands are *consumed* from the tableau. The functions are then *simplified*, and the simplified versions are *produced*—returning to their respective places in the tableau. The addition of the intervening simplification step is one of the key differences between SequenceL and other models or language approaches.

CONSUME-SIMPLIFY-PRODUCE—Execution Cycle

      p

AFTER

      mul([2,2])

CONCURRENT WITH

      mul([4,3])

CONCURRENT WITH

      mul([6,]1])

CONCURRENT WITH

      'NULL'

The boldface messages in the traces are produced by the interpreter to indicate its findings about computations that can be performed in parallel versus those that must be completed in sequential fashion. The sequential computations are based on dependencies discovered among computations. That is, sequential computations are functions not followed by fully computed operands. Parallel computations have no existing dependencies and are guaranteed to be noninterfering. Notice that nested parallelisms will ultimately fall out and be identified. This will be more readily observed in a later example. Finally, the first simplification step (seen in the preceding box) does nothing more than instantiate the function parameters with their respective operands. The *consume-simplify-produce* execution strategy combines a dynamic data flow and a mathematical distribution of functions and operators with a built-in Prolog-like assert and retract. The tableau now appears as

tableau = [p, [mul([2,2]), mul([4,3]), mul([6,1])]]

The next consume-simplify-produce step performs the specified parallel multiplications and produces the results in the tableau.

CONSUME-SIMPLIFY-PRODUCE—Execution Cycle

     p

CONCURRENT WITH

     [4,12,6]

The result is the new tableau, "tableau = [p, [4,12,6]]." Finally, the function "p" can execute.

CONSUME-SIMPLIFY-PRODUCE—Execution Cycle

    plus([4,12,6])

CONCURRENT WITH

    'NULL'

The relevant simplification results in the instantiation of "p" 's parameter. In the next step, the plus operator is distributed among the corresponding elements of the operand singleton sequences, forming a summation of the three elements:

CONSUME-SIMPLIFY-PRODUCE—Execution Cycle

    [22]

The final execution cycle results in no change in the tableau, which is the halting condition for the interpreter:

> **CONSUME-SIMPLIFY-PRODUCE—Execution Cycle**
>
> [22]

The functions "m" and "p" are given to demonstrate the use of function signatures in SequenceL's data-flow execution strategy. A more straightforward solution to the problem is to simply place the desired operations and their operands in the tableau, as reflected in the following trace.

> **initial tableau** = [plus([mul([2,2]), mul([4,3]), mul([6,1])])]
>
> **CONSUME-SIMPLIFY-PRODUCE—Execution Cycle**
>
> plus([4,12,6])
>
> **CONSUME-SIMPLIFY-PRODUCE—Execution Cycle**
>
> [22]

DISTRIBUTION OF OPERATORS

In the previous example, the programmer explicitly specifies, in the initial tableau, the computations that can be performed in parallel, so that a static definition of the computation results. In other words, the programmer has identified *what* is to be done in parallel. *Perhaps the greatest complexity in the development of parallel codes is the identification of the computations that can be parallellized.* Much effort on the part of the programmer is expended in identifying the computations that can be performed in parallel and in testing the codes to make certain that they execute correctly.

SequenceL's semantic allows for a dynamic determination of iterative and parallel control flow. Parallelisms are determined automatically by the language interpreter. Once identified, the data flow execution (i.e., the consume-simplify-produce strategy) ensures parallel execution.

The original definition of SequenceL did not have the simplification steps. Instead, functions were fully evaluated once they became eligible for execution. The introduction of the simplification step was a crucial change in the language semantic and garnered no syntactic change whatsoever. With the simplification step came an interaction with the execution strategy and the SequenceL language constructs. This interaction allows for a distribution of operators and their associated operands, in turn allowing for the discovery of more parallelisms in a problem solution.

SequenceL's constructs (regular, irregular, and generative) [Cooke, 1996] interact with the stepwise consume-simplify-produce execution strategy in a subtle yet powerful way. In particular, the fact that operators operate on sequences and produce as results only sequences allows for the consistent and appropriate distribution of operators among constituent operands during a simplification step. This feature of the language, combined with the stepwise consume-simplify-produce execution strategy, results in a significant capability to automatically parallelize complicated problem solutions.

Consider as an example the SequenceL matrix multiply function:

Function $mm(s1(n,*),s2(*,m)) = \{$ plus(mul([s1(i,*),s2(*,j)]))$\}$
   Taking [i,j] **from** cartesian_product([gen([1, $\cdots$,n]),gen([1, $\cdots$,m])])

This SequenceL function is a symbolic representation of the natural-language specification of the matrix multiply. The matrix multiply specification is as follows:

for each *i/j*th position in the resultant matrix, form the sum of the products obtained by multiplying the corresponding elements in the *i*th row and the *j*th column of the respective operand matrices.

Compare the simplicity of the SequenceL function with a concurrent solution in Java, shown in Figure 10.6, which exploits only a subset of the parallelisms that are possible. The complete set of inherent parallelisms is not specified by the SequenceL programmer but is ultimately discovered during the SequenceL function execution.

The matrix multiply function and an initial tableau,

initial tableau $= [mm,\ [[1,2,3],[4,5,6],[7,8,9]],[[1,2,3],[4,5,6],[7,8,9]]]$

are the only items the programmer must specify in order to solve this problem. The parallelisms seen in the following trace are identified during the function's execution. This trace is taken directly from the current version of the SequenceL interpreter. Referring back to the natural-language specification, one must specify how the i,jth values are obtained. A Cartesian product of the ranges of values each subscript can be assigned forms the set of legal i,j value pairs. The ranges of values serving as arguments to the Cartesian product are *generated* by the expression *[gen([1, $\cdots$,n]),gen([1, . . . ,m])]*. The values for n and m are acquired when the function's arguments are consumed from the tableau. These values are acquired based upon the function signature $mm(s1(n, *),s2(*,m))$, which obtains the row dimension of *s1* and the column dimension of *s2*. Since n and m are both 3, the result of the generative operations is a two-dimensional sequence, $[[1,2,3],[1,2,3]]$, which serves as the

```
class mm3 extends Thread{
private int[][] m;
private int rs, cs, k;
public int n, s;

mm3(int r, int c, int[][] mat, int i)                                          {
        rs=r;
        cs=c;
        n=i;
        m=mat;}

public void run()    {
        s = 0;
        for (k=0;k<=m.length−1;k++)
                { s += m[rs][k] * m[k][cs]; }
}

public static void main (String args[]) {
        int i,j,k,r,c,g;
        r = 3;
        c = 3;
        int[] row = new int[r];
        int[] col = new int[c];
        int[][] m = new int[r][c];
        int[][] mr = new int[r][c];

        m[0][0] = 2; m[1][0] = 4; m[2][0] = 6; m[0][1] = 3; m[1][1] = 5;
        m[2][1] = 7; m[0][2] = 1; m[1][2] = 1; m[2][2] = 1;

        mm3 mat[] = new mm3[r*c];

        g = 0;
        for (i=0;i<=c−1;i++)
                for (j=0;j<=r−1;j++)
                        {mat[g] = new mm3(j,i,m,g);
                        g++; }

        for(i=0;i<=(r*c)−1;i++)
                {mat[i].start();}

        for(i=0;i<=(r*c)−1;i++)
                {try {mat[i].join(); }
                catch (InterruptedException ignored) { }                       }

        System.out.println("The answer is: ");

        for(i=0;i<=(r*c)−1;i++)
                {System.out.println("i= " + i + " " +mat[i].s);}

}
```

FIGURE 10.6   Concurrent matrix multiply in Java.

operand of the Cartesian product operation, seen in the trace shown in the following box.

CONSUME-SIMPLIFY-PRODUCE—Execution Cycle

cartesian_product
AFTER
gen
AFTER
$[1, \cdots, 3]$
CONCURRENT WITH
gen
AFTER
$[1, \cdots, 3]$

CONSUME-SIMPLIFY-PRODUCE—Execution Cycle

$[[1,1],[1,2],[1,3],[2,1],[2,2],[2,3],[3,1],[3,2],[3,3]]$

The fact that operators operate only on sequences and produce only sequences provides a seamlessness in problem specification and execution. This seamless relationship from results to arguments—and the fact that sequences can represent any conceivable data structure, including binary ones—combines with an operator semantic that can deal with operands of varying dimension (i.e., levels of nesting) and cardinality in a consistent and predictable manner.

In the present example, when the row and column combinations are available, they are distributed among nine copies of the matrix multiply function. The distribution of the functions with their separate values of i and j are the result of the next consume-simplify-produce step, resulting in nine functions that can be executed in parallel. Notice that the nested parallelisms are identified insofar as the nine additions will take place only after the nine multiplies are performed in parallel:

CONSUME-SIMPLIFY-PRODUCE—Execution Cycle

plus   **AFTER**   mul([[1,2,3],[1,4,7]])
CONCURRENT WITH
plus   **AFTER**   mul([[1,2,3],[2,5,8]])
CONCURRENT WITH

plus	**AFTER**	mul([[1,2,3],[3,6,9]])
CONCURRENT WITH		
plus	**AFTER**	mul([[4,5,6],[1,4,7]])
CONCURRENT WITH		
plus	**AFTER**	mul([[4,5,6],[2,5,8]])
CONCURRENT WITH		
plus	**AFTER**	mul([[4,5,6],[3,6,9]])
CONCURRENT WITH		
plus	**AFTER**	mul([[7,8,9],[1,4,7]])
CONCURRENT WITH		
plus	**AFTER**	mul([[7,8,9],[2,5,8]])
CONCURRENT WITH		
plus	**AFTER**	mul([[7,8,9],[3,6,9]])

It turns out that the nine multiplies are further simplified. SequenceL's *regular* construct applies operators to the corresponding components of the operand sequences. In this case, the simplification step naturally results in a further distribution of the multiply operator, so that each of the nine multiplies results in three pairwise multiplies. The net result, in this example, is that 27 multiplies can theoretically be performed in parallel, as is seen in the next consume-simplify-produce step:

CONSUME-SIMPLIFY-PRODUCE—Execution Cycle

plus   **AFTER**
mul([1,1])   **CONCURRENT WITH**
mul([2,4])   **CONCURRENT WITH**
mul([3,7])
CONCURRENT WITH
plus   **AFTER**
mul([1,2])   **CONCURRENT WITH**
mul([2,5])   **CONCURRENT WITH**
mul([3,8])
CONCURRENT WITH
plus   **AFTER**
mul([1,3])   **CONCURRENT WITH**
mul([2,6])   **CONCURRENT WITH**
mul([3,9])
CONCURRENT WITH
plus   **AFTER**
mul([4,1])   **CONCURRENT WITH**
mul([5,4])   **CONCURRENT WITH**

mul([6,7])
CONCURRENT WITH
plus   **AFTER**
mul([4,2])   **CONCURRENT WITH**
mul([5,5])   **CONCURRENT WITH**
mul([6,8])
CONCURRENT WITH
plus   **AFTER**
mul([4,3])   **CONCURRENT WITH**
mul([5,6])   **CONCURRENT WITH**
mul([6,9])
CONCURRENT WITH
plus   **AFTER**
mul([7,1])   **CONCURRENT WITH**
mul([8,4])   **CONCURRENT WITH**
mul([9,7])
CONCURRENT WITH
plus   **AFTER**
mul([7,2])   **CONCURRENT WITH**
mul([8,5])   **CONCURRENT WITH**
mul([9,8])
CONCURRENT WITH
plus   **AFTER**
mul([7,3])   **CONCURRENT WITH**
mul([8,6])   **CONCURRENT WITH**
mul([9,9])

The next simplification step produces a sequence of products for each of the nine additions that have been waiting to execute:

CONSUME-SIMPLIFY-PRODUCE—Execution Cycle

plus([1,8,21])   **CONCURRENT WITH**
plus([2,10,24])   **CONCURRENT WITH**
plus([3,12,27])   **CONCURRENT WITH**
plus([4,20,42])   **CONCURRENT WITH**
plus([8,25,48])   **CONCURRENT WITH**
plus([12,30,54])   **CONCURRENT WITH**
plus([7,32,63])   **CONCURRENT WITH**
plus([14,40,72])   **CONCURRENT WITH**
plus([21,48,81])

After the additions are performed (in parallel), the final result is the result of the matrix multiply:

CONSUME-SIMPLIFY-PRODUCE—Execution Cycle

[[30,36,42],[66,81,96],[102,126,150]]

Two significant distributions took place in this example. The first distribution was of unique *i,j* values among copies of the matrix multiply function. Next, the multiplication operator was distributed among corresponding components of the operand sequences. The entire trace of the execution is captured in the lattice structure depicted in Figure 10.7.

This example demonstrates all of the SequenceL constructs except for the irregular. The next example will describe the irregular construct and the only manner in which recursion exists in SequenceL.

RECURSION

Recursion in SequenceL is accomplished through the consume-simplify-produce execution strategy when a function places itself in the tableau. Consider the following recursive function and its execution trace:

Function succ(*s*1) = { [succ,plus([*s*1,[1]])] **when** <([*s*1,[4]]) **else** *s*1 }

One of SequenceL's constructs, the *irregular construct*, which selectively applies operators to operand sequences, is demonstrated here. As long as the argument

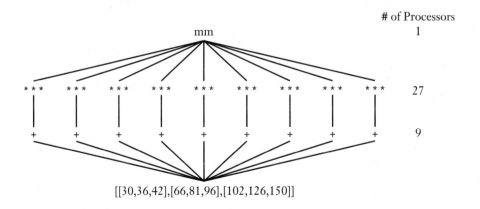

FIGURE 10.7 Lattice of matrix multiply.

*s*1 is less than 3, the function will reassert itself (the only form of recursion in SequenceL) and *s*1 + 1, to the tableau. When the condition is not satisfied, the final value of *s*1 is asserted:

---

initial tableau = [succ, [2]]
CONSUME-SIMPLIFY-PRODUCE—Execution Cycle
[[succ, plus([[2],[1]])], when, <([[2],[4]]), else, [2]]

CONSUME-SIMPLIFY-PRODUCE—Execution Cycle
succ   **AFTER**   plus([[2],[1]])

CONSUME-SIMPLIFY-PRODUCE—Execution Cycle
succ   [3]

CONSUME-SIMPLIFY-PRODUCE—Execution Cycle
[[succ, plus([[3],[1]])], when, <([[3],[4]]), else, [3]]

CONSUME-SIMPLIFY-PRODUCE—Execution Cycle
succ   **AFTER**   plus([[3],[1]])

CONSUME-SIMPLIFY-PRODUCE—Execution Cycle
succ   [4]

CONSUME-SIMPLIFY-PRODUCE—Execution Cycle
[[succ, plus([[4],[1]])], when, <([[4],[4]]), else, [4]]

CONSUME-SIMPLIFY-PRODUCE—Execution Cycle
[4]

From a run-time reliability standpoint, the approach to recursion in SequenceL is highly desirable. A deep stack of activation records is never produced as it is in conventional approaches to recursion. Recursion never results in more than one layer of activations. Functions do not call themselves. Instead they place themselves and the next state of their arguments in the shared-memory tableau. Therefore, as seen in our example, the states are maintained at the level of the tableau.

STATUS AND CONCLUSIONS

SequenceL is a small, high-level language that provides an abstraction suitable for automatically generating most sequential, iterative, and parallel program structures. (See Figure 10.8 for the language grammar.) The language is based

$A \rightarrow$ integer | real | string
$L \rightarrow$ A,L | E,L | A
$E \rightarrow$ [ ] | *[L]* | s(integer)
$V \rightarrow$ id | id*(M)*
$O \rightarrow$ + | − | / | * | abs | sqrt | cos | sin | tan | log | mod | reverse |
            transpose | rotateright | rotateleft | cartesianproduct
$M \rightarrow$ *,M | T,M | * | T
$T \rightarrow$ E | *[T*]* | V | $O(T)$ | V(map*(M)*) | $T(M)$ | gen*([T, $\cdots$,T])*
$RO \rightarrow$ < | > | = | >= | <= | <> | integer | real | var | operator
$R \rightarrow$ $RO(T)$ | and*(R$^+$)* | or*(R$^+$)* | not*(R$^+$)*
$B \rightarrow$ T^+ | T^+ when R else B
$C \rightarrow$ [ ] | taking *[V$^+$]* from T
$F \rightarrow$ id*(V$^+$)* where next = *{B}* C
$U \rightarrow$ V,U | E, U | V | E
$P \rightarrow$ {{F^+ } U}

P is a program, U is initial tableau
F^+ in P is a list of callable functions
S(integer) in E is a specification of the number of levels of nesting specified for an input
One to many ($^+$) and zero to many ($*$) has implied delimiters when necessary, usually commas

....

FIGURE 10.8   SequenceL Grammar

on a simple execution strategy that follows a stepwise *consume, simplify,* and *produce* process, halting when no further simplification is possible. The language can represent the Universal Turing Machine.

The working prototype interpreter has allowed us to develop and compare SequenceL codes (and their implied parallelisms) with Java or C/MPI counterpart codes. We began the language experiments with the *matrix multiply* problem presented in this chapter.

These initial experiments led us to conclude that the matrix multiply represents a fairly straightforward problem solution insofar as the parallel paths behave independently of one another. In other words, once the parallelisms are known, the paths can be spawned and joined together with each path contributing its part of the final solution without knowledge of what the other paths are computing. It became clear to us that we needed to explore a problem solution in which there are intermediate results that need broadcasting.

We settled on the *forward processing* in the *Gaussian elimination solution* of systems of linear equations for the next experiment. With three or more equations, intermediate results must be known to all paths in order to produce the final result. In this experiment, SequenceL behaves beyond expectations, finding more parallelisms than were thought to exist.

Finally, we noticed that in terms of scheduling, both the matrix multiply and the Gaussian codes are examples of problems for which static a-priori schedules can be generated. The paths of execution can be determined according to the size of the matrix in the matrix multiply and the number of equations in the Gaussian code. The need for a problem that requires dynamic scheduling led us to the *quicksort*. The quicksort provided the insight that in problems requiring dynamic scheduling, the number and schedule for the parallel paths are determined on the fly, regardless of the method used to choose the pivot. Again, SequenceL performed beyond our expectations.

It is our belief that each of these problems—the matrix multiply, the forward processing in Gaussian elimination, and the quicksort—are good representatives of possibly distinct, large classes of parallel problems. These initial experiments are described in Cooke and Andersen's article, "Automatic Parallel Control Structures in SequenceL" (2000).

Currently, the formal definitions and a prototype interpreter for SequenceL have been completed. The interpreter alone is a fairly handy tool in helping one design parallel codes and schedules using more traditional approaches, particularly Symmetric Multi Processing–based codes in Java. Our intent is to develop a compiler that will produce such codes and their schedules automatically. We remain confident that SequenceL problem solutions will allow us to find the inherent (or natural) parallelisms that exist in a given problem solution.

REFERENCES

J. Bishop. "The effect of data abstraction on loop programming techniques." *IEEE Trans. Soft. Eng.* SE-16, no. 4 (April 1990): 389–402.

Daniel E. Cooke and A. Gates, "On the development of a method to synthesize programs from requirement specifications." *International Journal on Software Engineering and Knowledge Engineering* 1, no. 1 (March 1991): 21–38.

Daniel E. Cooke, Elif Demirors, Onur Demirors, Ann Gates, Bernd Kraemer, Murat M. Tanik. "Languages for the specification of software." *Journal of Systems and Software* 32 (1996): 269–308.

Daniel E. Cooke. "An introduction to SEQUENCEL: A language to experiment with nonscalar constructs." *Software Practice and Experience* 26, no. 11, (November 1996): 1205–1246.

Daniel E. Cooke. "SequenceL provides a different way to view programming." *Computer Languages* 24 (1998): 1–32.

Daniel E. Cooke and Per Andersen. "Automatic Parallel Control Structures in SequenceL." *Software Practice and Experience* 30, no. 14 (November 2000): 1541–1570.

Daniel E. Cooke and Vladik Kreinovich. "Automatic parallelisms in SequenceL for supercomputing applications." *Science of Computer Programming*. In press.

K. Hammond and G. Michaelson. *Research Directions in Parallel Functional Programming.* London: Springer-Verlag, 1999.

H. Mills and R. Linger. "Data-structured programming: Programming without arrays and pointers." *IEEE Trans. Soft. Eng.* SE-12, no. 2 (February 1986): 192–197.

R. S. Nikhil and Arvind. *Implicit Parallel Programming in pH.* San Francisco: Morgan Kaufmann, 2001.

Index